Chinese Patent Law

Chinese Patent Law

A Practical Guide

Edited by
Yongbo Li
Fanwen Kong
Yang Yang

Wolters Kluwer

Published by:
Kluwer Law International B.V.
PO Box 316
2400 AH Alphen aan den Rijn
The Netherlands
E-mail: international-sales@wolterskluwer.com
Website: lrus.wolterskluwer.com

Sold and distributed by:
Wolters Kluwer Legal & Regulatory U.S.
7201 McKinney Circle
Frederick, MD 21704
United States of America
E-mail: customer.service@wolterskluwer.com

ISBN 978-94-035-3263-9

e-Book: ISBN 978-94-035-3264-6
web-PDF: ISBN 978-94-035-3265-3

Editors

Fanwen Kong, Senior Partner, started practicing as an attorney at law in 2005 after over 10 years of working as a Neurological Surgeon and then as a patent attorney in 2007. Mr. Kong focuses his practice mainly on patent litigations and patent invalidations in the technical fields, e.g., machinery, design, biochemistry, and chemistry, representing more than forty international and domestic clients. Mr. Kong has a profound understanding of the Chinese patent system through years of case handling in difficult and complex settings. Many of his cases have been selected as Typical Cases by the Supreme People's Court.

Mrs. Yang Yang is an attorney in the antitrust/competition compliance and litigation team. She is also an attorney in the patent litigation team. She has extensive experience in the pharmaceutical sector and internet-related sectors.

Yongbo Li, Senior Partner, practices intellectual property law in China, familiar with the international intellectual property rights protection mechanism, the Sino-US intellectual property trial mechanism, and the development of new information technology. Mr. Li has been involved in the multinational company's patent, trademark, unfair competition, business secrets, cyber-squatting, network communication, technology contract negotiations, and other IP issues. With the development of new technologies, Mr. Li focuses on cases about the field of advanced technology including data communication, Internet technology, network download, search engine, software patents, chip patents, biological medicine patents, and the research about intellectual property abuse in the antitrust field. He is familiar with the investigation procedures of the United States international trade commission 337 and has good communication and cooperation with foreign lawyers.

Contributors

Dang Li has been dedicated to patent agency business since 2009 and once worked for a well-known domestic integrated circuit company in R&D. Currently, Mrs. Dang is focusing on patent invalidation, patent administrative litigation, and patent infringement litigation, as well as patent search, analysis, patent strategy, and early warning. Mrs. Dang was engaged in the patent application agency business for many years, during which she got comprehensive and rich practical experience in patent applications, replying to OA, reexamination, and invalidation. Up to now, Mrs. Dang has dealt with nearly 1,000 patent application cases from a large number of well-known domestic enterprises.

Ge Xiaomei has been engaged in Intellectual property law practicing for 10 years since 2011. Mrs. Ge has a profound understanding of the Chinese patent system and anti-unfair competition law system. She represents companies in patent invalidation proceedings, patent infringement litigation as well as patent administrative proceedings with a focus on machinery, electronics, and computer science, and telecommunication patent-related disputes. She has successfully dealt with hundreds of patent applications, patent strategy counsel for a large number of clients. She has also accumulated rich and solid experience in trade secrets protection. Given her excellent performance and earnest attitude in solving complex and difficult patent cases, she is highly praised by domestic and foreign clients. In this project, Mrs. Ge invests much time and effort from drafting to the completion of the series report and acts as a major contributor.

Gu Runfeng is a partner and Attorney at Law at Unitalen Law Office. He got a Bachelor of Engineering from the Hebei University of Technology and has been engaged in intellectual property matters for more than 20 years. Before joining Unitalen in February 2003, Mr. GU used to serve as a lawyer in a foreign IP firm. In his legal experience, Mr. GU has handled lots of legal affairs involving Trademark, Copyright, Patent, unfair competition, etc., especially in difficult and complex patent reexamination & invalidation cases. Regarding patent legal affairs, he has dealt with some influential cases, such as patent invalidation and administrative litigation case of IRST SAMURAI, patent right case of Changsha Zoomlion Heavy Industry Science & Technology, patent infringement case between Kohler Company and Hai De Fu company, patent invalidation case between Electrolux and Haier, patent infringement case between XinFei company and a famous Korean company, as well as well-known trademark cases of Houdy, New Oriental, etc. As being interviewed by many media organizations for IP cases, such as CCTV, BTV, Guangming Daily, China Intellectual Property News, etc., Mr. GU has strong social influence in the IP field. Besides, he also participated in writing Trademarks and Patent Agents-Full Memoir of Chinese Lawyers Handling Cases, Intellectual Property Strategy and Practice, and so on.

He Yibo is Attorney at Law and Patent Attorney at FAIRSKY, based in Beijing. He got a Master of Pharmacology from Peking Union Medical College and a Master of Laws from the Renmin University of China. Mr. He engaged in intellectual property law work in 2010, who served as a patent examiner and re-examiner in the State Intellectual Property Office for nine years before joining FAIRSKY. Mr. He has profound experiences in patent search, patent stability and FTO analysis, patent invalidation proceeding, patent administrative enforcement, patent administrative litigation, patent infringement litigation, technology secret litigation and antitrust litigation, etc. One of the reexamination cases handled by him was awarded as one of the top ten cases of 2017 patent reexamination/invalidation.

Lu Weiting is both Attorney at Law and Patent Attorney, and as a Master of Science and Master of Law, owns both technical background majoring in Machinery and juristical background focusing on Intellectual Law. Mrs. Lu is primarily engaged in patent infringement litigations, patent administrative litigations, technology secret infringement litigation, as well as non-litigation proceedings, such as patent administrative enforcement, patent invalidation, and reexamination. Since her graduation from UIBE in 2012, Mrs. Lu has focused on patent cases in various fields including motor vehicles, rail vehicles, medical treatment, environmental protection, and textiles. Clients represented by Mrs. Lu include well-known domestic and foreign enterprises, such as CRRC Group, Mindray Medical, Neusoft Medical, Neusoft Group, Haier, BCS AG, VMI Holland, etc. Invalidation case of ROLLERCOASTER and invalidation case of A GRAPHICAL USER INTERFACE FOR MOBILE COMMUNICATION DEVICES handled by her were awarded as two of the top ten cases of 2019 and 2020 patent reexamination/invalidation of CNIPA.

Sun Changlong is a partner at Unitalen Law Office and a Patent Law Subcommittee member of the Beijing Lawyers Association. He has profound practical experience in the fields of patent civil litigation, administrative litigation, commercial secret infringement litigation, and patent application, reexamination, and invalidation. With over 20 years of experience in dealing with patent legal affairs since 2001, Mr. SUN has handled thousands of patent applications, hundreds of patent review and invalidation cases, and several dozens of typical patent infringement litigations and patent administrative litigations. Among these cases, cases concerning patent infringement and patent confirmation of automobile antennas, in which Mr. SUN was an agent of Chongqing Lifan Motors, were selected as "2017 Supreme People's Court Annual Report Cases" and "2019 Supreme People's Court Annual Report 60 Selected Typical Cases." Moreover, Mr. SUN used to participate in the writing of the book *Analysis of Typical Cases of Intellectual Property Rights*, and a lot of his professional articles were included in books like *China Inventions and Patents, Intellectual Property Strategy and Practice.*

Wang Meng has been engaged in the intellectual property law business since 2010. He is both an Attorney at Law and a Patent Attorney. He is familiar with the technical fields of electronics, machinery, networks, computers, and communications. He currently focuses on handling patent infringement litigation, patent invalidation, and patent administrative litigation. Mr. Wang also has extensive experience in trade secret litigation. The China Patent Reexamination Commission (CNIPA) once ranked the ROLLERCOASTER patent invalidation case represented by Mr. Wang as one of the top ten patent reexamination invalidation cases in 2019.

Wang Rong graduated from Shandong Normal University with a Bachelor of Science in Computer Science in 2011 and graduated from Southwest University of Political Science and Law in 2014 with a Master of Law. After graduation, Lawyer Wang Rong has been engaged in the field of intellectual property, especially the field of patents and has the qualifications of lawyers and patent agents at the same time. At present, Lawyer Wang Rong's main practice areas are patent invalidation, patent analysis, and patent litigation. He has accumulated many years of working experience in the patent field. In addition, Lawyer Wang has also acted as an agent of disputes on trademarks, copyrights, unfair competition, and technical secrets, providing clients with a full range of intellectual property services.

Zhang Junjie is licensed to practice law in China as an attorney. Mr. Zhang has been active in the areas of patent infringement and validity analysis with respect to invention, utility model, and design patents. He is especially adept in technical litigation in the fields of mechanics, electronics, and computer science. Two invalidation cases represented by Mr. Zhang were respectively awarded by CNIPA as two of the top ten patent invalidation and reexamination cases of 2019 and 2020. Mr. Zhang holds a Master's in Posts and Telecommunications from Beijing University and a Bachelor's in Communication Engineering from Tianjin University. After attaining his Master's, Mr. Zhang worked as a patent examiner in China Patent Office. Then, he worked as a patent agent in a big law firm, where he helped many international companies with patent prosecution in China. Mr. Zhang's prior experiences in roles of both patent examiner and patent agent have given him valuable insight applicable in both prior art searching and patent prosecution work.

Zhang Qiulin is both Attorney at Law and Patent Attorney, and as Master of Science and Master of Law, owns both technical background majoring in Organic Chemistry and juristical background focusing on Intellectual Law. Mr. Zhang has worked for CHIPSCREEN for two years in the research and development of new drugs and started practicing intellectual property law in 2006. He mainly practices and has profound experiences in patent invalidation, patent administrative enforcement, patent administrative litigation, patent infringement litigation, and technology secret litigation. Invalidation case of AMEC and invalidation case of ROLLERCOASTER handled by him were awarded as one of the top ten cases of 2018 and 2019 patent reexamination/invalidation of CNIPA, and vanillin case of ZHOGNHUA CHEMICAL represented by him gained the highest compensation of RMB 159 million among trade secret misappropriation cases tried by Chinese courts so far.

Summary of Contents

Table of Contents

CHAPTER 1

Assertion of a Claim: Systematic Introduction to Chinese Patent Law and Rules and Patent Infringement Litigations

Wang Rong & Ge Xiaomei

Patent rights are different from general civil rights. They are based on administrative authorization, and the scope of protection is subject to the content of the claims recorded in the patent documents. After the patent is granted, its scope of protection can be adjusted through amendments in the invalidation procedure and will change as a result of the invalidation procedure. Then, in a patent infringement lawsuit, how should the right holder as the plaintiff choose the basis of the right to sue? When the scope of protection of patent rights changes, how can we claim to change the basis of rights? This chapter combines extensive court decisions and a systematic introduction to Chinese patent law and rules to explain these issues.

§1.01 BASIC RULES

Interpretation of the Supreme People's Court on Several Issues concerning the Application of Law in the Trial of Patent Infringement Dispute Cases **(hereinafter referred to as "*Judicial Interpretation I*") provides that**

Article 1 The People's court shall, based on the claim asserted by the right holder, determine the scope of protection of a patent in accordance with paragraph 1 of Article 59 of the Patent Law. Where the right holder alters the claim asserted by him before the end of court debate of the first instance, the People's court shall permit such alteration.

Where the right holder asserts that the scope of protection of a patent should be determined according to a dependent claim, the People's court shall determine the scope of protection of the patent according to the additional technical features described in the dependent claim and the technical features described in the claim referred to by it.

***Interpretation of the Supreme People's Court on Several Issues concerning the Application of Law in the Trial of Patent Infringement Dispute Cases* (hereinafter referred to as "*Judicial Interpretation II*")**

Article 1 Where there are two or more claims in a statement of claims, the patentee shall specify in the written complaint the claims based on which it initiates an action against the alleged infringer for infringement upon its patent right. Where there is no such record, or the record is unclear in the written complaint, the people's court shall require the patentee to specify the relevant information. Where, after explanations, the patentee still fails to specify the relevant information, the People's court may rule to dismiss the action.

§1.02 INTERPRETATIONS OF THE BASIC RULES

The determination of a claim is the fundamental work of a patent infringement lawsuit. Article I of the *Judicial Interpretation I* specifies that the patentee can choose one or more claims before the end of court debate of the first instance to determine the protection scope of the patent into which the alleged infringing technical solution falls. Article I of the *Judicial Interpretation II* provides that in practice, where the patentee does not specify in the written complaint the claims based on which it initiates an action, the people's court shall require the patentee to specify the relevant information through explanations. Where, after explanations, the patentee still fails to specify the chosen claims, requirements to initiate an action are not satisfied, and the action shall be dismissed by ruling in accordance with the law.

According to the above provisions, when initiating an action against the patent infringement:

(1) the patentee shall first consider choosing the independent claim as the right basis, and then consider the dependent claim;
(2) the patentee shall specify the claims based on which it initiates an action in the written complaint or pretrial conference;
(3) the patentee may alter the asserted claims before the end of court debate of the first instance;
(4) where, after explanations of the court, the patentee still fails to specify the claim to be protected, the people's court may rule to dismiss the action;
(5) the waived claims on one's initiative in the invalidation procedure shall not serve as the right basis for infringement action; the claims that are maintained valid through the invalidation procedure may serve as the right basis for continuing the trial of the infringement action;
(6) the patentee may alter the asserted claims from "the date of receipt of the decision of invalidation" to "the end of court debate of the first instance," and

if the time limit is exceeded, the patentee shall actively contact the court to explain the situation and apply for another court session; and

(7) the number of claims infringed by the alleged infringing product will not affect the amount of compensation for infringement.

§1.03 APPLICATIONS OF THE BASIC RULES: DISPUTES AND ISSUES ARISEN UNDER THE RULES

[A] When Initiating an Action, the Patentee as a Plaintiff Should Assert the Related Claims as the Right Basis as Fully as Possible

The determination of a claim is the fundamental work of a patent infringement action, the prerequisite for the court hearing and for parties to respond to the action, and also the key element to decide whether the patentee can win the patent infringement action. In the patent infringement action, patent invalidation is a common countermeasure of the defendant. Therefore, in order to avoid the possible impact of partial invalidation of the patent involved in the infringement action, the patentee should assert the related claims on the right basis as fully as possible.

For example, in the following case, the patentee only asserts Claim 1 as the right basis in the first instance, and the Court of First Instance determines that the infringement is established. However, the patent involved was declared invalid during the second instance of the infringement action. The patentee then asserted that the alleged infringing product still fell within the protection scope of the amended Claim 1 (i.e., the original Claim 2). Both the Court of Second Instance and the court of retrial did not support the assertion.

Case 1: In an infringement dispute over a utility model patent between Hunan HuaHui New Energy Co. Ltd. (Huahui Company) and Dongguan Liyuan Battery Ltd. (Liyuan Company) ((2017) Yue Min Zhong No. 1086), in the first instance, Huahui Company sought to protect Claim 1 of the patent involved, the Guangzhou Intellectual Property Court of First Instance holds that the infringement of Liyuan Company is established.

In the second instance, a part of the patent involved is declared invalid. The original Claim 1 is deleted, and the patent is maintained valid on the basis of the amended Claims 1-2. Huahui Company held that the alleged infringing product still constituted infringement even compared with the amended Claim 1. In this regard, the Guangdong High Court of Second Instance holds that since Claim 1 of the patent involved claimed by Huahui Company is declared invalid, the right basis for Huahui Company to initiate the action is lost. Therefore, the judgment of the first instance is revoked, and the action initiated by Huahui Company is dismissed. Huahui Company was not satisfied with the judgment of the second instance and filed a request for retrial.

After retrial, the Supreme Court believes that the protection scope of the claim on which Huahui Company relies in the action of first instance of the case is obviously different from that of the amended Claim 1. Therefore, it is appropriate for the Court of Second Instance to determine that the right basis for Huahui Company to initiate the action has been lost and to rule that the action is dismissed in accordance with Article 2 of the *Interpretation II*. Therefore, the retrial request of Huahui Company is dismissed.

The author holds that it is reasonable for the court to dismiss the plaintiff's action where the right basis claimed by the plaintiff has been lost for the reasons such as patent invalidation. It is because no comparison is performed in the first instance on whether the alleged infringing solution infringes Claim 2, and there is no opportunity for the defendant to express a defense on whether the original Claim 2 is infringed in the first instance; at this time, if the patentee is allowed to alter the right basis in the second instance, the action interests of the defendant will be affected.

Note: when filing a patent infringement action, the patentee shall assert the related claims, including dependent claims, as fully as possible; and the infringement comparison shall be as detailed as possible to minimize the impact of partial invalidation of the claim due to the invalidation procedure on civil action.

Otherwise, in the event that the claim claimed by the patentee in the first instance is invalidated, and the claim, which may cause establishment of infringement but is not asserted in the action, is maintained, the patentee will face adverse risks that the maintained claims may not be claimed in this case. Although there is a relief measure for the patentee to institute a separate action, this undoubtedly consumes action time and increases action costs.

[B] The Number of the Claims Infringed by the Alleged Infringing Product Will Not Affect the Amount of Compensation

Each claim is a complete technical solution, so the patentee may choose one or more claims as the right basis for the assertion of the infringement action. As long as the alleged infringing technical solution falls within the protection scope of one of the claims, the infringement is constituted, and the amount of compensation for infringement does not vary with the number of claims of patent infringed by the alleged infringing solution.

Case 2: In an infringement dispute over a utility model patent between IZUMI-COSMO LIMITED (Japan) and Guangzhou Grandview Crystal Screen Co. Ltd., Beijing Ren He Shi Ji Technology Co. Ltd. ((2008) Gao Min Zhong Zi No. 941), the appellant holds: the Court of First Instance determines the amount of compensation for infringement on the basis of Claim 5 and Claim 12 of the patent involved. In the second instance, the appellant filed a request for patent invalidation, and the appellee deleted the original Claim 5. Therefore, the technical solution adopted by the alleged infringing product only falls within the original Claim 12, and thus the amount of compensation should be reduced.

In this regard, the Beijing High Court believes: in this case, the IZUMI-COSMO LIMITED explicitly asserts that the amount of compensation shall be determined according to the statutory compensation method. The Court of First Instance determines the amount of compensation discretionarily, taking into account factors such as the type of the patent involved, nature, and infringement circumstances of Grandview Crystal Company. Although the IZUMI-COSMO LIMITED waived the original Claims 1-6 in the examination process of patent invalidation on its initiative, the alleged product is still the product that infringes the patent involved. Moreover, the amount of compensation for infringement shall not vary with the number of claims of the patent infringed by the alleged product. Therefore, the amount of compensation determined by the Court of First Instance is appropriate.

When calculating the amount of compensation for infringement, the court should consider the actual losses suffered by the patentee or the benefits obtained by the infringer due to infringement, which is related to the cost, selling price, and quantity of the whole product. And the amount of compensation should not be determined by the number of the asserted claims.

[C] The Technical Solution Waived Initiatively in the Invalidation Procedure Shall Not Serve as the Right Basis in the Infringement Action

In the patent infringement action, a request for the invalidation of the patent involved is the conventional countermeasure of the defendant. In patent invalidation procedure, the patentee may alter the protection scope of the patent by amending the claim, and the specific methods for amending the claim are generally limited to deletion of a claim, deletion of a technical solution, further definition of a claim, and an amendment to an obvious error.

The Intellectual Property Court of the Supreme Court specified in the following case: in the invalidation administrative procedure of the patent involved, where the patentee initiatively waives a claim based on which the right is asserted in a civil infringement case by deleting the claim, no matter whether the validity of the administrative decision recording the waiver is finally determined, the waived claims have no possibility of restoration. The waived claims cannot be reincorporated in the protection scope of the patent in the dispute over the patent infringement. The right basis on which the infringement action is initiated no longer exists, and the relevant action request can be dismissed by judgment.

Case 3: In an infringement dispute over a utility model patent between Shunfang Pipe Co. Ltd. (Shunfang Company) and Shandong Yanggu Dasheng Pipe Co. Ltd (Dasheng Company), Shandong Zhuorui Dasheng Pipe Co. Ltd. (Zhuoda Company) ((2019) Zui Gao Fa Zhi Min Zhong No. 145), Shunfang Company takes Claims 1-3 as the right basis. During the second instance, Dasheng Company and Zhuoda Company submitted an examination decision of the request for invalidation for the patent involved, stating: Shunfang Company amended the claims in the invalidation procedure by deleting Claims 1 and 2 and combining Claims 3 and 4 into a new Claim 1. The China Intellectual Property Administration declares invalidation of the whole patent involved based on the amended Claim 1.

In this regard, the Intellectual Property Court of the Supreme Court of Second Instance believes: from the subjective aspect, Shunfang Company's initiative deletion of Claims 1-3 is regarded as its recognition that Claims 1-3 do not meet the substantive conditions for granting patent rights from the date of filing, that is, Claims 1-3 should not have been allowed. From the objective aspect, Shunfang Company's initiative deletion of Claims 1-3 complies with the provisions of Section 4.6 of Chapter 3 of Part IV of *the Guidelines for Patent Examination* and has been accepted by the China Intellectual Property Office. Even if Decision No. 41399 is revoked in administrative proceedings, Claims 1-3 can no longer serve as the basis for its assertions according to the principle of estoppel. In the case that Shunfang Company only takes Claims 1-3 as the basis for its assertions and Claims 1-3 have been waived on its initiative, in accordance with the provision of Article 1 of the *Judicial Interpretation I*, the basis for the protection scope of the patent rights based on which Shunfang Company files the action no longer exists, and its request of action is established.

The author holds that this case corresponds to the amendment of claims by deleting; that is, the patentee waives the claimed technical solution by deleting a claim. Furthermore, since the deletion of a technical solution leads to the waiver thereof, the rule of adjudication will also apply to the amendment method of deletion of the technical solution.

Note: The patentee should be cautious about amendments of the claim in the invalidation procedure. In particular, the deletion of a claim and the deletion of a technical solution will result in the impossibility of restoration of the waived technical solution. No matter whether the decision of invalidation is finally effective or revoked, the waived technical solution cannot be claimed again in an infringement case.

[D] The Part of Claims That Are Maintained Valid in the Invalidation Procedure May Serve as the Right Basis for Continuing the Trial of an Infringement Action

Maintaining the validity of a patent can be divided into two circumstances: one is to maintain the validity of claims on the basis of patented texts; the other is to maintain the validity of the patent on the basis of amended claims. No matter whether the amendment to the claim is involved or not, where the patentee asserts that the claim maintained valid in the invalidation procedure is taken as the right basis, the people's court shall allow the assertion. The detailed analysis is as follows:

> On the one hand, where the patent involved is maintained valid on the basis of the original claims, the patentee can claim rights in the infringement action on the part maintained valid, which is no doubt in judicial practice. For example, the Intellectual Property Court of the Supreme Court has made it clear in the following case that if the parallel technical solutions in the claims are declared invalid in part, the patentee may continue to claim the rights according to the valid part.
>
> Case 4: In a dispute over the infringement of a utility model patent between Shenzhen Yunchongba Technology Ltd and Shenzhen Laidian Technology Co. Ltd ((2019) Zui Gao Fa Zhi Min Zhong No. 350), the Intellectual Property Court of the Supreme Court of Second Instance indicates that where, during the patent

> infringement action, a corresponding part of one or more parallel technical solutions in the claims of the patent involved is declared invalid while the corresponding part of the remaining parallel technical solutions is still valid, and the patentee continues to claim the rights according to the part of claims that is still valid, the people's court may dismiss the action on the claims that are declared invalid, and at the same time hear and make a judgment on the claims that are maintained valid.
>
> On the other hand, there are different arguments in practice on whether the patentee can claim the right in the infringement action in the case that the patent involved is maintained valid on the basis of the claims amended by further definition. An opinion is that the amendment method of "further definition of the claims" will generate a new technical solution that is not clearly published in the claims of the allowed texts. If the patentee is allowed to claim rights based on the new technical solution that is not clearly published in the granted text, the expected interests of the public will be exceeded, and the interests of the defendant will be directly harmed.

It can be found that this opinion is obviously untenable through a simple analysis.

Section III of Chapter IV of the *Guidelines for Patent Examination* specifies that: "where a patent right is declared invalid in part, the part of the patent right so invalidated shall be deemed non-existent from the date of filing, and the part of the patent right that are maintained valid (including the amended claims) shall be deemed existent from the date of filing at the same time." Accordingly, it can be known that:

(1) no matter how the claim is amended, the claims that are maintained valid shall be deemed existent from the date of filing; and
(2) the amendments in the invalidation phase will not exceed the scope of the original claims and description of the patent; that is, the amended claims do not violate the principle of publicity of rights and do not infringe upon the public interests.

Accordingly, the patentee shall be allowed to assert the new claims formed in the invalidation procedure in the infringement action, and the original trial procedure should be continued.

Case 5: In an infringement dispute over a patent for invention between Shenyang Sky Air-Ship Digital Printing Equipment Co. Ltd and Qingdao Hanze Electric Co. Ltd ((2019) Zui Gao Fa Zhi Min Zhong No. 161), during the first instance, the patent involved is declared invalid in part, and the patent is maintained valid on the basis of the claims that are amended by the patentee in the method of further definition. The Jinan Intermediate Court of First Instance dismisses the plaintiff's action on the basis that the content of Claim 1 was altered and that the right basis on which the Sky Air-Ship Company files the action was lost.

In this regard, the Intellectual Property Court of the Supreme Court of Second Instance believes: although a certain claim based on which the patentee asserted the protection scope previously is declared invalid, there are other claims that are maintained valid in the patent involved. And in particular, in the case that the original claims are amended, and the protection scopes thereof are further defined, the people's court shall give the patentee the procedural right to re-clarify the claim based on which the protection scope is claimed and continue the trial on the claim re-clarified by the patentee.

As can be seen, the Intellectual Property Court of the Supreme People's Court also clarifies the following rules in the above case: where, in the first instance of a dispute over patent infringement, the claim based on which the patentee claims the patent is declared invalid, but the involved patent is maintained valid on the basis of the remaining original claims or the amended new claims, the patentee shall be allowed to re-clarify the claims based on which the patent is claimed. If the patentee chooses the currently valid claims to claim the patent right, the Court of First Instance shall continue the trial; and after explanations, if the patentee still insists on claiming the right based on the claim that has been declared invalid, the Court of First Instance may rule to dismiss the action.

[E] The Patentee May File a Petition to Alter the Right Basis "From the Date of Receipt of the Decision of Invalidation"

As mentioned above, the patentee may alter the right basis in the infringement action according to the decision of invalidation that maintains the validity of the patent. When can the patentee claim to alter the claims? Does the patentee need to wait for the effective date of the decision of invalidation?

The parties of the invalidation procedure may, within three months from the date of receipt of the decision of patent invalidation, institute legal proceedings in the Beijing Intellectual Property Court. In other words, the decision of invalidation does not take effect from the date when the decision is made, or the decision is received but should take effect after the final judgment of the second instance of administrative action is made. However, based on the above theoretical basis that the new claims are still within the original protection scope and are valid from the date of filing, there is no doubt that the patentee may claim to alter the right basis from the date of receipt of the decision of invalidation without waiting for the effective date of decision of invalidation.

Case 6: In a dispute over the royalties of the patent for invention during the temporary protection period and infringement of a patent for invention between LG Innotek Co. Ltd., and Nidec (Dongguan) Ltd., and Beijing Zhongnan Shuanglv Technology Co. Ltd. ((2015) Jing Zhi Min Chu Zi No. 338), in response to the request for invalidation filed by the defendant Nidec Ltd., the Patent Reexamination Board makes a decision of invalidation as follows: the patent is maintained valid on the basis of Claims 1-69 amended by LG Innotek Co. Ltd. After that, in the pretrial conference, LG Innotek Co. Ltd. further clarified the claimed right basis based on the claims that were maintained valid.

In this regard, Beijing Intellectual Property Court of First Instance holds: the patent involved is still in the validity period when the alleged infringing product is manufactured and sold, and the decision of invalidation involved also decides to maintain the patent involved valid on the basis of Claims 1-69 submitted by LG

Company on July 6, 2015. Therefore, *in the case that there is no evidence to prove that the relevant administration or judicial procedures has made negative evaluations on the validity of the patent involved, the patent involved shall be protected as a valid patent in this case.*

In particular, when hearing this case, the court also heard the patent invalidation administrative dispute concerning the decision of invalidation of the patent involved at the same time. The court fully heard the opinions of Nidec Ltd., the Patent Reexamination Board, and LG Company during the hearing of the administrative dispute and combined the dispute determination such as the interpretation of a claim, the determination of the protection scope involved in the administrative case into the trial process of the case, and tried the case on the basis that the correctness of the decision of invalidation was finally determined.

Accordingly, the patentee may alter the claimed right basis according to the claims that are maintained valid from the date of receipt of the decision of invalidation and does need to wait for the effective date of the decision of invalidation.

[F] The Patentee Shall Try to Claim the Alteration of the Right Basis "Before the End of Court Debate of the First Instance"

Article 1 of the *interpretation I* specifies that where the patentee needs to alter the right basis, the alteration shall be made before the end of court debate of the first instance. As mentioned above, if the patentee claims the alteration of the claimed claims before the end of court debate of the first instance, the amended claims are still within the protection scopes of the original claims and are further defined. Therefore, the litigious rights of the defendant are not deprived or restricted, and the original trial procedure should be continued. There is no dispute on this opinion in practice.

The question is: what impact will be generated if the patentee's application for the alteration of the right basis is made after the end of court debate of the first instance? The explanation will be made below with reference to Case 5.

Case 5: In the above infringement dispute over a patent for invention between Shenyang Sky Air-Ship Digital Printing Equipment Co. Ltd and Qingdao Hanze Electric Co. Ltd ((2019) Zui Gao Fa Zhi Min Zhong No. 161), the Jinan Intermediate Court of First Instance holds: before the declaration of invalidation of the patent involved, the Sky Air-Ship Company explicitly takes the original Claim 1 before the amendment as its claimed protection scope before the end of court debate. However, after the decision of invalidation was made, the content of Claim 1 of the involved patent has been altered. Therefore, the right basis on which the Sky Air-Ship Company filed the action was lost, and thus the plaintiff's action was dismissed. Sky Air-Ship Company was not satisfied with the judgment of the first instance and filed an appeal.

In this regard, the Intellectual Property Court of the Supreme Court holds: after the patent right involved is declared invalid in part, as long as the original court has not made a judgment, the original court shall explain to the patentee, Sky Air-Ship Company, in accordance with the law, allowing the patentee, Sky Air-Ship Company, to specify the claims of which the protection scope is claimed within the scope of the claims that are maintained valid. However, the original court did not give the patentee, Sky Air-Ship Company, the procedural right to re-clarify the claims and directly ruled to dismiss the action of Sky Air-Ship Company without explanations, which is an error in the application of the law.

From the grounds for the judgment of this case, it can be seen that the time point when the decision of invalidation is made in this case may be after the end of the court debate of first instance and before the first-instance judgment is made. In the case, the Intellectual Property Court of the Supreme Court holds that it is inappropriate to directly dismiss the plaintiff's action and that as long as the original court has not made a judgment, the original court should explain to the patentee and allow the patentee to alter the right basis.

Note: It is beneficial for the patentee to extend the time point for the patentee to alter the right basis before the first-instance judgment is made. In practice, if the plaintiff receives a decision of invalidation that has an impact on the infringement assertions after the first instance hearing, the plaintiff should actively contact the judge, explain the situation, apply to the court for opening another court session, and apply for the alteration of right basis.

[G] Is the Provision of Punitive Damages Applicable When a New Claim Formed by an Amendment in an Invalidation Procedure Is Taken as the Right Basis?

When the patentee takes the new technical solution formed by the amendment in the invalidation procedure as the right basis, and the sued infringer claims that the new technical solution is not recited in the claims before the infringement occurs, should the sued infringer be deemed to have no malice and thus should the liability for damages be reduced discretionarily? The author has not found any relevant judgment to discuss this issue and only summarizes different academic opinions as follows.

One opinion is that the new technical solution formed by the amendment will not affect the determination of damages. The reasons are as follows: the new technical solution that is maintained is valid from the date of filing. Since the amendment does not exceed the scope of the original claims and description of the patent, the new technical solution has the same publicity effect as the granted text. In addition, due to the publicity effect of the granted text, the defendant cannot defend that he does not know the existence of the patent right. Since the *Guidelines for Patent Examination* clearly specifies the amendment method of further definition, and the new technical solution is amended in accordance with the public granted text, the defendant should fulfill his reasonable duties of foresight and care. Therefore, it cannot be used as a favorable defense that the newly amended technical solution is not clearly stated in the announcement text for grant of patent.

Another opinion is that the defendant can be deemed to have no intention of infringement subjectively when the new technical solution formed by the amendment is claimed. The reasons are as follows: based on the principle of publicity of claims, the protection scope of each claim is determined. In an infringement action, if the plaintiff claims the new claim amended in the invalidation procedure as the right basis, while the newly formed technical solution does not exist in the announcement text for grant of a patent, the defendant does not have a subjective intention in the infringement, and thus the application of punitive damages is excluded.

According to The WTO Agreement on Trade-Related Aspects of Intellectual Property Rights (TRIPS) agreement, the subjective factors of the infringer are not considered in determining whether the infringer infringed the patent right but can be taken as consideration factors of compensation. Article 71 of the *Patent Law of the People's Republic of China,* newly revised in October 2020, added a system of punitive damages. The application of punitive damages requires two conditions: one is the subjectively intentional infringement, and the other is the objectively serious circumstances. The author holds that in the case that the plaintiff claims rights based on the new technical solution formed by the amendment, the defendant may try to put forward the defense in the case that the provision of punitive damages should not be applied according to the above second view.

§1.04 CONCLUSION

The chapter analyzed how the patentee chooses the right basis and alters the right basis when defending its patent rights, discusses the above issues based on corresponding judicial cases, and gives corresponding suggestions for defending rights.

Although the number of claims infringed by the alleged infringing product will not affect the amount of compensation, the patentee should assert relevant claims as the right basis as fully as possible in consideration of the stability of a patent. When the patent is challenged by the invalidation procedure, the claim waived on the patentee's initiative shall not serve as the right basis, while the part that is maintained valid can serve as the basis for the continuation of an infringement action. The patentee may claim the alteration of the right basis "from the date of receipt of the decision of invalidation" to "the end of court debate of the first instance." When the time point is exceeded, the patentee needs to actively communicate with the court to explain the relevant situation and apply for another court session.

This chapter also introduced the potential impact on the application of the newly added provision of punitive damages in the *Chinese Patent Law* from the perspective of taking the new claim that has not appeared in the granted text as the right basis, which provides a reference for parties in different status in litigation.

CHAPTER 2

Application of the Rule "Ruling to Dismiss the Action and Initiating a Separate Action": A Report Series on Law Interpretation and Case Study Related to Patent Infringement

Zhang Qiulin & Ge Xiaomei

This chapter mainly discusses the impacts on the patent infringement action at different trial procedures or stages when the claims of the patent are declared invalid in the invalidation procedure, that is, the application of the system "ruling to dismiss the action and initiating a separate action" in judicial practice since it was introduced in judicial interpretation II in 2016. In addition, this chapter also discusses the handling procedures of corresponding matters, such as provisional measures, facts, and evidence determined in the original trial, after the action is ruled to be dismissed and a separate action is initiated. This chapter includes seven judicial cases in total.

§2.01 BASIC PROVISIONS OF LAWS

***Interpretation (II) of the Supreme People's Court on Several Issues Concerning the Application of Law in the Trial of Patent Infringement Dispute Cases* (hereinafter referred to as "*Judicial Interpretation II*")**

Article 2 Where the claims of a patentee in a patent infringement action are declared invalid by the Patent Reexamination Board, the people's court hearing the patent infringement dispute case may rule to dismiss the action which is initiated based on such invalid claims.

Where there is evidence proving that the decision of declaring the invalidation of the aforesaid claims is set aside by an effective administrative judgment, the patentee may initiate a separate action.

Where the patentee initiates a separate action, the limitation of action for patent infringement shall be calculated from the date when the written administrative judgment as mentioned in paragraph 2 of this Article is served.

§2.02 INTERPRETATION OF THE ARTICLES OF LAW

In the patent infringement dispute cases, the patentee brings an action against the defendant's infringement, and the defendant usually files an invalidation request to the China National Intellectual Property Administration. Based on the current litigation structure of the separation of civil and administrative trials, in cases where the claims asserted by the patentee in the patent infringement action are declared invalid by the Patent Reexamination Board, the court usually suspends the civil action to wait for the outcome of administrative action for determining the ownership of the patent according to the provision "the case involved is dependent upon the outcome of the trial of another case that has not been concluded" as prescribed in Article 150(5) of the *Civil Procedure Law*, which causes a relatively long trial period for the patent infringement dispute cases.

The system of "ruling to dismiss the action first and initiating a separate action" designed in the Article fully considers the fact that the proportion for change of the invalidation decision of the Patent Reexamination Board by the administrative action for determining the ownership of the patent is low. After the Patent Reexamination Board makes a decision to announce the patent right invalid, the court hearing the patent infringement dispute case may rule to dismiss the action without waiting for the final outcome of the patent administrative action, and the patentee can resort to the judicial relief by initiating a separate action. The purpose of the system is to improve the efficiency of the trial of patent infringement action and alleviate the impact of the relatively long trial period as much as possible.

> According to the above provisions, the conditions for applying the provision of "ruling to dismiss the action and initiating a separate action" are as follows:
> (1) the patentee includes the patentee and the interested parties such as the licensee;
> (2) the claims asserted in the infringement are invalidated by the Patent Reexamination Board;
> (3) the provision that the people's court may (not shall) rule to dismiss the action initiated by the patentee means that where the patentee fails to change the asserted claims timely, the court may rule to dismiss the action based on the invalidated claims;
> (4) where the decision of declaring the invalidation of the claims is set aside by an effective administrative judgment, the patentee may initiate a separate action; and
> (5) the starting point of the limitation varies between patentee and licensee:
>
> for the patentee, the limitation shall be counted from the date of service of the effective judgment of the administrative action of patent invalidation; and

for other interested parties, the limitation shall be counted from the day when the effective judgment is known or should be known to other interested parties.

SECTION III ISSUES/DISPUTES ARISING IN THE LAW APPLICATION

§2.03 THE APPLICATION OF THE SYSTEM "RULING TO DISMISS THE ACTION AND INITIATING A SEPARATE ACTION" IN DIFFERENT TRIAL PROCEDURES

Although the provision is that the action "may" (not shall) be ruled to be dismissed, it is found from the retrieval of relevant cases that since the implementation of the judicial interpretation in 2016, in the case that the claims asserted by the patentee are invalidated in the invalidation procedure, most plaintiffs chose to withdraw the actions on their initiative, or the court ruled to dismiss the actions, and the circumstances of ruling to suspend the actions are rare.

[A] In the Case That the Patent Involved Is Invalidated in the First Instance Procedure, the Patentee May Withdraw the Action on His Initiative, or the Court May Rule to Dismiss the Action

In the case that the claims asserted in the infringement are invalidated by the Patent Reexamination Board in the first instance, the plaintiff usually chooses to withdraw the action on his initiative, and the court usually approves such withdrawal. In the case that the patent involved is "recovered" in the subsequent patent invalidation administrative procedure, the patentee may refile an action according to Article 214 of the *Interpretation of the Supreme People's Court on the Application of the Civil Procedure Law of the People's Republic of China.*[1]

In the above circumstance, if the patentee does not withdraw the action and still asserts rights based on the invalidated claims, the Court of First Instance may dismiss the action according to the Article. In the case that the patent involved is "recovered" in the subsequent patent invalidation administrative procedure, the patentee may initiate a separate action according to the Article.

Case 1: In an infringement dispute over a patent right between JiangSu General Protecht Co. Ltd (GP Company) and Bull Group Co. Ltd. (Bull) et al. ((2018) Su 01 Min Chu No. 3440, etc., and (2020) Zui Gao Fa Zhi Min Zhong No. 227, etc.), GP company filed ten patent infringement actions against Bull related to socket safety to the Nanjing Intermediate Court in December 2018, with a claimed amount of CNY 999 million. The

1. Article 214 of the *Interpretation of the Supreme People's Court on the Application of the Civil Procedure Law*: where, after the plaintiff withdraws an action or the People's court deems that the plaintiff has withdrawn the action, the plaintiff institutes another action for the same claims, the People's court shall accept the action.

series of cases involve two patents: the patent for invention ZL201010297882.4 "Support slide-type safety door" and the patent for utility model ZL201020681902.3 "Safety protection device for power socket." In July 2019, the China National Intellectual Property Administration made decisions of invalidation No. 40759 and 40829 to declare the above two patents to be completely invalid.

In five actions related to the patent for invention ZL201010297882.4 "supporting sliding safety door," GP Company applied for withdrawing the action to the Court of First Instance on the grounds that the patent was declared invalid. In July 2019, the Nanjing Intermediate Court of First Instance issued a *Civil Ruling* to approve GP Company's application for withdrawal of the action.

In another five actions related to the patent for utility model ZL201020681902.3 "Safety protection device for power socket," the Nanjing Intermediate Court of First Instance dismissed the action of the GP Company. GP Company filed an appeal, requesting the revocation of the *Civil Ruling* of the first instance and remand of the case back to Nanjing Intermediate Court for retrial. In this regard, the Intellectual Property Court of the Supreme People's Court made a final ruling on April 20, 2020, to dismiss the appeal of GP Company and uphold the original ruling.

To sum up, if the claims for the infringement asserted are declared invalid in the first instance procedure, the plaintiff may voluntarily withdraw the action, or the court may rule to dismiss the action. In either case, where the decision of declaring the invalidation of the aforesaid claims is set aside by an effective administrative judgment, the patentee may initiate a separate action.

Note: in the case that the patent involved is partially invalidated and the claims maintained valid can still cover the alleged infringing object, the patentee should first compare the solutions of the alleged infringing object, upon receiving the decision of invalidation involved, and check whether to change the right basis or not, contact the court hearing the patent infringement dispute as soon as possible to propose new claims for the assertion of infringement, based on the claims that are maintained valid. If the right basis claimed is not changed in time, the Court of First Instance will dismiss the action of the patentee based on the invalidated claims.

Therefore, for the sake of prudence, when the action is filed, or the court is in the first informal session, the patentee shall propose as many claims as possible for the assertion of the right against the alleged infringing object, no later than the close of court debate of the first instance; and the patentee shall timely change the claims for the assertion of infringement when the claims are partially invalidated.

[B] In the Case That the Patent Involved Is Declared Invalid in the Second Instance Procedure, the Court may Rule to Dismiss the Action and Concurrently Set Aside the First-Instance Judgment, and May Suspend the Action in Some Circumstances

On the one hand, where the claims asserted by the patentee are declared invalid in the second instance procedure, it indicates that the patent infringement action is still faced with the influence of the unstable validity of rights. Therefore, the Court of Second

Instance may rule to dismiss the action of the patentee. When the court rules to dismiss the action of the patentee, it should concurrently revoke the first-instance judgment.

Case 2: In an infringement dispute over a patent right for utility model between Hunan HuaHui New Energy Co. Ltd. (Huahui Company) and Dongguan Liyuan Battery Ltd. (Liyuan Company) ((2017) Yue Min Zhong No. 1111), the patent involved was partially invalidated in the second instance procedure, wherein the asserted Claim 1 is invalidated. The Court of Second Instance ruled to revoke the first-instance judgment and dismiss the action of the patentee. The patentee applied for a retrial to the Supreme People's Court, and the Supreme People's Court dismissed the retrial petition of the patentee.

In this case, the asserted Claim 1 by the patentee is invalidated in the second instance procedure, and the Court of Second Instance applies the provision "ruling to dismiss the action first and initiating a separate action" according to the Article to dismiss the action of the plaintiff in the original trial and revoke the first-instance judgment.

On the other hand, in the case that the Court of First Instance has determined that the infringement is established and the procedure of patent infringement action is drawing to a close, and the Court of Second Instance revokes the original judgment and rules to dismiss the action, it will cause the judicial procedure to be restarted from the first instance, which is a waste of judicial resources. In particular, the Intellectual Property Court of the Supreme People's Court was established in China on January 1, 2019; it unifies the right to hear civil and administrative patent cases. Under such circumstance, if the patent right is invalidated in the second instance, the attorney may put the decision of invalidation and relevant evidence as new evidence for examination, and the court may rule to dismiss the action or suspend the trial of the second instance according to the specific circumstances of the case.

[C] In the Case That the Patent Involved Is Declared Invalid in the Second Instance Procedure, If the Patentee Applies for Withdrawing the Action, the Consent of the Other Party Shall Be Required

In the case that the claims for the assertion of infringement are declared invalid by the Patent Reexamination Board in the second instance, if the plaintiff of the original trial applies for withdrawing the action, the consent of the other party shall be required. If the other party agrees with the withdrawal and the national interests, social public interests, and the legitimate rights and interests of others are not harmed, such withdrawal may be approved.

Case 3: In an infringement dispute over a patent right for utility model between Ningbo Norman Electronic Technology Co. Ltd. (Norman Company) and Jindong Copy Service Agency in Mazhang District of Zhanjiang City ((2019) Zui Gao Fa Zhi Min Zhong No. 75), the Guangzhou Intellectual Property Court determined in the first instance that the Jindong Copy Service Agency constituted the infringement and should bear the liability of compensation. During the second instance, the claims asserted by

Norman Company in the first instance were declared invalid by the China National Intellectual Property Administration. Therefore, Norman Company applied for withdrawing the action to the Court of Second Instance. Upon the inquiry of the court, Jindong Copy Service Agency did not agree with Norman Company's withdrawal of the action. The Intellectual Property Court of the Supreme Court ruled to revoke the first-instance judgment and dismiss the action of Norman Company in the second instance.

In this case, the patent involved was invalidated in the second instance procedure, and the patentee applied for withdrawing the action, but the other party did not agree, so the Court of Second Instance ruled to revoke the first-instance judgment and dismiss the action of the patentee. According to the provisions of the Article, the patentee may initiate a separate action after the patent right is restored to be effective. *Note:* If the other party agrees that the patentee withdraws the action, according to the provision of Article 338 of the *Interpretation of the Supreme People's Court on the Application of the Civil Procedure Law of the People's Republic of China*,[2] if the patentee refiles an action after the patent involved is restored to be effective, the people's court shall not accept such action. Therefore, from the perspective of subsequent refiling, if the patent involved is invalidated in the second instance procedure, the patentee should carefully take the initiative to withdraw the action.

[D] If the Patent Involved Is Determined to Be Invalid by the Administrative Judgment of the Court, the Provision "Ruling to Dismiss the Action and Initiating a Separate Action" May Be Applied by Reference

The Article clarifies that if the claims asserted by the patentee in the infringement action are declared invalid by the Patent Reexamination Board, the provision "ruling to dismiss the action and initiating a separate action" may be applied. Then, if the patent involved is determined by the final administrative judgment of the Supreme Court that it does not possess the substantive granting requirements of a patent, can the provision "ruling to dismiss the action and initiating a separate action" be applied?

Case 4: In an infringement dispute over a patent right for invention between CAO Guilan, HU Meiling, JIANG Li, JIANG Haotian and Chongqing Lifan Automobile Sales Co. Ltd., Chongqing Lifan Passenger Vehicle Co. Ltd., Wieson Automotive Co. Ltd., Nanjing Jiuhuashan Automobile Maintenance Co. Ltd., Lifan Industry (Group) Co. Ltd, Hangzhou Yafan Automobile Co. Ltd. ((2018) Su Min Zai No. 47), the patent involved is the patent right for invention ZL200710019425.7 "Shark fin type antenna." The

2. Article 338 of the *Interpretation of the Supreme People's Court on the Application of the Civil Procedure Law of the People's Republic of China*: If, in the procedure at second instance, the plaintiff in original trial applies for withdrawal of an action, the People's court may approve the application upon consent of other parties without damaging the interests of the state, public interests or the legitimate rights of others. Where withdrawal of the action is approved, the People's court shall rule to concurrently revoke the first-instance judgment. Where the plaintiff in original trial brings an action again after he or it withdraws the original action in the procedure at second instance, the People's court shall not accept such action.

original China National Intellectual Property Administration made examination Decision No. 25637 to maintain the validity of the patent involved. Lifan Company was not satisfied with the sued decision of invalidation and filed an administrative action, and repeatedly failed in the Beijing Intellectual Property Court of First Instance and the Beijing High Court of Second Instance. In December 2019, the Supreme Court retried the case and held that the determination in the sued decision regarding that Claim 1 involves an inventive step is incorrect, and revoked the decision involved ((2019) Zui Gao Fa Xing Zai No. 268).

The Jiangsu Provincial High People's Court held in the retrial that the provision "ruling to dismiss the action first and initiating a separate action" aims at avoiding the long trial period and idling procedures in actions of civil infringement of the patent. Although the Patent Reexamination Board made the sued decision to maintain the validity of the patent right involved, the decision was set aside by the final administrative judgment made by the Supreme People's Court. Judging from the judgment grounds of the administrative judgment, the Supreme People's Court revoked the sued decision on the basis that Claim 1 of the patent involved does not involve an inventive step, which is the substantive granting requirement of a patent. Considering the following factors, this case meets the conditions for applying the Article by reference, and the action of CAO Guilan et al. based on Claim 1 of the patent involved is dismissed.

In this case, the Jiangsu High Court made it clear that if a patent was determined by the final administrative judgment of the Supreme Court that it did not possess substantive granting requirements, the provision "ruling to dismiss the action and initiating a separate action" may be applied by reference, and the reasons are as follows: although the Patent Reexamination Board is the subject for determining the validity of the claims of a patent, the Supreme Court, as the judicial organ that conducts judicial review of the invalid examination decision according to the law, has the right to make a relevant determination on whether the claims of the patent meet the substantive granting requirements of a patent. Therefore, this circumstance can refer to applying the provision "ruling to dismiss the action and initiating a separate action."

Case 5: In an infringement dispute over the patent right for design between Beijing Century Beking Furniture Co. Ltd. and Yiyi (Tianjin) Furniture Co. Ltd. (Yiyi Company) et al., Yiyi Company filed a request for invalidation of the patent right involved, and the Patent Reexamination Board made a decision of invalidation to maintain the validity of the patent right involved. Yiyi Company was not satisfied with the decision and filed an administrative action to Beijing Intellectual Property Court. The first-instance judgment determined that the patent involved should be invalid. The Court of First Instance held that the legal effect that the people's court revoked the decision to maintain the validity of the patent involved made by the Patent Reexamination Board is the same as the legal effect of the Patent Reexamination Board's declaration of invalidation of the patent involved. In the case that the decision made by the Patent Reexamination Board to maintain the validity of the patent involved has been revoked by the Court of First Instance, the action of the plaintiff shall also be dismissed in accordance with the above provision. The Court of Second Instance upheld the first-instance judgment on the same grounds.

It can be seen that if the patent involved is determined to be invalid by the court, the provision "ruling to dismiss the action and initiating a separate action" specified in this chapter may be applied by reference.

[1] *Handling of Corresponding Matters after the Action Is Ruled to Be Dismissed*

[a] *If the Action Is Dismissed by Ruling, the Provisional Measures Shall Be Lifted*

According to the following legal provisions, if the plaintiff's action is ruled to be dismissed, the provisional measures shall be lifted:

> Article 23 of the *Provisions of the Supreme People's Court on Several Issues Concerning the Handling of Property Preservation Cases by the People's Courts* prescribes that: After a people's court takes a property preservation measure, under any of the following circumstances, the preservation applicant shall apply for removal of preservation in a timely manner: (4) Another people's court does not accept the action instituted, permits the withdrawal of the action, or deems that the action has been withdrawn; and (5) An action instituted or the claims in the action are dismissed by an effective judgment or ruling of another people's court.

Case 6: In an infringement dispute over the patent right between Qualcomm Incorporated (Qualcomm Company) and Apple Electronics Products Commerce (Beijing) Co. Ltd., Apple Computer Trading (Shanghai) Co. Ltd., Apple Trading (Shanghai) Co. Ltd., and Fuzhou Taihe Branch of Apple Electronics Products Commerce (Beijing) Co. Ltd. (Apple Company) (...), Qualcomm Company applied to Fuzhou Intermediate People's Court on July 10, 2018, for ordering Apple Company to stop the behavior of infringing patent rights. On November 30, 2018, Fujian High Court ruled that Apple Company should immediately cease importing, offering to sell, and selling infringing products iPhone 6s, iPhone 6s Plus, iPhone 7, iPhone 7 Plus, iPhone 8, iPhone 8 Plus, and iPhone X (excluding products manufactured by Pegatron Corporation) which infringe the patent involved.

On April 17, 2019, Qualcomm Company and Apple Company announced a settlement, withdrew all lawsuits between the two companies worldwide, and reached a six-year direct licensing agreement. In July 2019, the China National Intellectual Property Administration issued the decision to announce the patent involved ZL200480042119.X (named "Mobile terminal and method with ergonomic imaging functions") in regard to which the Apple products were banned to be sold by the Fuzhou Intermediate People's Court, to be completely invalid.

In this case, after the sales ban was issued, both parties quickly reached a settlement, which was due to the powerful deterrent force of the behavior ban on the parties. In judicial practice, in some cases involving evidence preservation or property preservation, after the patent involved is declared invalid, if the court decides to dismiss the plaintiff's action, the corresponding preservation measures should also be lifted.

Note: If the court preserving the property is different from the court hearing the patent infringement action, the property preservation measures shall be lifted upon the application of the applicant. On the contrary, the property preservation measures shall be automatically lifted.

[2] After the Action Is Ruled to Be Dismissed, the Facts and Evidence Materials Determined in the Original Trial Shall Be Properly Kept

Since the Court of Second Instance ruled to dismiss the action from procedure based on the invalidation of the patent and did not respond to the first-instance judgment, the evidence already determined in the first-instance judgment should not be simply rejected, especially for the contents confirmed by the parties in the trial transcripts, which generally have binding force on the parties in a separate action.

Case 7: In an infringement dispute over a patent right for invention between Yulong Computer Telecommunication Science (Shenzhen) Co. Ltd. (Yulong Company) and Xiaomi Communications Co. Ltd, Xiaomi Inc., Xiaomi Home Commercial Co. Ltd. ((2019) Zui Gao Fa Zhi Min Zhong No. 507), the patent involved was completely invalidated in the first instance, and the Court of First Instance ruled to dismiss the action of the patentee. The plaintiff in the original trial, Yulong Company, was not satisfied with the ruling and filed an appeal, in which the plaintiff in the original trial stated that the case belongs to the case where the action should be suspended, not the case where the action should be dismissed. If the action of the case is dismissed, once the court revokes the decision of invalidation, Yulong Company can only file an action again, which will undoubtedly increase the burden on the patentee. There may even be a risk of damage or loss of the evidence preserved, resulting in that it may be impossible for infringement comparison even if an action is refiled in the future, which is not conducive to the protection of intellectual property rights.

In this regard, the Intellectual Property Court of the Supreme Court of Second Instance held that the provision (Article 2 of the *Judicial Interpretation II*) designed the system "ruling to dismiss the action first and initiating a separate action" to mitigate the impact, which is conducive to improving the efficiency of hearing the patent infringement action, while not affecting the litigation rights of the patentee. In this case, the claims of the patent involved based on which Yulong Company filed an action have been declared invalid by the China National Intellectual Property Administration, and the original court's ruling to dismiss the action of Yulong Company complies with the above provision. If the above decision of invalidation is finally revoked by the effective administrative judgment, Yulong Company may initiate a separate action to continue to claim rights against Xiaomi Communication Company et al., and there is no adverse effect to the litigation rights and substantive rights of Yulong Company. Whether the evidence materials involved will be damaged or lost is unknown, and even if there is such a possibility, it is the risk of evidence preservation and providing that should be borne by the parties, which is irrelevant to whether the action is ruled to be dismissed.

Note: The time point for the patentee to file a separate action is when the decision to declare the above claims invalid is revoked by an **effective** administrative judgment. In view of the fact that some cases may require 2-3 years or longer to obtain the effective judgment due to the undergoing of the first instance, second instance, or even retrial of administrative action. During this period, the patentee should properly keep the evidence and exhibits which involve infringement so as to prevent the damage or loss of evidence from causing obstacles to the subsequent litigation and rights protection.

In addition, for patent infringement disputes involving chemicals with a strict quality guarantee period, in order to avoid as much as possible the adverse consequences caused by "ruling to dismiss the action and initiating a separate action" due to the invalidation of the patent right involved, the patentee should try his best to persuade the Court of First Instance to fix the technical solutions of the alleged infringement object. In this way, even if the patent involved is declared invalid in the first instance, there will be no consequence that the alleged infringing product cannot be used due to damaging, lost, or out of the expiry date because the technical solutions of the alleged infringing object have been fixed.

§2.04 CONCLUSION

In the case that the patent involved is invalidated, in the first instance procedure, the Court of First Instance may rule to dismiss the action of the patentee according to this law, or the patentee may voluntarily withdraw the action; in the second instance procedure, the withdrawal of the action of the patentee requires the consent of the other party. If the other party does not agree, the Court of Second Instance may rule to revoke the first-instance judgment, dismiss the action of the patentee, and suspend the action under exceptional circumstances. This chapter also provides the cases in which the provision "ruling to dismiss the action and initiating a separate action" are applied by reference when the patent involved is determined by the administrative judgment of the Supreme Court that it does not possess the substantive requirements for patent granting. This chapter also discusses the handling procedures of corresponding matters after the action is ruled to be dismissed.

CHAPTER 3

Ruling to Suspend the Action for Obvious Violation of Article 26.3 and Article 26.4: A Report Series on Law Interpretation and Case Study Related to Patent Infringement

Zhang Qiulin & Ge Xiaomei

The structure of the separation of civil and administrative trials is the current state of the patent infringement procedure and right determination procedure in China. In a circumstance where the description cannot interpret the claims due to conflicts in the patent documents, it should be first judged whether "the unique understanding" can be obtained. If "the unique understanding" can be obtained, an interpretation should be made according to such understanding; and if not, a right determination procedure of the patent administrative department is required. Only if the party concerned makes it clear that he will not initiate an administrative procedure can the court determine the protection scope according to the reciting of the claims.

§3.01 BASIC PROVISIONS OF LAWS

***Interpretation (II) of the Supreme People's Court on Several Issues concerning the Application of Law in the Trial of Patent Infringement Dispute Cases* (hereinafter referred as "*Judicial Interpretation II*")**

Article 3 provides that where any patent right is requested to be declared invalid because the description cannot be used to interpret the claims due to an obvious violation of Article 26.3 and 26.4 of the Chinese Patent Law, and the case does not fall within the scope of the circumstances as prescribed in Article 4 of this Interpretation, the people's court that tries the patent infringement dispute case shall generally rule to suspend the action; or where the patent right is not requested to be declared invalid during a reasonable period, the people's court may, according to the reciting in the claims, determine the protection scope of the patent.

Article 8 of Several Provisions of the Supreme People's Court on Issues concerning the Application of Law in the Trial of Cases on Patent Dispute provides that the plaintiff who institutes a patent infringement action alleging infringement upon the patent for utility model before October 1, 2009 may provide the search report made by the patent administrative department of the State Council. The plaintiff who institutes a patent infringement action alleging infringement upon the patent for utility model or design on or after October 1, 2009 may provide the patent assessment report made by the patent administrative department of the State Council. As required for the trial of a case, the people's court may require the plaintiff to submit the search report or the patent assessment report. Where the plaintiff fails to submit the report without any justifiable cause, the people's court may render a ruling to suspend the action or rule to order the plaintiff to assume potential adverse consequences.

Where the defendant in a case involving a dispute over infringement upon a utility model or design patent requests suspension of the action, the defendant shall file a request for declaring invalidation of the plaintiff's patent during the period of submitting a statement of defense.

Article 9 of Several Provisions of the Supreme People's Court on Issues concerning the Application of Law in the Trial of Cases on Patent Dispute provides that where, in a case involving a dispute over infringement upon a utility model or design patent, the defendant files a request for declaring invalidation of the patent during the period of submitting a statement of defense, the people's court trying the case shall suspend the action. However, under any of the following circumstances, the people's court may rule not to suspend the action:

(1) the search report or patent assessment report provided by the plaintiff does not contain any cause that leads to the invalidation of the patent for utility model or design;
(2) evidence provided by the defendant is sufficient to prove that the technology used by the defendant is in common knowledge;
(3) the defendant's evidence or reason for a request for declaring invalidation of the patent is apparently insufficient;
(4) the people's court otherwise deems that the action shall not be suspended.

Article 10: Where, in a case involving a dispute over infringement upon a utility model or design patent, the defendant files a request for declaring invalidation of the patent after the period of submitting a statement of defense ends, the people's court trying the case shall not suspend the action unless it deems the suspension necessary after review.

Article 11: Where, in a case involving a dispute over infringement upon a patent for an invention or over infringement upon a patent for utility model or design which has been sustained by the Patent Reexamination Board, the defendant files a request for declaring invalidation of the patent during the period of submitting a statement of defense, the people's court trying the case may rule not to suspend the action.

§3.02 INTERPRETATION OF THE PROVISIONS

Although the system of ruling to dismiss the action and initiating a separate action provided in Article 2 of the *Judicial Interpretation II* has made active exploration in improving the efficiency of action, subject to the current legal provisions, it cannot fundamentally solve the problem of long trial period caused by the "separation of civil and administrative trials."

Therefore, Article 3 of the *Judicial Interpretation II* stipulates that in a circumstance where a patent obviously violates Article 26.3 or 26.4 of the Chinese Patent Law and should be declared invalid, the court trying the patent infringement case can only first make an explanation to the party concerned and inform him to initiate the patent invalidation declaration procedure unless it pertains to the circumstances specified in Article 4 of the *Judicial Interpretation II*. If the invalidation procedure is initiated, the patent infringement action shall generally be suspended. Of course, if, by comparison, the alleged infringement technical solution does not fall within the protect scope of the patent right, it is not necessary to suspend the action, and the court can directly judge that the defendant does not infringe the patent right. Only if the patent right is not requested to be declared invalid within a reasonable period of time can the people's court determine the protection scope of the patent according to the reciting of the claims. The obvious violation mentioned in this chapter refers to that the claims and the description are totally inconsistent, constituting a substantive contradiction in the technical solution so that the description cannot be used to interpret the claims. In other circumstances where the claims are not supported by the description, this chapter shall not be applied to avoid excessive interference of the infringement procedure in the invalidation procedure and the resulting problem of inconsistent judgment standards.

According to the above provisions, if the claims cannot be interpreted by the description due to the contradiction in the patent documents:

(1) first of all, it should be judged whether "the unique understanding" regarding the ambiguity can be obtained;
(2) if the unique understanding can be obtained, the reciting of the claims shall be corrected according to such understanding; if not, the following steps shall be carried out;
(3) after preliminary infringement comparison, if it can be concluded that the alleged infringement solution does not fall within the protection scope of the patent right, the court may be requested to make a direct determination of non-infringement without applying for suspension of the action;
(4) if there is any risk of infringement, the invalidation procedure should be initiated for the patent involved, and a request for suspension of the action should be made to the court trying the infringement dispute case;

(5) if no invalidation request is made within a reasonable period of time, the protection scope of the patent may be determined according to the reciting of the claims.

If the protection scope of the patent still cannot be determined according to the reciting of the claims, what should be done? There are no clear provisions in the current effective judicial interpretation documents. Article 5 of the *Judicial Interpretation II (Draft for Comments)* stipulated that the action could be dismissed in such cases, but it was not written in the *Judicial Interpretation II*. The No. 55 guidance case issued by the Supreme Court points out that for the patent right having an obviously unclear protection scope, the alleged infringement technical solution shall not be deemed to constitute infringement. In practice, we find that the court trying a patent infringement dispute case is very cautious in determining whether the claims are clear, and the application of the rules established in the No. 55 guidance case is strictly limited.

Article 59 of the Chinese Patent Law provides that the extent of protection of the patent right for invention or utility model shall be determined by the terms of the claims. The description and the appended drawings may be used to interpret the content of the claims. This chapter is further refined by Article 2 of *the Interpretation of the Supreme People's Court on Several Issues concerning the Application of Law in the Trial of Patent Infringement Dispute Cases*. That is to say, the claims and the description and the drawings shall be naturally harmonious and consistent. If necessary, it is a common practice to interpret the claims by observing and shifting among the claims and the description as well as the drawings in determining the protection scope of the claims in the patent infringement action. Taking a step back, if ambiguity exists in the claims but the unique understanding can be obtained, the ambiguity can be corrected by using the unique understanding according to Article 4 of the *Judicial Interpretation II*. Moreover, if the description cannot be used to interpret the claims due to the obvious violation of Article 26.3 and Article 26.4 of the Chinese Patent Law, the protection scope of the claims can be determined only according to the reciting of the claims based on Article 3 of the *Judicial Interpretation II*. Finally, if the protection scope of the claims is obviously unclear, according to the No. 55 guidance case, the alleged infringement technical solution cannot be determined to constitute infringement. It can be seen from the above discussion that the above four circumstances are common, rare, very rare and barely seen, respectively, and there is a strict order of application among the above circumstances.

§3.03 ISSUES/DISPUTES ARISING IN THE LAW APPLICATION

[A] The Protection Scope of the Claims Is Determined According to the Reciting of the Claims in the Circumstances of Obviously Being Insufficient in Disclosure, Being Not Supported by the Description, and Being Unclear

Case 1: In an infringement dispute over a patent for utility model between Chuangqun Machinery Co. Ltd. and Dongguan Dianzhen Machinery Co. Ltd. ((2014) Yue Gao Fa Min San Zhong Zi No. 1212), after comprehensive analysis, Guangdong Higher People's Court first denied the application of Article 4 of the *Judicial Interpretation II*: on the basis of reading the whole patent literature involved in the case, those skilled in the art cannot be obviously aware of the existence of the defect, nor can they obtain the only correct interpretation after correction of the defect, failing to accurately determine the technical solution and the protection scope of the patent involved. Therefore, the "shift lever" recited in Claim 2 of the patent involved cannot be identified as the ambiguity specified in the judicial interpretation, to which provisions of Article 4 of the *Judicial Interpretation II* cannot be applied. On the contrary, according to Article 3 of the *Judicial Interpretation II*, Guangdong Higher People's Court deems that the protection scope of the patent shall be determined based on the reciting of the claims. The asserted Claim 2 defines that the clamping claws are pushed and pulled by the shift lever to move close to or apart from each other. Since the technical solution of the alleged infringement product does not include the technical feature that "the clamping claws are pushed and pulled by the shift lever to move close to or apart from each other," it does not fall within the protection scope of the patent involved.

Case 2: In an infringement dispute over a patent for utility model between Hangzhou CHIC Intelligent Technology Co. Ltd. and Zhejiang Luqi Intelligent Technology Co. Ltd. and Shenzhen Ruiyi Innovation Technology Co. Ltd. ((2018) Yue Min Zai No. 245), Guangdong Higher People's Court applied the second-best, i.e., Article 3 of the *Judicial Interpretation II*. Specifically, one of the disputes between the two parties lies in whether the alleged infringement product possesses the technical feature "a power supply, a controller and a plurality of sensors fixed on the inner cover" of Claim 1, especially whether the number of the power supply and the controller therein is one. First, based on the provision of Article 59 of the Chinese Patent Law, the court deems that it is difficult to reach the conclusion that the number of the "power supply and controller" in the above technical feature must be defined to one, in this case, no matter from the disclosure of Claim 1 and the description of the patent involved or from the purpose of the invention. Then, the court applies Article 3 of the *Judicial Interpretation II* as the second-best: even if the beneficial effect disclosed in the description present in the patent of this case is redundant and cannot be used to interpret the claims, in the circumstance that the defendant has filed twice the request for declaring invalidation of the patent and voluntarily withdrawn it twice, resulting in that the patent right in this case is still valid, the protection scope of the patent can be determined according to the reciting of the claims. Claim 1 of the patent involved does not define the number of the power supply and controller. To sum up, it is appropriate to judge in the first and second instance that the determination that the number of the power supply and controller of the alleged infringement product accused is more than one does not affect the determination that it falls within the protection scope of the patent right.

[B] The Claims Are Obviously Unclear and Cannot Be Protected

An accurate definition of the protection scope of the patent right is the prerequisite to determine whether the alleged infringement technical solution constitutes infringement. If there are obvious defects in the writing of the claims, and the specific meaning of the technical terms in the claims cannot be determined in combination with the description and the drawings of the patent involved and the common knowledge in the art as well as the related prior art, resulting in that the protection scope of the patent cannot be accurately determined, it is impossible to make a meaningful infringement comparison between the patent and the alleged infringement technical solution. Therefore, for the patent right having an obvious unclear protection scope, it cannot be determined that the alleged infringement technical solution constitutes infringement.

Case 3: In an infringement dispute over a patent for utility model between BAI Wanqing and Chengdu Nanxunpin Marketing Service Center, Shanghai Tianxiang Industry Co. Ltd. ((2012) Min Shen Zi No. 1544, No. 55 guidance case issued by the Supreme People's Court), according to the description of the patent involved and the relevant evidence provided by BAI Wanqing, it is difficult for those skilled in the art to determine the specific scope or meaning of "high magnetic conductivity" in the technical feature C of Claim 1, and it is impossible to determine the protection scope of Claim 1 and make a meaningful infringement comparison between Claim 1 and the alleged infringement product. Therefore, it is appropriate to determine in the second-instance judgment that BAI Wanqing fails to prove that the alleged infringement product falls within the protection scope of the patent involved with evidence.

[C] A Request for Declaring Invalidation Is Filed Beyond the Defense Period, and an Application for Suspending the Action Is Made

According to the provisions of Articles 10 and 11 of *Several Provisions of the Supreme People's Court on Issues concerning the Application of Law in the Trial of Cases on Patent Dispute*, the defendant shall file a request for declaring invalidation of the patent involved during the defense period. If the defendant fails to in time or neglect to file the request for declaring invalidation during the defense period, he can continue to file the request for declaring invalidation according to Article 3 of the *Judicial Interpretation II*, and further try to apply to the people's court for suspension of the action by taking the following as one of the reasons for invalidation: the disclosure in the description is obviously insufficient, the claims are obviously not supported by the description, or the claims are obviously unclear.

§3.04 CONCLUSION

The ambiguity in the claims can be corrected by using the unique understanding according to Article 4 of the *Judicial Interpretation II*. The final application of Article 3 of the *Judicial Interpretation II*, on the one hand, physically requires that the disclosure in the description is obviously insufficient, the claims are obviously not supported by the description, or the claims are obviously unclear, and on the other hand, procedurally depends on whether the request for declaring invalidation is filed within a reasonable period of time. The result of the application is either to decide to suspend the action or to determine the protection scope of the patent according to the reciting of the claims.

CHAPTER 4

Eclectic Interpretation Principle

He Yibo & Ge Xiaomei

Defining the protection scope of claims of a patent is a precondition and basis for conducting technical comparison and determining if the accused infringing technical solution falls within the protection scope of claims of the patent. The accurate delimitation of the protection scope of claims depends on the interpretation of claims. RiCh, the former chief judge of the United States Court of Appeals for the Federal Circuit, once said, "the name of the game is claim" for modern patent laws. This chapter is the start of the second part of the Report Series, "Interpretation of the Protection Scope of Claims," in an attempt to reveal the rules of the game (rules on interpretation of claims) with detailed and typical cases. This chapter discusses eleven judicial cases for the "Eclectic Interpretation Principle."

§4.01 BASIC PROVISIONS OF LAWS

***Interpretation of the Supreme People's Court on Several Issues concerning the Application of Law in the Trial of Patent Infringement Dispute Cases* (hereinafter referred to as "*Interpretation I*")**

Article 2 The people's court shall determine the content of a claim as provided for in paragraph 1 of Article 59 of the Patent Law according to the description of the claim and in consideration of the understanding of the claim by persons of ordinary skill in the art after reading the Description and Drawings.

***Patent Law of the People's Republic of China* (hereinafter referred to as "*Patent Law*")**

Article 59 The extent of protection of the patent right for invention or utility model shall be determined by the terms of the claims. The description and the appended drawings may be used to interpret the claims.

Several Provisions of the Supreme People's Court on Issues concerning the Application of Law in the Trial of Cases on Patent Disputes (2015 Amendment)

Article 17 "The extent of protection of the patent right for invention or utility model shall be determined by the terms of the claims. The description and the appended drawings may be used to interpret the claims" as mentioned in paragraph 1 of Article 59 of the Patent Law means that the extent of protection of the patent shall be determined by the extent determined by all technical features recited in the claims, and shall also include the extent determined by the features that are equivalent to these technical features.

§4.02 INTERPRETATION OF THE PROVISIONS

There are two relatively extreme theories about the interpretation of claims. The first is the central definition principle, according to which the patent system protects an inventive concept, and the claims are only an example of that inventive concept. Therefore, the interpretation of claims should not be confined to the literal meaning of claims but should focus on the technical solutions recited in the claims and provide a comprehensive understanding of the overall concept of the invention and creation through the Description and Drawings so as to expand the protection scope to that expected by the patentee. The second is the peripheral definition principle, according to which the patentee has defined the boundary of invention and creation in the claims, and the words of the claims should be strictly and faithfully interpreted, whose literal meaning is the protection scope of the patent.

On the basis of drawing lessons from foreign legislation examples, Article 2 of the *Interpretation I* clarifies the eclectic interpretation principle that has always been adhered to in the patent trial practice of our country. That is, the claims can neither be interpreted in full accordance with the literal meaning thereof nor can the claims be regarded as technical guidance that can be interpreted at will. A middle way between the above two extreme interpretation principles should be taken so that the interpretation of the claims can not only reasonably protect the interests of the patentee but also make the social public clearly determine the boundary of the patent. In fact, the application and limitation of the doctrine of equivalents are derived from this interpretation principle.

In addition, "persons of ordinary skill in the art" is contained in the chapter. First, "persons of ordinary skill in the art" is a legal fictitious person, which is an abstract concept. The persons of ordinary skill in the art refer to the technical personnel with the average knowledge level of the technical field to which the patent belongs when the infringement occurs and are neither a technical expert in the field nor a person who does not understand the technology. Second, although according to the explanation by the drafters, the introduction of the concept is based on the provisions of Article 26.3

of the Patent Law, the meaning of the concept is different from that of "person skilled in the art" in the *Guidelines for Patent Examination 2010*. "Persons of ordinary skill in the art" is distinguished from the "person skilled in the art" in the patent confirmation procedure in that the former takes "when the infringement occurs" as the time node for delimitation of knowledge level, while the latter takes "the patent application date or priority date" as the time node. Finally, based on the current search results, in judicial practice, the Supreme People's Court currently has no ruling/order involving the aforementioned time node difference.

§4.03 POTENTIAL ISSUES/DISPUTES ARISING IN THE LAW APPLICATION

[A] If There Are Different Understandings of the Content of the Claims, the Interpretation Shall Be Made According to the Description and Drawings

Case 1: In the case of infringement dispute over a patent for utility model between Guangzhou New GEP Decoration Material Co. Ltd. and FU Zhihong and Taishan Xianqu Building Materials Co. Ltd. ((2010) Min Shen Zi No. 871 Civil Ruling Paper issued by the Supreme People's Court[1]), the key to determining whether the accused infringing product falls within the protection scope of the patent involved lies in how to understand the meaning expressed by the feature "a composite layer of magnesium gelling bamboo, wood, plant fiber" in Claim 1, that is, whether the commas indicate a coordinating relation or a selective relation.

In this regard, the Guangzhou Intermediate People's Court has held in the first instance that, as understood according to the common meaning, the composite layer is a mixture made of magnesium gel, bamboo, wood and plant fiber, namely, the parallel use of such three materials as bamboo, wood and plant fiber. However, in the examples of the Description of the patent, the composite layer is given a specific meaning, namely, a mixture made of magnesium chloride, magnesium oxide, and bamboo fiber or wood bran or plant fiber. One of the three materials, namely bamboo, wood and plant fiber, is selected. In accordance with the principle that the disclosure of Claim 1 mentioned above has priority, in this case, the protection scope of the patent shall be determined by the technical content recited in Claim 1, that is, the composite panel is made by parallel use of the three materials, namely, bamboo, wood and plant fiber.

However, the Higher People's Court of Guangdong Province has held in the second instance that if there are different understandings of the content recited in the claims, the claims can be interpreted based on the Description. In this case, the composite layer is further explained and specified in the examples of the Description of the patent; that is, the selective relation exists between the three materials, namely bamboo, wood and plant fiber.

1. Case 2 of Annual Report of the Supreme People's Court on Intellectual Property in 2010.

The Supreme People's Court has supported the judgment of the second instance in the retrial and has held that, based on the written expression of the relation between "bamboo, wood, plant fiber" in Claim 1 of the patent, it is difficult to determine whether the relation between the three is "and" or "or," and the interpretation should be conducted based on the relevant content disclosed in the Description. It has been disclosed in the examples of the Description of the patent that: "Magnesium gelling plant fiber layer is a mixture made of magnesium chloride, magnesium oxide, and bamboo fiber or wood bran or plant fiber." Accordingly, the disclosure of "bamboo, wood, plant fiber" in Claim 1 of the patent should cover the selective relation, that is, the composite layer comprises one of bamboo, wood and plant fiber, rather than it must comprise all the three materials.

In this case, the Supreme People's Court has clearly pointed out that if there are different understandings of the content of the claims, which lead to disputes over the protection scope of the claims, the Description and Drawings can be used to interpret the claims.

[B] The Interpretation of the Claims Shall Be Guided by the Conformity with the Purpose of the Invention and the Possibility to Realize the Technical Solution of the Invention

Case 2: In the case of infringement dispute over a patent for invention between Shenzhen Dunjun Technology Co. Ltd. and Shenzhen Tenda Technology Co. Ltd., Jinan Lixia Hongkang Electronic Product Operation Department, etc. ((2019) Zui Gao Fa Zhi Min Zhong No. 147), the parties have differed on the understanding of the feature "a first uplink HTTP message before the portal business user equipment fails the authentication" in Step A of Claim 1 of the patent involved.

In this regard, the Intellectual Property Court of the Supreme People's Court has held in the second instance that the eclectic interpretation principle should be observed in the interpretation of claims of a patent. For the specific application of the eclectic interpretation principle, it should be recognized that: first, the claims are the basis for defining the protection scope of a patent, and the Description and Drawings can be used to explain the relevant contents of the claims. The explanatory function of the Description and Drawings on the claims is reflected in helping the persons of ordinary skill in the art to accurately understand the content of the claims, but the Description and Drawings cannot replace the status and role of the claims in the process of defining the protection scope of the patent. Second, the interpretation of relevant technical terms or technical features in the claims should follow the principle of internal evidence precedence. If the relevant technical terms or technical features in the claims have been specially stated in the Description of the patent, the interpretation should be made in accordance with such special statements; if not, the interpretation should be made in accordance with the common understanding of the persons of ordinary skill in the art. Finally, the interpretation of the claims should be made on the basis of an overall understanding of technical solutions claimed in the claims of the patent of the persons of ordinary skill in the art in conjunction with the specific context of the claims to rationally define the protection scope of the claims, and be guided by the conformity with the purpose of the invention and the possibility to realize the technical solution of the invention.

According to the above-mentioned interpretation principles and rules, the "first uplink HTTP message" in Claim 1 of this case should be interpreted as the first uplink HTTP message sent to the access server by the user equipment that has not passed authentication and should not be interpreted as the first message in the process of the user equipment establishing a Transmission Control Protocol (TCP) "three-way handshake" connection with the actual website to be visited, for the following reasons:

First, the text in Step A of Claim 1 explicitly defines "HTTP message" and does not mention "TCP connection," "TCP three-way handshake message," and the like. To understand the "first uplink HTTP message" in Step A of Claim 1 as the first message in the three-way handshake process of establishing a TCP connection, a special statement is required in the Description and Drawings, and the adoption of this interpretation should ensure that the overall technical solution claimed in the patent involved meets the inventive purpose of the patent involved. However, in the contents disclosed in the Description and Drawings of the patent involved, there is no special statement regarding the "HTTP message" as defined in Step A of Claim 1. Therefore, the meaning of the "HTTP message" defined in Step A of Claim 1 should be interpreted according to the common understanding of the persons of ordinary skill in the art.

Second, in the field of network communication, HTTP and TCP are concepts that are connected to each other and have their own independent meanings. HTTP is located at the application layer, and HTTP messages refer to messages that use the HTTP protocol; TCP is located at the transport layer, and TCP messages refer to messages that use the TCP protocol. The persons of ordinary skill in the art will not regard any TCP handshake message as a message per se of application layer protocol, such as the HTTP protocol. If the "first uplink HTTP message" in Claim 1 of the patent involved is understood as "the first message in the three-way handshake process of establishing a TCP connection," it would violate the basic cognition of the persons of ordinary skill in the art.

Third, according to the overall design idea of the invention disclosed on pages 5/9 to 6/9 of the Description of the patent involved in conjunction with the definite disclosure in Step 3 on page 7/9 of the Description of the patent, the persons of ordinary skill in the art can understand that the "first uplink HTTP message" submitted directly to the "virtual Web server" in Step A of Claim 1 should obviously be interpreted as an "HTTP message," and it is unlikely to be interpreted as "the first of the TCP three-way handshake messages." This is because the "virtual Web server" (such as the virtual "www.sina.cn" Web server) analyzes the received "first uplink HTTP message" and virtualizes it into a message containing redirection information that the website that the user wants to access returns to the underlying hardware of the access server. If the "first uplink HTTP message" received by the "virtual Web server" is interpreted as the first of the TCP three-way handshake messages, then the message returned by the "virtual Web server" to the underlying hardware of the access server in the next step will necessarily be the second of the TCP three-way handshake messages. However, since the TCP three-way handshake messages cannot carry the redirection information, this will result in that in the technical solution of the patent involved, the "virtual Web server" will fail to, after receiving the first of the TCP three-way handshake messages, execute the step of "virtualizing it into a message containing redirection information that the website that the user wants to access returns to the underlying hardware of the access server," thereby leading to the failure to realize the entire patented technical solution. This further confirms that in Step A of Claim 1 of the patent involved, the "first uplink HTTP message" can only be an HTTP message and cannot be any TCP handshake message.

In this case, the Supreme People's Court has clearly pointed out the specific rules in application of the eclectic interpretation principle: first, the claims are the basis for defining the protection scope of a patent, and the Description and Drawings can be used to explain the relevant contents of the claims. Second, the interpretation of relevant technical terms or technical features in the claims should follow the principle of internal evidence precedence. Finally, the interpretation of the claims should be made on the basis of a general understanding of technical solutions claimed in the claims of the patent of the persons of ordinary skill in the art in conjunction with the specific context of the claims to rationally define the protection scope of the claims, and be guided by the conformity with the purpose of the invention and the possibility to realize the technical solution of the invention.

[C] The Disclosure of the Technical Effect in the Description Has an Interpretative Effect on the Relevant Technical Features of the Claims

Case 3: In the case of infringement dispute over a patent for invention between XIAO Yong and Shenzhen Seno Light Limited ((2019) Zui Gao Fa Min Shen No. 365[2]), the focus of the dispute between the two parties has involved the determination of the technical feature "a ring slot in a pluggable electrical connection to the LED light bar (2)" in Claim 1 of the patent involved. In this case, XIAO Yong has alleged that the meaning of the technical feature in the patent involved is clear, while the disclosure of the technical effect in the Description is introduced in the second-instance judgment to interpret the technical feature and the application of the law is incorrect.

In this regard, the Supreme People's Court has held in the retrial that *the first is about the necessity of interpretation of the claims.* The claims describe patented technical solutions in the form of written and digital recording of technical features. Based on the ambiguity and limitations of language and text, if the claims are not interpreted in a specific context, it will be difficult to accurately define the technical solutions to be expressed. Therefore, *in the process of determining the protection scope of a patent, the meanings of the claims should not be determined solely based on the claims themselves, regardless of whether the terms of the claims are literally clear. The second is about the timing of introducing the Description and Drawings to interpret the*

2. Case 3 of Annual Report of the Supreme People's Court on Intellectual Property in 2019.

claims. The content of the claims is an abstraction and generalization of the Description, and the content of the Description is a further explanation and description of the claims; that is, the Description creates the specific context in which the claims are applicable. Therefore, *in the process of interpreting the claims, it is necessary to systematically and comprehensively understand the technical solutions claimed by the patent based on the Description, and on this basis, to make an accurate determination of the technical features recited in the claims. The last is about the interpretive effect of the technical effects disclosed in the Description on the relevant technical features of the claims and the influence of the same on the application of the doctrine of equivalents.* Generally, what is described in the claims are the technical solutions defined by the technical features, namely, the composition of the invention, and the purpose of the invention and the related technical effects are disclosed in the Description. The beneficial effects reflected by the disclosure of technical effects in the Description are generally the progress made by the patent over the prior art. Due to the limitation of the patentee's knowledge of the prior art and the limitation of the patent examination department's search of the prior art, the technical effects disclosed in the Description can only serve as a reference for the interpretation of the claims. *For the disclosure of the technical effect of a specific technical feature of the claims in the Description, it is necessary to consider whether the technical effect is actually caused by the technical feature, the significance level of the technical effect and other factors, thereby making a synthetic determination of whether the technical feature in the claims should be limited by the technical effect disclosed in the Description.* When the doctrine of equivalents applies in infringement litigation, the technical effects that are clearly disclosed in the Description and can be determined by those skilled in the art should be considered.

Regarding the disputed technical feature, the claims only define that the connection relation between the light bar and the ring slot is a pluggable electrical connection and does not specifically define how to realize the pluggable electrical connection. However, it is clearly disclosed in the technical effect portion of the Description of the patent involved that: "Compared with the prior art, the LED lighting lamp of the present invention has the following advantages: ... Due to the structure of pluggable electrical connection between the LED light bar and the slot, the maintenance and trouble clearing of the LED lighting lamp are convenient. When one or several LED lamp beads are damaged, the lamp beads can be repaired or replaced by pulling out the corresponding LED light bar, without affecting the use of other LED light bars, so that the maintenance and use costs are minimized." According to the common understanding of those skilled in the art, the "pluggable electrical connection" of the patent involved can indeed achieve the above technical effects. Therefore, in the interpretation of the disputed technical feature, the above technical effects should be considered. In the inquiry procedure organized by the court, after confirmation by both parties, the corresponding technical feature of the accused infringing technical solution is that the LED light bar does not contact the ring slot in the plugging and unplugging process, while the electrical connection and fixation are achieved by soldering. The resulting technical effect is that when the light bar fails, the solder structure needs to be destroyed before the replacement and maintenance of the light bar. Therefore, the technical feature of the accused infringing technical solution that the fixation and electrical connection between the LED light bar and the ring slot are achieved through soldering is neither identical with nor equivalent to the disputed technical feature of the patent involved, and thus the accused infringing technical solution does not fall within the protection scope of the patent involved.

In this case, the Supreme People's Court has identified that: in the process of determining the protection scope of a patent, the meanings of the claims should not be determined solely based on the claims themselves, regardless of whether the terms of the claims are literally clear. For the determination of whether the relevant technical features of the claims should be limited by the technical effects disclosed in the Description, it is necessary to comprehensively consider whether the technical effects are actually caused by the technical features, as well as the significance level of the technical effects and other factors. On this basis, if the doctrine of equivalents applies, the technical effects that are clearly disclosed in the Description and can be determined by those skilled in the art should be considered.

[D] In Determination of the Definitive Effect of the Technical Effect, It Should Be Considered Whether the Technical Effect Is Actually Caused by the Technical Feature

Case 4: In the case of infringement dispute over a patent for utility model between Zhejiang Luqi Intelligent Technology Co. Ltd., etc., VS Hangzhou Chic Intelligent Technology Co. Ltd. ((2017) Zui Gao Fa Min Shen No. 3993 Civil Ruling Paper issued by the Supreme People's Court), the key to determining whether the accused infringing product falls within the protection scope of the patent involved is whether the beneficial effects disclosed in the Description of the patent involved have a limiting effect on the interpretation of technical features relating to the power supply and controller in Claim 1.

The relevant technical features of Claim 1 are: "a power supply, a controller and a plurality of sensors fixed on the inner cover, and an inductive switch fixed to a side of the inner cover facing away from the pedal area for sensing whether the blocking member moves." Luqi Company has argued that it is restricted in the Description of the patent in this case that there is one power supply and one controller, while the accused infringing product has a different number of power supply and controller. The accused infringing product has more than one inductive switch. Consequently, it has been argued that the accused infringing product does not fall within the protection scope of the patent.

In this regard, the Supreme People's Court has held that paragraph 33 of the Description of the patent involved discloses "The power supply and the controller are disposed in two parts of the vehicle body, respectively. Therefore, one power supply and one controller can control the two hub motors simultaneously, the assembly is easier, the wiring is more convenient, and more space is saved. Meanwhile, the weights on both sides of the vehicle body are better balanced thus to improve the self-balance of the vehicle body … ." In consideration of the context of this paragraph, it can be known that the above disclosure pertains to the beneficial effects of the technical solution of the patent involved. *Since none of the dependent claims of the patent involved sets further restrictions on the number of power supply and controller, those skilled in the art, upon reviewing the Description and Drawings, cannot and should not consider that the above-mentioned beneficial effects are produced by the technical solutions defined by the dependent claims of the patent involved, but should consider that the above-mentioned beneficial effects are produced by the technical solution defined by the independent claim of the patent involved.* If this is not the case, there is absolutely no need to disclose such beneficial effects in the Description. Furthermore, negating the limiting effect of beneficial effects on the interpretation of technical features neither is conducive to enhancing the publicity of granted patent documents and the predictability of patent right boundaries nor is favorable to improving the drafting quality of patent documents. Therefore, for the interpretation of the technical features of the number of power supply and controller in Claim 1 of the patent involved, the beneficial technical effects disclosed in paragraph 33 of the Description should be considered, and on this basis, the number of power supply and controller in the accused infringing product should be ascertained. On this basis, the Supreme People's Court has ordered the Higher People's Court of Guangdong Province to re-examine the case.

The Higher People's Court of Guangdong Province has formed a separate collegiate panel for retrial according to the law ((2018) Yue Min Zai No. 245 Civil Judgment), and held that: according to the disclosure of Claim 1, it does not define the number of power supply and controller. The relevant statement in paragraph 33 of the Description only proposes that the position arrangement can achieve the beneficial effect of using only one power supply and one controller for carrying out the control, but it does not limit the technical means in Claim 1 of the patent in this case that one and only one power supply and controller must be used. Even if the statement in this paragraph is construed as proposing an implementation solution of using only one power supply and one controller, it is just an example of the invention, and the illustrative description in the Description and Drawings cannot limit the protection scope of the patent. In this case, Luqi Company has not provided any evidence to prove that if the number of power supply and controller is not limited to one, the inventive purpose of the patent involved that "No operating lever required, relative rotation, and control of the balance car by only the feet" cannot be achieved. *Therefore, it is difficult to conclude in this case that the number of "power supply and controller" must be limited to one, no matter from the disclosure of Claim 1 and the Description of the patent involved or from the purpose of the invention.* In addition, as determined from the content of paragraph 33 of the Description of the patent, in this case, this paragraph summarizes multiple means and solutions for achieving beneficial effects, including the space arrangement of the inner cover and electronic component, the distribution of wheels, the position of the motor, and the like. The arrangement position of the inner cover, the position of the motor, etc., *are all related to the contents of dependent claims rather than Claim 1. Therefore, paragraph 33 of the Description is not a special interpretation or limitation of Claim 1. Even if some of the content of this paragraph cannot be included in the dependent claims, it lacks a legal basis to consider this part of the content as a limitation on Claim 1.*

In this case, the Supreme People's Court has held upon examination that the technical effects disclosed in paragraph 33 of the Description could not and should not be considered to be produced by dependent claims but should be identified to be produced by the independent claim. Furthermore, it has been held that for the interpretation of relevant technical features, the beneficial effects disclosed in the Description should be considered. The Supreme People's Court ordered a retrial by the Higher People's Court of Guangdong Province. The Higher People's Court of Guangdong Province has held that the above technical effects are related to the contents of dependent claims rather than Claim 1. That is, disagreeing with the Supreme People's Court, the Higher People's Court of Guangdong Province has held that the above disclosure of technical effects should not restrict the protection scope of the claims.

[E] The Content Disclosed in the Description Shall Not Be Used to Deny the Clear Meaning of the Terms of the Claims

Case 5: In the case of dispute over patent infringement between Xi'an Qinbang Telecom Material Co. Ltd. and Wuxi Longsheng Cable Material Factory and Shanghai Xisheng Cable Material Co. Ltd. ((2012) Min Ti Zi No. 3[3] Civil Judgment issued by the Supreme People's Court), one of the focal points of the dispute between the two parties is the understanding of the meaning of the technical feature "such that a surface of plastic film forms a 0.04-0.09 mm thick uneven rough surface" recited in Claim 1.

As to this technical feature, the retrial respondent Xi'an Qinbang Company has alleged that, as can be known from the examples of the Description of the patent involved, the technical feature "such that a surface of plastic film forms a 0.04-0.09 mm thick uneven rough surface" recited in Claim 1 of the patent refers to the thickness of the plastic film, not the thickness of the uneven rough surface of the plastic film surface. There is no expression of "the thickness of the uneven rough surface of the plastic film surface" in the art. The corresponding technical feature of the plastic film layer used by the petitioner for retrial is equivalent to the above-mentioned technical feature.

In this regard, the Supreme People's Court does not support interpreting the thickness as the thickness of the plastic film itself for the reason that the thicknesses of 0.04 mm, 0.09 mm and 0.07 mm disclosed in the examples of the Description of the patent all are thicknesses of plastic film, and the reasons are as follows:

> The first is about the relationship between the term in the technical feature "such that a surface of plastic film forms a 0.04-0.09 mm thick uneven rough surface" as recited in Claim 1 and the common terminology in the art. The meanings of the terms created by the patent drafter should be determined from the perspective of those skilled in the art based on the special meanings understood by those skilled in the art upon reviewing the claims, Description and Drawings. The common terms in the art cannot be used to replace the

3. Case 2 of Annual Report of the Supreme People's Court on Intellectual Property in 2012.

special terms of the patent drafter simply on the grounds that the special terms are not commonly used in the art.

The second is about the relationship between the technical feature "such that a surface of plastic film forms a 0.04-0.09 mm thick uneven rough surface" recited in Claim 1 and the thickness of plastic film mentioned in the examples of the Description of the patent in this case. For the interpretation of the meanings of the terms in the claims, according to the general principle of text interpretation, the same terms used in the claims should be considered to have the same meanings and different terms to have different meanings. Each term in the claims has its own independent meaning and should not be interpreted as redundant. Of course, the above-mentioned principle is only a guide rather than a rigid rule. Interpreting the meanings of the terms of the claims should be done in consideration of the common understanding of those skilled in the art upon reviewing the claims, the Description and the Drawings. Claim 1 of the patent, in this case, uses the expression "such that a surface of plastic film forms a 0.04-0.09 mm thick uneven rough surface." This expression emphasizes the surface structure of the surface unevenness of the plastic film and its numerical values, which are different from the thickness values of plastic films used in the examples. In the absence of further explanation and instruction in the Description, it should be considered that the two have different meanings.

The third is about the statement made by the patentee in the process of patent invalidation. In its observations, Xi'an Qinbang Company has explicitly denied that the Description of the patent, in this case, discloses "the thickness of the plastic film is maintained at 0.04-0.09 mm," indicating that in the invalidation procedure, it did not think that the technical feature "such that a surface of plastic film forms a 0.04-0.09 mm thick uneven rough surface" means "the thickness of the plastic film is 0.04-0.09 mm."

The fourth is about the boundary of interpretation of the claims. When the persons of ordinary skill in the art can clearly determine the meanings of relevant expressions in the claims and the Description does not specifically define the meanings of the terms of the claims, the understanding of the contents of the claims by the persons of ordinary skill in the art should prevail. The contents of the Description should not be used to deny the disclosure of the claims so as to achieve the result of a substantive amendment to the claims and make the interpretation of the claims in the patent infringement litigation procedure an additional opportunity for the patentee to amend the claims. Otherwise, the publicity and delimitation effects of the claims on the protection scope of the patent will be impaired, and the patentee will hence undeservedly obtain a protection scope that should not be covered by the claims. Of course, the obvious errors that can be immediately learned by the persons of ordinary skill in the art upon reviewing the Description and Drawings should be excluded.

In Claim 1 of the patent, in this case, the meaning of "such that a surface of plastic film forms a 0.04-0.09 mm thick uneven rough surface" is clear and complete, which means that the thickness of the uneven rough surface of the plastic film surface is 0.04-0.09 mm. Under this circumstance, upon reviewing the claims and the Description, it is difficult for the persons of ordinary skill in the art to form an understanding that the expression "such that a surface of plastic film forms a 0.04-0.09 mm thick uneven rough surface" in Claim 1 should actually be "the thickness of plastic film is 0.04-0.09 mm." Although the numerical range of "0.04-0.09 mm" in the expression "such that a surface of plastic film forms a 0.04-0.09 mm thick uneven rough surface" is relatively close to and overlaps with the numerical value of the thickness of the plastic film in the examples, it is unjustified to simply take this as a reason to think that the expression is obviously wrong, and further correct the thickness of the uneven rough surface of the plastic film surface to the thickness of the plastic film.

In this case, the Supreme People's Court has clarified the boundary of interpretation of claims: when the persons of ordinary skill in the art can clearly determine the meanings of relevant expressions in the claims and the Description does not specifically define the meanings of the terms of the claims, the understanding of the contents of the claims by the persons of ordinary skill in the art should prevail. The contents of the Description should not be used to deny the disclosure of the claims. However, if there are obvious errors in the expression of specific terms in the claims, and the persons of ordinary skill in the art can clearly, directly and unambiguously modify the meanings of the specific terms in the claims based on the corresponding disclosure in the Description and Drawings, the specific terms should be interpreted according to the revised meaning.

[F] The Technical Solutions Containing the Technical Defects to Be Overcome by the Patent Cannot Be Included in the Protection Scope of the Claims

Case 5: In the case of dispute over patent infringement between Xi'an Qinbang Telecom Material Co. Ltd. and Wuxi Longsheng Cable Material Factory and Shanghai Xisheng Cable Material Co. Ltd. ((2012) Min Ti Zi No. 3[4] Civil Judgment issued by the Supreme People's Court), one of the focal points of the dispute between the two parties is whether the bonding mode of plastic film and metal foil tape surface in the accused infringing process is identical with or equivalent to the corresponding technical feature "perform uneven non-pure plane bonding for a plastic film and a metal foil tape surface" recited in Claim 1.

In this regard, the Supreme People's Court has held in the retrial that, for the determination of the meanings of the terms in the claims, care should be taken not to include the technical solutions that contain the technical defects to be overcome by the patent into the protection scope of the claims. According to the disclosure of the Description of the patent, the existing process method is defective in that the bonding

4. Case 2 of Annual Report of the Supreme People's Court on Intellectual Property in 2012.

for the plastic film and the metal foil tape layer is pure-plane bonding, that is, the surface of the plastic film bonded to the metal foil tape and the surface of the metal foil tape are planes. In order to overcome this defect, it is necessary to require that at least one of the two bonding surfaces of the plastic film and the metal foil tape is uneven. Therefore, for the feature "perform uneven non-pure plane bonding for a plastic film and a surface of a metal foil tape" recited in Claim 1 of the patent, the interpretation should be that the bonding mode for the plastic film and the surface of the metal foil tape is "uneven non-pure plane bonding"; that is, at least one of the two bonding surfaces of the plastic film and the metal foil tape is uneven.

From the facts ascertained in this case, for the composite aluminum-plastics tape manufactured by Wuxi Longsheng, the petitioner for retrial, the plane bonding under traditional technology is adopted between the plastic film layer and the aluminum foil tape, that is, the surface of the plastic film bonded to the metal foil tape and the surface of the metal foil tape are planes, which are bonded together by the mutual extrusion between the steel roller conveying the plastic film and the extrusion roller driving the metal foil tape. According to the disclosure of the Description of the patent regarding the defect of the prior art, the pure-plane bonding for the plastic film and the metal foil tape surface is the technical defect to be overcome by the patent in this case. Thus, the plane bonding between the plastic film layer and the aluminum foil tape adopted in the accused infringing process, which is a means of prior art, is neither identical with nor equivalent to the technical feature "perform uneven non-pure plane bonding for a plastic film and a metal foil tape surface" recited in Claim 1.

It should be noted that the interpretation principle "the interpretation of the claims shall not include the technical solutions containing the defects or deficiencies of the prior art to be overcome by the patent" is likewise reflected in Article 3.1.3.3, which relates to the understanding of technical features, of *Guide for the Trial of Patent Infringement Dispute Cases*, an operating specification for case trial formulated by the Higher People's Court of Jiangsu Province in November 2010, and in Article 2 of *Guidelines for Patent Infringement Determination (2017)* of Beijing High People's Court.

[G] The Technical Solutions That Cannot Achieve the Purpose of the Invention Shall Not Be Included in the Protection Scope of the Claims

Case 6: In the case of infringement dispute over a patent for invention between Dyson Technology Limited VS Suzhou Su-Vac Electric Motor Co. Ltd. ((2017) Zui Gao Fa Min Shen No. 1461 Civil Ruling Paper issued by the Supreme People's Court), the key to determining whether the accused infringing product falls within the protection scope of the patent involved is whether the "power source" in the claims of the patent includes the "power lead," while the accused infringing product exactly uses a power lead.

Regarding the technical feature "power source," Dyson, the petitioner for retrial, has alleged that if the "power lead" in the Description of the patent is narrowly interpreted as a "wire for transmitting electrical energy," and thereby "AC power source" is excluded from the scope of "power source" recited in the claims, it does not conform to the general understanding of the Description of the patent by those skilled in the art, and also violates a basic common sense of life. Based on the aforementioned misinterpretation of the concepts of "power source" and "power lead," the protection scope of the patent will be unreasonably limited.

In this regard, the Supreme People's Court has held that, in a broad sense, the meaning of the term "power source" includes both DC power and AC power. However, the Description of the patent involved in this case does not specify the "power source." Therefore, whether the "power source" in the claims of the patent involved is the power source in the above-mentioned broad meaning should still be determined based on the understanding of the claims by the persons of ordinary skill in the art upon reviewing the Description and Drawings. The court has held that the above-mentioned broad understanding is inapplicable, and the specific reasons are as follows: firstly, according to the Description of the patent involved, in order to achieve the purpose of easy and comfortable manipulation, in the patent involved, the handgrip is arranged at a reasonable position between the airflow generator (including the motor and the fan assembly) and the power source, so that the resultant moment between the centers of mass of components is smaller. Therefore, only when the power source is a power source device with a certain weight can the inventive purpose of the patent involved be satisfied and the corresponding technical effect be achieved. Moreover, the Description of the patent involved discloses in paragraph [0027] that: "Further, the hand-held vacuum cleaner need not be fitted with a rechargeable power source. Standard batteries or a power lead could be used." It can be seen that the Description of the patent involved strictly distinguishes between the rechargeable power source, standard battery, and power lead, and the above three are all power sources in a broad sense. However, as determined from the overall disclosure in the Description of the patent involved, at least the technical solution of the power lead cannot achieve the inventive purpose of the patent involved. Therefore, it cannot be included in the protection scope of the claims as a specific technical solution, nor can the "power source" in the claims be interpreted as including a "power lead" accordingly.

In this case, from the perspective of the purpose of the invention, the Supreme People's Court has held that the interpretation of the claims should meet the purpose of the invention, and technical solutions that could not achieve the purpose and effects of the invention should not be included into the protection scope of the claims by interpretation. The technical solution of the "power lead" does not meet the purpose of the invention of the patent involved. Therefore, it is considered that it cannot be included in the protection scope of the claims as a specific technical solution.

Case 7: In the case of infringement dispute over a patent for utility model of Ningbo Dayang Industry & Trade Co. Ltd. VS WenZhou SORBO Technology Co. Ltd. ((2018) Zui Gao Fa Min Shen No. 4880 Civil Ruling Paper issued by the Supreme People's Court), the key to determining whether the accused infringing product falls within the protection scope of the patent involved is whether the USB charging port of the accused infringing product is identical with or equivalent to the technical feature "a light bulb seat connecting with a mouth of a light bulb" of Claim 2 of the patent involved.

As to the technical feature "a light bulb seat connecting with a mouth of a light bulb," Dayang Company, the petitioner for retrial, has alleged that the meaning of "a light bulb seat connecting with a mouth of a light bulb" is clear and definite, and the contents of the Description and Drawings need not and should not be used to limit the protection scope of the patent involved. The contents of the Description and Drawings cannot be used to limit the protection scope of the patent involved, and it cannot be determined that the existing mouth of a light bulb only includes the forms of "being threaded" and "being provided with a snap-fit structure," but not the form of "USB interface." That is, the petitioner for the retrial of this case has tried to use common knowledge to interpret the "USB interface" as a specific form of the "mouth of a light bulb" in Claim 2.

In this regard, the Supreme People's Court has held that: the title of the subject matter of the patent involved is a "mosquitocidal light bulb" comprising a light bulb seat connecting with a mouth of a light bulb and lighting elements. Those skilled in the art can know from the contents of paragraphs [0003], [0004], [0016] and [0021] of the Description that the technical problem to be solved by the patent involved is to provide a mosquitocidal light bulb that can kill insects and which can be directly connected with an existing mouth of a light bulb. With the light bulb seat directly connected with an existing mouth of a light bulb, the mosquitocidal light bulb achieves the technical effect of "directly replacing the ordinary light bulb functioning on existing wire arrangements and making it not necessary to change the existing wire arrangements and switch controls." Accordingly, it can be determined that the "a light bulb seat connecting with a mouth of a light bulb" should be a conventional light bulb seat for connecting a mouth of a light bulb and fixing the light bulb, and does not include other forms of light bulb seats that cannot be connected with an existing mouth of a light bulb.

The accused infringing product is a mosquito killer lamp that can be used directly. Although the accused infringing product can be used in the USB direct external power supply working mode, it cannot be directly connected with an existing mouth of a light bulb, nor can it achieve the technical effect of "replacing the ordinary light bulb functioning on existing wire arrangements and making it not necessary to change the existing wire arrangements and switch controls." The two are obviously different in technical means, functions and effects. Therefore, it has been held in the second-instance judgment that the USB interface of the accused infringing product is not equivalent to the technical feature "a light bulb seat connecting with a mouth of a light bulb" of the patent involved, and it is appropriate to give a judgment that the accused infringing product does not fall within the protection scope of the patent involved.

In this case, the Supreme People's Court, based on the technical problem to be solved by the present invention, namely, "can be directly connected with an existing mouth of a light bulb," and the achievable technical effect has concluded that "a light bulb seat connecting with a mouth of a light bulb" should be a conventional light bulb seat, while the accused infringing product could not achieve the technical effect, and thus does not fall within the protection scope of the claim involved.

[H] The Illustrative Description of the Description and Drawings Shall Not Be Used to Limit the Protection Scope of the Claims

Case 8: In the case of infringement dispute over a patent for invention between XU Yongwei and Ningbo Huatuo Solar Technology Co. Ltd. ((2011) Min Ti Zi No. 64[5]) (hereinafter referred to as the patent infringement case of "solar flashlight"), both parties have a dispute over two technical features recited in Claim 1: the first is "the solar cell panel and an outside transparent cover that protects the solar cell panel form a *detachable* component," and the second is "the component can be installed and fixed on a mounting hole on an outer surface of the cylinder body through a *detachable connection structure.*" One of the focal points of the dispute between the two parties is: since the rear end cover of the accused infringing product cannot be opened manually, does it mean that it does not have the "detachable" feature in the claim of the patent?

In this regard, the Supreme People's Court has held in the retrial that the role of the claims is to define the boundary of the patent right, and the Description and Drawings are mainly used to clearly and completely describe the patented technical solutions so that those skilled in the art can understand and implement the patent. One of the best ways to teach those skilled in the art to implement the patent is to provide embodiments. However, the embodiments are merely for illustrating the invention because the Patent Law does not require, nor can it require that the Description enumerates all specific ways of implementing the invention. Therefore, when the Description and Drawings are used to interpret the claims, the illustrative description of the Description and Drawings shall not be used to limit the protection scope of the patent. Otherwise, the protection scope of the patent will be unreasonably limited, which is contrary to the legislative intent to encourage invention and creation.

First, in this case, the "rear end cover" of the flashlight is not recited in the claims of the patent but is only mentioned in the embodiments of and the Drawings for the Description. As mentioned above, it is incorrect to regard the "rear end cover" as one of the bases for defining the protection scope of the patent in this case.

Second, according to the description of the Description, the opening and closing of the rear end cover does not have the same meaning as the two "detachable" mentioned in the claims and the Description. The description of the detachable connection structure in the patent examination files further proves that the rear end cover is not a component of the "detachable connection structure" disclosed in the patent in this case.

Third, even the effect of the "rear end cover" on the feature "detachable" of the patent is considered based on the reading of the Description and other patent documents; it is impossible to conclude that the opening and closing of the rear end cover is only achieved manually.

In summary, the fact that the rear end cover of the accused infringing product cannot be opened manually does not mean that it does not have the "detachable" feature in the claims of the patent.

5. Case 1 of Annual Report of the Supreme People's Court on Intellectual Property in 2011.

In this case, the Supreme People's Court has firstly clarified the effect of the claims of defining the boundary of the patent right and the interpretive effect of the Description and Drawings on the patented technical solutions and then pointed out that: when the Description and Drawings are used to interpret the claims, since the embodiments are merely for illustrating the invention, the illustrative description of the Description and Drawings shall not be used to limit the protection scope of the patent.

Case 9: In the case of infringement dispute over a patent for invention between Huawei Technologies Co. Ltd. and ZTE Corporation ((2015) Min Shen Zi No. 2720 Civil Ruling Paper issued by the Supreme People's Court[6]), one of the keys to determining whether the accused infringing product falls within the protection scope of the patent involved is whether the protection scope of the patent involved could be construed as a way of "turning on a dynamic host configuration protocol (DHCP) relay" in the illustrative description of the Description and Drawings.

In this regard, the Supreme People's Court has held that, first, Claim 1 of the patent involved does not recite the feature "whether a DHCP relay is turned on," and none of the features implicitly requires an exchange to turn on the DHCP relay. Therefore, according to the content of the text description of Claim 1, the implementation method for preventing IP address cheating is not limited to the situation where the exchange "turns on the DHCP relay." Second, according to the background art disclosed in the Description of the patent involved and the available prior art, in the process of using the DHCP server for dynamic address allocation, "whether a DHCP relay is turned on" is a possible situation, depending on whether the DHCP server and the user terminal are in the same network segment. Therefore, Claim 1 of the patent involved does not explicitly exclude the situation where "a DHCP relay is not turned on," and the networking mode may also involve a situation where the DHCP relay is not turned on. If the protection scope of the patent involved is construed as the mode of "turning on a DHCP relay" as illustrated in the Description and Drawings, the protection scope of the patent will be unreasonably limited.

Although the patent involved does not include the specific network application environment of the patented method as a technical feature in Claim 1, the patented method cannot be implemented without regard to the specific network application environment. With the overall consideration of the disclosure of the relevant dependent claims, the Description and the Drawings, according to the common understanding of the persons of ordinary skill in the art, it should be confirmed that turning on the DHCP relay to allow the DHCP server to provide services to user terminals that are not in its network segment should be the most reasonable, common and popular operating environment and mode of operation for implementing the patented method involved, and also preset by Huawei, as the patentee, as an ideal network application environment for the patented method involved.

In this case, the Supreme People's Court has made an elaboration, as consistent with that of the foregoing case, of the interpretative effect of the Description and Drawings on the claims, that is, the illustrative description of the Description and

6. Case 3 of Annual Report of the Supreme People's Court on Intellectual Property in 2015.

Drawings shall not be used to limit the protection scope of the patent. Moreover, the Supreme Court has also pointed out, in this case, that: the most reasonable, common and popular operating environment and mode of operation for implementing the patented method, although not written as a technical feature in the claims, should be considered in the determination of infringement involving process patents.

[I] The Dimensional Parameters Obtained by Measuring the Drawings for the Description Shall Not Be Used to Define the Protection Scope of the Claims

Case 10: In the case of infringement dispute over a patent for utility model between Amphenol East Asia Electronics Technology (Shenzhen) Company and Shenzhen Shinning Electronics Co. Ltd. ((2011) Min Shen Zi No. 1318[7] Civil Ruling Paper issued by the Supreme People's Court), the key to determining whether the accused infringing product preserved by the Court of First Instance falls within the protection scope of the patent, in this case, is whether the accused infringing product has the technical feature "locating slot."

As to this technical feature, Shenzhen Shinning Electronics Co. Ltd., the petitioner for retrial, has argued that the interpretation should be made according to the Description and Drawings to determine the protection scope of Claim 1. The accused infringing product has only a large notch, the width of which is much larger than the thickness of the left end of the trapezoidal groove frame. It has no positioning function for the left end of the trapezoidal groove frame, let alone the fixing function. The feature "an end cover is provided with a locating slot that can fix an end of a trapezoidal groove frame of the plug-in body" is not adopted, while the traditional large-notch structure before the improvement is used. Consequently, this large-notch structure is neither identical with nor equivalent to the locating slot structure of the patent in this case. That is, the petitioner for the retrial of this case has tried to define the width of the "locating slot" in Claim 1, according to the dimensions shown in the Drawings for the Description, to be approximately equal to the thickness of the left end of the trapezoidal groove frame.

In this regard, the Supreme People's Court has held that in the technical solution claimed in Claim 1 of the patent, in this case, the matching relationship between the end cover, the housing and the trapezoidal groove frame is that the end of the trapezoidal groove frame in the plug-in body is fixed through the locating slot and that the end cover and the housing are connected by a snap. Claim 1 defines that the end cover is matched with the trapezoidal groove frame through the locating slot and contains the technical feature that the end cover can be connected to the housing by a snap. The thickness of the locating slot and the thickness of the left end of the trapezoidal groove frame are not defined. Although the width of the locating slot shown in the Drawings for the Description of the patent, in this case, is approximately equal to the thickness of the left end of the trapezoidal groove frame, the dimensional

7. Case 3 of Annual Report of the Supreme People's Court on Intellectual Property in 2012.

parameters obtained by measuring the Drawings for the Description shall not be used to define the technical features of the claims for the reason that the protection scope of a patent for invention or utility model is subject to the contents of the claims. The Description is the basis of the claims, and the claims are based on the Description and use the technical features that constitute the technical solution of the invention or utility model to indicate the protection scope of the patent as claimed. Only the technical features recited in the claims can define the protection scope of the claims. The technical features disclosed in the Description but not recited in the claims cannot be used to limit the protection scope of the claims. ... The meaning of "locating slot" in the claims of the patent, in this case, is clear and definite, and the Description does not specifically define the meaning of "locating slot." Consequently, the contents defined by the claims themselves shall prevail, and the petitioner cannot, based on "the Description and Drawings can be used to interpret the contents of the claims," use the interpretation of the locating slot as an excuse to incorporate the contents not recited in the claims into the claims, and include the thickness of the locating slot measured in the Drawings for the Description into the claims, so as to achieve the purpose of substantially revising the claims by means of the Description.

In this case, the Supreme People's Court has clarified that: the dimensional parameters not recited in the claims but obtained only by measuring the Drawings for the Description generally shall not be used to define the protection scope of the claims. Only the technical features recited in the claims can define the protection scope of the claims. The technical features described in the Description but not recited in the claims cannot be used to limit the protection scope of the claims.

§4.04 CONCLUSION

Article 2 of the *Interpretation I,* as a rule, applies throughout the interpretation of the claims in the patent infringement litigation procedure. It is optional, but not necessary, to use the Description and Drawings to interpret the claims. If any technical feature recited in the claims is not clear in content, the Description and Drawings can be introduced for the further interpretation of the claims. And the Description and Drawings are in a subordinate position and can only be used for the interpretation of the claims. The protection scope cannot be expanded according to the Description and Drawings, which may infringe on the public interests.

During the specific interpretation of the claims, each part of the Description should be considered, such as inventive purpose, beneficial effect and the like. However, it should be noted that different parts of the Description may vary in the functions on the interpretation of the claims. For example, when the portion of detailed embodiments is considered, the illustrative description is generally not used to limit the protection scope of the claims. Similarly, the information in the Drawings should also be considered during the interpretation of the claims, while the dimensional parameters obtained by measuring the Drawings for the Description cannot be used to define the technical features of the claims.

CHAPTER 5
Principle of Internal Interpretation Priority

He Yibo & Ge Xiaomei

The rule of internal interpretation is a basic principle for interpreting a claim as internal evidence takes precedence over external evidence. The seemingly clear rule substantively has unclear boundaries in the process of application. Since reference books, textbooks and a general understanding of persons of ordinary skill in the art are required for interpretation only when internal interpretation is unclear, the question is how to perform internal interpretation. As understood by the author, internal interpretation is also an understanding based on the knowledge level of those skilled in the art. Therefore, substantively, comprehensive use of internal evidence and external evidence is common in the claim interpretation. This chapter discusses nine (9) court decisions.

§5.01 BASIC PROVISIONS OF LAWS

***Interpretation of the Supreme People's Court on Several Issues concerning the Application of Law in the Trial of Patent Infringement Dispute Cases* (hereinafter referred to as "*Judicial Interpretation I*")**

Article 3 The people's court may interpret a claim based on the Description, the Drawings, relevant claims in the Claims and the patent examination dossier. If the Description has any special definition on the wording of a claim, such a particular definition shall apply.

If the meaning of a claim still cannot be clarified by the approaches above, the claim may be interpreted according to reference books, textbooks and other common knowledge literature and the common understanding on the part of persons of ordinary skill in the art.

***Interpretation (II) of the Supreme People's Court on Several Issues concerning the Application of Law in the Trial of Patent Infringement Dispute Cases* (hereinafter referred to as "*Judicial Interpretation II*")**

Article 6 A people's court may interpret a claim of the patent involved in a case by using any other patent which has a divisional application relationship with the patent involved in the case and its patent examination dossier or effective patent granting and confirmation judgment documents.

A patent examination dossier includes written materials submitted by the patent applicant or the patentee in the process of patent examination, reexamination and invalidation, the Office Action, meeting minutes, oral hearing records, effective examination decisions on the patent reexamination request and on the invalidation declaration request of a patent, among others, made by the patent administrative department of the State Council and its Patent Reexamination Board.

§5.02 INTERPRETATION OF THE PROVISIONS

Article 3 of the *Judicial Interpretation I* provides an operation guideline of claim interpretation from a micro-level. The Description, the Drawings and the related claims of the Claims, all as parts of the patent granting documents, are most closely related to the claim and are usually the best guideline to clarify the wording in dispute. In addition, although the patent examination dossier is not an integral part of the patent granting documents, it can be consulted by the public, and the wording of the claim should have the same meaning in the patent examination process and in the infringement litigation. Therefore, the patent examination dossier also performs an important function in the interpretation of a claim. With respect to the above "internal evidence," some reference books and textbooks and the like are called "external evidence" since they are not included in the relevant patent documents and dossier of the Patent Office. External evidence is generally used only when internal evidence is insufficient to interpret a claim clearly. Of course, this does not mean that each of the above interpretation means must be used in the interpretation of the claim. If the meaning of a claim can be clarified by using the Description only, other interpretation means are no more required.

According to the above legal provisions, the following principles should be followed in claim interpretation:

(1) the Description, the Drawings, the related claims and the examination dossier are internal evidence for claim interpretation;
(2) where a term of the claims has a specific meaning in the Description, the wording of the claims should be interpreted according to the definition in the Description;
(3) where the wording of the claims is not specifically defined in the Description, it should be commonly interpreted according to the general meaning understood by persons of ordinary skill in the art;
(4) Claim Differentiation is a principle but cannot be applied rigidly;

(5) the patent examination dossier plays an important role in claim interpretation; and
(6) the meaning of an applicant-created technical term of the claims in the overall technical solution shall be defined by comprehensively using internal evidence.

§5.03 DISPUTES ARISING IN THE LAW APPLICATION

[A] The Description, the Drawings, the Related Claims and the Examination Dossier Are Internal Evidence for Claim Interpretation

Case 1: In an infringement dispute over a patent for utility model between SUN Shouhui and Qingdao KFC Co. Ltd., Yum China Holdings, Inc. et al. ((2009) Min Shen Zi No. 1622[1]), one of the focuses in dispute, in this case, is the interpretation of the feature "comprising a trapezoidal end face frame body" in Claim 1.

SUN Shouhui held in retrial that the feature "comprising a trapezoidal end face frame body" means that "an end face in the frame body is trapezoidal" rather than that the structure of the whole frame body is trapezoidal, such that Claim 1 does not define the structural shape of the frame body.

In this regard, the Supreme People's Court held in retrial that: in the patent infringement litigation, to determine the protection scope of a patent, the definition made by the patentee, in the patent granting and invalidation procedures in order to ensure obtaining a patent right or to maintaining the validity of a patent right, also should be considered. First, from the literal content of Claim 1, according to the general understanding, the word "a" in the feature "comprising a trapezoidal end face frame body" in Claim 1 is used to modify and define the "frame body" rather than the "trapezoidal end face," not to define the number of the "trapezoidal end face." Therefore, the feature "comprising a trapezoidal end face frame body" actually means "being a frame body having a trapezoidal cross-section." Second, from the related disclosure of the frame body in the Description and the Drawings of the patent, the Description discloses that "the structure thereof is a frame 2 having a trapezoidal cross-section." According to the general understanding, the number "2" herein indicates the sign 2 in Figure 1 and refers to the "frame" instead of "cross-section" or "end face" because it is placed after the word "frame." Third, from the application of the term "trapezoidal" in two claims of SUN Shouhui's patent, the word "trapezoidal" in the "trapezoidal end face frame" recited in Claim 2 is obviously used to define the cross-section of the frame body as a trapezoid. According to the basic principle that the same technical term used in different claims should be interpreted as a term with the same meaning, the word "trapezoidal" in Claim 1 should also be interpreted as a

1. This case is the Case 1 in the Intellectual Property Annual Report of the Supreme People's Court in 2010.

definition of the frame body. In addition, according to the Observations made by the patentee SUN Shouhui in the invalidation procedure of his patent, SUN Shouhui took the effect "this design of a trapezoidal end face can save materials to the greatest extent" as a reason why his patent involves an inventive step compared with Evidence 1 in the patent invalidation procedure. It is also based on the above reason that the Patent Reexamination Board determined that SUN Shouhui's patent involves an inventive step and decided to maintain that his patent was valid. The above Observations of SUN Shouhui in the invalidation procedure are binding in this case. The feature "comprising a trapezoidal end face frame body" in Claim 1 of SUN Shouhui's patent shall be determined as that the simple toothpaste extruder itself claimed by the patent is a frame body having a trapezoidal cross-section. Otherwise, SUN Shouhui's patent does not involve an inventive step relative to Evidence 1 in the invalidation procedure. It is not inappropriate that the people's courts of the first and second instances both held that a strict interpretation shall be made to the first technical feature of Claim 1 of SUN Shouhui's patent, that is, "trapezoidal end face frame body."

In this case, the Supreme Court clarified several principles to be followed when interpreting the claims, including: (1) the Description and the Drawings can be used to interpret a claim; (2) a term in the claims should be generally understood in case that the Description makes no special explanation; (3) a relevant technical term used in different claims should be interpreted as a term with the same meaning; and (4) the definition of the protection scope of the patent, made by the patentee in the patent granting and invalidation procedures to ensure obtaining a patent right or maintaining the validity of a patent right, should be considered.

[B] Where a Term of the Claims Has a Specific Meaning in the Description, the Wording of the Claims Should Be Interpreted According to the Definition in the Description

Case 2: In an infringement dispute over a patent for invention between Fujian Duoleng Steel Group Co. Ltd and Qidong Baling Steel Shot Co. Ltd ((2010) Min Shen Zi No. 979[2]), the focus of the dispute between the two parties is whether the technical feature of the alleged infringement method has the necessary technical feature "two-stage crushing" in the patent involved.

In this regard, the Supreme People's Court held in retrial the following opinions: there is no clear definition of "two-stage crushing" in the relevant industrial field. However, the Description of the patent involved discloses "the invention adopts two-stage crushing: a jaw crusher for coarse crushing and a compound crusher for fine crushing. The invention does not break steel beads into steel sand but breaks a cutting material into steel sand. The cutting material is not as small and uniform in particle size as the steel beads. In the present invention, the coarse and large cutting material is crushed into small pieces using a jaw crusher, and then finely crushed into steel sand."

2. This case is the Case 3 in the Intellectual Property Annual Report of the Supreme People's Court in 2010.

The disclosure of the Description of the patent involved indicates the specific meaning of the term "two-stage crushing," and such definition clarifies the protection scope of Claim 1 of the patent involved. Therefore, the meaning of the wording in the claims should be understood according to the definition in the Description. The term "two-stage crushing" should be understood as a "two-stage crushing" wherein coarse crushing is performed first and fine crushing is performed later.

In this case, the Supreme People's Court held that: although there is no clear definition of "two-stage crushing" in the relevant industrial field, the disclosure of the Description of the patent involved indicates that the term has a specific meaning, and such definition clarifies the protection scope of Claim 1 of the patent involved. Therefore, the meaning of the wording in the claims should be understood according to the definition in the Description.

Case 3: In an infringement dispute over a patent for invention in *Beijing Chaoyang District Maizidian Fuli Plastic Products Factory et al. v. Shaanxi Xin Run Real Estate Co. Ltd* (A Civil Ruling of the Supreme People's Court (2015) Min Shen Zi No. 2604), one of the keys to judge whether the alleged infringement product falls within the protection scope of the patent involved is whether the inner wall of the alleged infringement product has the technical feature of a smooth surface.

Regarding this technical feature, the petitioner for retrial, Fuli Factory, held that: as for whether the surface is smooth or not in dispute, the surface finishes formed by removing the surface material (turning, boring, planning, milling, grinding, etc.) are different from those formed by not removing the surface material (casting, forging, stamping, mold forming, cold pressing, etc.). The racket frame of the alleged infringement product is a surface formed by a mold, which pertains to the processing method with the material not removed and is coarser than the process with the surface material removed. That is, the petitioner for retrial, in this case, attempts to use the general understanding of persons of ordinary skill in the art to interpret the word "smooth" in Claim 1 differently from the surface of the alleged infringement product. In this regard, the Supreme People's Court held that: in this case, Claim 1 of the patent involved recites that "the inner wall of the racket frame is a smooth surface." From the manufacturing process of the racket frame in the patent, a straight rod is sleeved by an air pipe and then wrapped with carbon cloth to form a hollow frame, and after the straight rod is pulled out, the hollow pipe is inflated and pressurized to make the hollow inner wall smooth. That is, the effect of a smooth inner wall is achieved by the patent product involved under the condition that the hollow pipe is inflated and pressurized (up to 8-9 kg). The word "smooth" herein shall be interpreted as relatively smooth, which pertains to the smoothness formed with the surface material not removed, instead of the smoothness formed by removing the surface material through the process of turning, boring, planning, milling, grinding, etc. The petitioner for retrial also argued that the racket frame of the alleged infringement product is a surface formed by a mold, which pertains to the surface formed with the material not removed. Based on the above, it is held that the forming process of this inner wall surface is the same as that of the inner wall surface of the present patent, and therefore, the inner wall of the alleged infringement product shall be relatively smooth as well.

In this case, the Supreme People's Court preferentially applied the contents of the Description related to the forming process of "an effect of a smooth inner wall" to interpret the feature "a smooth surface," but did not accept the claim of the petitioner for retrial that the interpretation should be based on the general understanding of persons of ordinary skill in the art.

[C] Where the Wording of the Claims Is Not Specifically Defined in the Description, It Should Be Interpreted According to the General Meaning Understood by Persons of Ordinary Skill in the Art

Case 4: In an infringement dispute over a patent for utility model between LUO Shizhong and Shenzhen Blue Eagle Hardware and Plastic Products Factory ((2011) Min Ti Zi No. 248[3]), one of the focuses in dispute between two parties is the understanding of the feature "both sides of the vertical large hole are provided with longitudinal holes penetrating through the center thereof" in the claims.

Shenzhen Intermediate People's Court held in the first instance that: the technical feature should be understood as "the longitudinal holes on both sides are on the same horizontal line with the center of the vertical large hole," and further held that they are different from the longitudinal holes which are arranged in an up-and-down dislocation manner on both sides of the vertical large hole in the sued product.

Guangdong High Court held in the second instance that the above conclusion cannot be derived uniquely from the literal meaning of the claims, and no corresponding explanation is made in the literal part of the Description. On the contrary, as can be known from an analysis of the technical solution of the patent involved, the requirement can be met as long as the longitudinal holes on both ends penetrate the center of the vertical large hole, respectively, and it is not a necessary means that the longitudinal holes on both sides are on the same horizontal line with the center of the vertical large hole to realize the above purpose.

In this regard, the Supreme People's Court held in retrial that the phase "penetrate through" is neither a professional technical term nor specifically defined in the Description of the patent involved. Therefore, it should be interpreted according to its general meaning. The *Modern Chinese Dictionary (5th Edition)* recites that the word "penetrate" means "pierce, run through and join," and the phrase "penetrate through" means "pass through and connect." That is, the feature "longitudinal holes are arranged on both sides of the vertical large hole penetrating through the center thereof" literally means that the longitudinal holes on both sides are connected and pass through the center of the vertical large hole. The vertical large hole is stereoscopic, and its center refers to its axial centerline, not the center of its axial centerline. To achieve this, the longitudinal holes on both sides of the vertical large hole can form a cross-shape structure with the vertical large hole on a straight line or a "Z"-shape structure with the vertical large hole by up-and-down dislocation. Since the vertical

3. This case is the Case 2 in the Intellectual Property Annual Report of the Supreme People's Court in 2011.

large hole and the longitudinal holes are both hollow, both the above two structures can realize that the longitudinal holes on both sides of the vertical large hole are connected and pass through the center of the vertical large hole. According to the reciting of the disclosure of the Claims and Description of the patent involved, the longitudinal holes on both sides of the vertical large hole are equipped with an elastic positioning clamp and a lock-up element, respectively, which realize locking and unlocking in cooperation with the rotating shaft installed in the vertical large hole. The above two structures can also achieve this purpose. Therefore, the technical feature regarding the structure of the lock body of the alleged infringement product falls with the literal scope of the claims of the patent involved, which is the same as that of the patent involved.

In this case, the Supreme People's Court held that: where the wording of the claims is not specifically defined in the Description, it should be commonly interpreted according to the general meaning understood by persons of ordinary skill in the art. The meaning of the wording shall not be simply defined and narrowed down to the content embodied by a specific embodiment provided in the Description.

Case 5: In an infringement dispute over a patent for invention in *Shenzhen Jixiang Tenda Technology Co. Ltd. v. Dunjun Technology Co. Ltd.* (A Civil Judgment of the Supreme People's Court (2019) Zui Gao Fa Zhi Min Zhong No. 147), the two parties have a different understanding of the feature "a first uplink HTTP message before a portal service user device passes authentication" in Step A of Claim 1 of the patent involved. The appellant Tenda Company held that "a first uplink HTTP message" in Step A of Claim 1 should be interpreted as the first TCP message in the process of establishing TCP "three-way handshake" connection between a user device and an actual website to be visited, thereby before the portal service user device passes authentication. However, Dunjun Company held that "a first uplink HTTP message" in Step A of Claim 1 refers to an HTTP message.

In this regard, the Intellectual Property Court of the Supreme People's Court held in the second instance that: first, the text recited in Step A of Claim 1 clearly defines an "HTTP message," but does not mention any "TCP connection," "TCP three-way handshake message," etc. To make "a first uplink HTTP message" in Step A of Claim 1 understood as the first message in the three-way handshake process of establishing a TCP connection, it requires specific disclosure in the Description and the Drawings. Moreover, the adoption of such interpretation shall ensure that the overall technical solution claimed by the patent involved conforms to the invention purpose of the patent involved. However, the "HTTP message" defined in Step A of Claim 1 is not specially described in the contents of the Description and the Drawings of the patent involved. Therefore, its meaning shall be interpreted according to the general understanding of persons of ordinary skill in the art.

Second, in the field of network communication, HTTP and TCP are concepts connected with but independent from each other in terms of meaning. A TCP three-way handshake message is the precondition of HTTP message transmission, but not an HTTP message itself. Message transmission by the application layer protocol (such as HTTP, etc.) all requires the precondition of a connection established by a TCP three-way handshake message on the transmission layer. However, persons of ordi nary skill in the art would not regard any TCP handshake message as an application layer protocol, such as the HTTP message itself. If "a first uplink HTTP message" in Claim 1 of the patent involved is understood as "the first message in the process of establishing a TCP three-way handshake connection," it would go against the basic cognition of persons of ordinary skill in the art.

In this case, the Intellectual Property Court of the Supreme People's Court clearly pointed out in the second instance that the interpretation of relevant technical terms or technical features in the claims should follow the principle of internal evidence priority. If the relevant technical terms or technical features of the claims have been specially described in the Description of the patent, interpretation shall be made according to the special description. If there is no special explanation in the Description, interpretation shall be made according to the general understanding of persons of ordinary skill in the art.

[D] Claim Differentiation Is a Principle but Cannot Be Applied Rigidly

According to the provision of Article 3 of the *Judicial Interpretation I*, relevant claims in the Claims can be used for interpretation. When using the relevant claims for interpretation, we should also note the "Doctrine of Claim Differentiation." According to the Doctrine of Claim Differentiation, the court shall interpret the multiple claims in each patent in a way that each claim has a different protection scope and none of the claims is redundant. That is, according to this doctrine, each claim with a different expression is presumed to be a different claim.

Case 6: In an infringement dispute over a patent for invention in *Free Motion Fitness, Inc. v. Changzhoushi Yingcai Metalwork Co. Ltd.*, Shanghai Jianda Fitness Equipment Co. Ltd. (A Civil Ruling of the Supreme People's Court (2014) Min Shen Zi No. 497[4]), Claim 1 defines "a resistance assembly," "a cable," etc. The additional technical feature of Claim 2 is "the cable consists essentially of a single cable." Free Motion Company claimed that according to the Doctrine of Claim Differentiation, Claims 1 and 2 of the patent involved should be interpreted differentially and "a cable" in Claim 1 is not "a single cable," which should be understood as one or more cables.

In this regard, the Supreme People's Court held in retrial that: the current laws, although Claim Differentiation has not been clearly provided in the regulations and judicial interpretations in China, it is necessary and reasonable in common situations to interpret different claims differentially as claims having different protection scopes. Article 20 of the Implementing Regulations of the Chinese Patent Law provides that the Claims shall have an independent claim and may also contain dependent claims. Considering the purpose of the patentee in drafting different claims, especially the purpose of drafting dependent claims based on independent claims, which is to define protection scopes of different levels to make the protect scopes of the patent clearer and

4. This case is the Case 1 in the Intellectual Property Annual Report of the Supreme People's Court in 2014.

more stereoscopic, generally speaking, different claims are presumed to have different protection scopes.

However, polysemy and synonyms may exist in the language. In addition, due to differences in drafting skills, subjective understanding and the like, the applicant may define one technical solution with different technical terms in different ways of expression, resulting in that the protection scopes of different claims are the same or substantively the same. Under this circumstance, undoubtedly, it is contrary to the objective facts to rigidly interpret the claims differentially. In this case, for those skilled in the art, "a cable" in Claim 1 is not substantially different from "a single cable" in Claim 2, which is only expressed in a different way. Therefore, it is not supported to interpret the word "a" in Claim 1 as one or more.

In this case, the Supreme People's Court pointed out that although laws in China have not made clear provisions on Claim Differentiation, it is necessary and reasonable to interpret different claims as claims having different protection scopes. That is, in general, different claims should be presumed to have different protection scopes. Meanwhile, the Supreme People's Court also pointed out that if the protection scopes of different claims are the same or substantively the same, interpretation differentiation should not be applied rigidly.

[E] The Patent Examination Dossier Plays an Important Role in Claim Interpretation

Case 7: In an infringement dispute over a patent for invention between HUANG Zhenbo and Quanzhou Jiurong Sanitary Development Co. Ltd, Nan'an Luncang Jiurong Plumbing Accessories Dealership ((2018) Zui Gao Fa Min Shen No. 5730[5]), Jiurong Company and Jiurong Plumbing Dealership claimed in retrial that the iron sand particles in the alleged infringement technical solution neither fill up nor form a honeycomb between the plastic inner valve core pipe and the metal faucet body and thus does not have any anti-cracking technical effect.

In this regard, the Supreme People's Court held in the retrial that in this case, according to Claim 1, "an antifreeze protective layer is filled up between the plastic inner valve core pipe and the metal faucet body..., ... the antifreeze protective layer is a honeycomb metal antifreeze protective layer formed by the aggregation of a plurality of metal particles." Combined with the disclosure of the Description and the determination of the above examination dossier, the phrase "fill up" refers to fully arranging the "antifreeze protection layer" in the cavity formed between the plastic inner valve core pipe and the metal faucet body, rather than filling the metal particles in the cavity without any gap. The "honeycomb" refers to a "honeycomb"-shaped layer structure formed by the aggregation of metal particles with gaps there between. Thus, it can achieve the purpose of using its own deformation to absorb the pressure of the plastic inner valve core pipe to prevent it from cracking due to the influence of water pressure

5. This case is the Case 2 in the Intellectual Property Annual Report of the Supreme People's Court in 2019.

and water temperature. Moreover, it can also realize the function of better adhering to the plastic inner valve core pipe and the metal faucet body as the honeycomb-state shell gradually evolves into a solid state after absorbing moisture for a long time. Whether the specific shape of the "honeycomb" is a regular polygon does not fall within the scope defined by the claims.

Looking back to the alleged infringement product, although the applicant deems that the iron sand particles filled between the plastic inner valve core pipe and the metal faucet body do not have the function of the technical solution of Claim 1 of the patent involved, the solid spherical metal particles can be regarded as "filling up" the cavity between the plastic inner valve core pipe and the metal faucet body, and the gaps between the particles can be regarded as a "honeycomb"-shaped layer structure. The above structure and material mean that they will objectively perform anti-cracking and moisture-absorbing functions.

In this case, the Supreme People's Court pointed out that a claim should be interpreted in consideration of the literal meaning thereof and the disclosure of the Description, especially the description regarding the technical effect, so as to accurately define the protection scope of the claim. Meanwhile, the relevant determination in the examination dossier can also be used to interpret the content of the claim. The wording of a claim should have the same meaning in the patent examination process and in the infringement litigation. Therefore, in infringement litigation, the patent examination dossier plays an important role in claim interpretation.

[F] The Meaning of an Applicant-Created Technical Term of the Claims in the Overall Technical Solution Shall Be Defined by Comprehensively Using Internal Evidence

Case 8: In an infringement dispute over a patent for utility model between Shanghai Gujian Lock Co. Ltd. and Shanghai Mode Lock Manufacturer ((2013) Min Ti Zi No. 113[6]), the main disputes between the two parties lie in whether the alleged infringement product has a telescopic linkage device, a telescopic rod arranged on one end of the telescopic linkage device, and a passage through which the telescopic linkage device extends outwards in Claim 1 of the patent involved. These disputes all relate to the understanding of the meaning of the telescopic linkage device.

In this regard, the Supreme People's Court held in retrial that the dispute between the two parties on the meaning of the telescopic linkage device is substantively originated from their different understandings of the working manner, function and effect of the telescopic linkage device in the technical solution of the patent involved. Therefore, the premise of judging whether the alleged infringement product falls within the protection scope of the patent involved is a correct understanding of the meaning of the telescopic linkage device in the overall technical solution of the patent involved.

6. This case is the Case 2 in the Intellectual Property Annual Report of the Supreme People's Court in 2014.

The telescopic linkage device is not a technical term existing in the art prior to the application date of the patent involved but a technical term created by the patent applicant. When the meaning of an applicant-created technical term is determined, the technical contents related to the technical term and disclosed in the Claims, the Description and the Drawings shall be taken into consideration comprehensively. If the technical term is clearly and explicitly defined or explained in the Claims or the Description, its meaning can be generally determined according to the definition or explanation. If the technical term is not clearly and explicitly defined or explained in the Claims or the Description, the working manner, function and effect related to the technical term shall be found out by combining the contents disclosed in the Description and the Drawings, such as the background art, technical problems, invention purpose, technical solution and technical effect related to the technical term, so as to determine the meaning of the technical term in the overall technical solution of the patent involved.

In the patent involved, the applicant of the patent neither defines nor explains the telescopic linkage device in the Claims and the Description. Therefore, *it is required to comprehensively consider the technical contents related to this technical term and disclosed in the Description and the Drawings to determine its meaning*. First, according to the background art, description of the invention, and technical effect of the patent involved, the invention purpose of the patent involved is to provide an idling burglar-proof lock device. The patent involved does not relate to the improvement of a lock bolt or latch itself in an ordinary lock, nor does it relate to the transformation of an ordinary lock by replacing the lock bolt or latch directly with the telescopic linkage device.

Second, according to the specific embodiment of the patent involved, the matching manner of the telescopic linkage device and the lock bolt or latch must be changed by changing the matching manner of the telescopic linkage device and the rotary pusher in the patent involved so as to achieve the purpose of locking and unlocking or burglar proofing by idling. The telescopic linkage device is an intermediate part arranged between the rotary pusher and the lock bolt or latch to push the lock bolt or latch to move. The telescopic linkage device and the lock bolt or latch are independent of each other and are not the same part. The patent involved does not disclose any technical content that the telescopic linkage device directly replaces the lock bolt or latch and directly performs the locking function.

Third, the QB/T3835-1999 Standard provided by Mode Lock Manufacturer, as a national industrial standard for terms of locks, can demonstrate the meanings of technical terms related to locks in the art prior to the application date of the patent involved and help those skilled in the art to understand the meaning of the telescopic linkage device in the patent involved. Section 3.2.2 of the QB/T3835-1999 Standard recites that "bolt: a part which directly performs the locking function in a lock" and Section 3.2.3 recites that "follower: a part which directly performs the function of pulling the bolt." Since the telescopic linkage device is a part of pushing the lock bolt or latch to move, the telescopic linkage device itself cannot directly perform the function of locking. Therefore, the telescopic linkage device does not conform to the definition of the "bolt" in the above standard, and it substantively pertains to the "follower" in the above standard.

To sum up, according to the background art, description of the invention, technical solution, and technical effect in the Description of the patent involved and the QB/T3835-1999 Standard, the telescopic linkage device in the patent involved is an intermediate part for pushing the lock bolt or latch to move. The telescopic linkage device and the lock bolt or latch are independent of and cooperate with each other so as to realize the invention purpose and technical effect of the technical solution of the patent involved. The claim of Gujian Company that the telescopic linkage device also has the function of the lock bolt is a lack of factual basis and is not supported by this court.

In this case, the Supreme People's Court pointed out that: on the one hand, based on objective requirements, the patent applicant should be allowed to use a technical term created by himself when drafting patent application documents. On the other hand, when using the technical term created by himself, the patent applicant is also obliged to clearly and accurately define, explain or describe this technical term in the Claims or the Description of the patent.

When interpreting a claim, the meaning of a technical term created by the patentee can generally be determined according to the definition or explanation in the Claims and the Description. If such explanation or definition is not available, the working manner, function and effect of the technical term shall be found out by combining the Claims and the relevant contents such as the background art, invention purpose and technical effect disclosed in the Description and the Drawings, to determine the meaning of the technical term in the overall technical solution.

Case 9: In an infringement dispute over a patent for invention in *Tatsuta Wire and Cable Co. Ltd. v. Guangzhou Fang Bang Electronics Co. Ltd.* (A Civil Ruling of the Supreme People's Court (2018) Zui Gao Fa Min Shen No. 5287), one of the keys to judge whether the alleged infringement product falls within the protection scope of Claim 8 of the patent involved is how to understand the "corrugated structure" in the claim.

Regarding this technical feature, the Supreme People's Court held that in this case that the feature "corrugated structure" should be understood based on the Description, the Drawings, relevant claims in the Claims, the patent examination dossier and the like according to law.

According to the relevant reciting of the Claims of the patent, Claim 8 recites three technical features, namely "an insulating layer having an arithmetic average roughness of 0.5-5.0 μm on a single surface," "a first metal layer formed on the single surface of the insulating layer," and "the first metal layer is formed in a way of forming a corrugated structure along the single surface of the insulating layer." Accordingly, an uneven shape naturally caused only by an uneven surface of the insulating layer and a corrugated structure in which the first metal layer is formed should be interpreted as two meanings.

As can be seen in combination with the relevant disclosure of the Description, the purpose of the present invention is to provide a shielding film for a printed wiring board, and a printed wiring board having a metal layer is not easily broken in repeated bending and sliding from a large bending radius to a small bending radius (1.0 mm). However, paragraph [0009] of the Description discloses that: "since the metal layer has a corrugated structure with a high bending property, it can provide a shielding film for a printed wiring board having a metal layer not easily broken in repeated bending and sliding from a large bending radius to a small bending radius (1.0 mm)." Therefore, the "corrugated structure" is an invention point that distinguishes the invention from the background art and realizes the invention purpose of the patent involved. This can be confirmed by the contents, such as "the corrugated structure which can form a more desired shape" and "the corrugated structure that forms a desired shape," especially emphasized in the Description. As shown above, the corrugated structure of the metal layer should have an obvious bending property. The shape of the metal layer is a corrugated structure which the patent involved expects to form and can form a more desired shape through controlling by a specific method, so as to more reliably achieve the effects of making the metal layer difficult to damage and maintaining the electromagnetic wave shielding properties. The same "corrugated structure" reflected in different forms in Figure 1 and Figure 13(a) of the Description of the patent also involved obviously indicates that it is the relatively regular "corrugated structure" with relatively continuous smooth fluctuation and high bending properties that conforms to the invention purpose.

Moreover, according to the facts found in the original trial, the petitioner for retrial Tatsuta Company clearly stated in the original trial that structures such as the serrated shape, the continuous concave-convex shape did not conform to the invention purpose.

Therefore, it is not improper for the original court to interpret the "corrugated structure" as one that "at least should be a relatively regular, relatively obvious and relatively smooth, continuously fluctuating structure, excluding an irregular fluctuation of the metal layer naturally caused by the uneven surface of the insulating layer and also excluding a roughly flat, serrated or continuous concave-convex structure without high bending properties" by combining the Description, the Drawings, the relevant claims of the Claims and the patent examination dossier.

In this case, the "corrugated structure" is not specially defined in the Claims and the Description of the patent involved. According to facts found in the original trial, both parties confirmed that the "corrugated structure" is not a common term in the field of the shielding film for the printed wiring board in the patent involved and does not have a unified meaning. On this basis, the Supreme People's Court held that the understanding of the "corrugated structure" in this case should be based on the Description, the Drawings, relevant claims in the Claims, the patent examination dossier and the like according to law.

§5.04 CONCLUSION

Article 3 of the *Judicial Interpretation I*, as a principle, is applicable to the process of claim interpretation through the whole patent infringement litigation procedure. Where the Description has a special definition on the wording of a claim, the special definition shall prevail. Where the Description does not have any special definition on the wording, other internal or external evidence is considered to interpret the claim. Internal evidence is preferred to interpret the claim over external evidence. External evidence is used only when the internal evidence fails to clarify the meaning of the claim.

Although the drafter of the judicial interpretations, when interpreting this Article, mentioned that if the meaning of a claim can be clarified by using the Description only, other interpretation means are no more required. However, in judicial practice, various types of internal evidence are often comprehensively used to interpret a claim.

When different claims are interpreted with the Doctrine of Claim Differentiation, generally speaking, different claims should be presumed to have different protection scopes. However, since polysemy and synonyms may exist in the language itself, the claims should be interpreted based on objective facts and cannot be rigidly interpreted differentially.

Finally, it should be noted that certain differences exist in the interpretation of claims with the Observations in patent granting and confirmation procedures and civil infringement procedures.

CHAPTER 6

The Principle That All Features Have the Defining Effect

Zhang Junjie & Ge Xiaomei

All the technical features recited in the claim have the defining effect, and the question of whether a feature pertains to the essential technical feature is no longer discriminated by the court which hears the infringement dispute. Such practice highlights the publicity function of the claims, improves the certainty of the protection scope of patent right, provides a clear legal expectation for the public, and also puts forward higher requirements for the patent document drafters. In addition, this chapter also discusses the defining effect of the title of the subject matter, as the preamble portion, on the protection scope of the claim.

§6.01 BASIC PROVISIONS OF LAWS

***Interpretation II of the Supreme People's Court on Several Issues concerning the Application of Law in the Trial of Patent Infringement Dispute Cases* (hereinafter referred to as "*Judicial Interpretation II*")**

Article 5 When a people's court determines the protection scope of a patent right, the technical features recited in the preamble portion and characterizing portion of an independent claim, and the reference portion and characterizing portion of a dependent claim shall all have the defining effect.

Related Articles of Laws

***Implementing Regulations of the Chinese Patent Law of the People's Republic of China* (hereinafter referred to as "*Implementing Regulations of the Chinese Patent Law*")**

Rule 21 An independent claim of an invention or utility model shall contain a preamble portion and a characterizing portion, and be presented in the following form:

(1) a preamble portion: indicating the title of the claimed subject matter of the technical solution of the invention or utility model, and those technical features which are necessary for the definition of the claimed subject matter but which, in combination, are part of the most related prior art;
(2) a characterizing portion: stating, in such words as "characterized in that ... " or in similar expressions, the technical features of the invention or utility model, which distinguish it from the most related prior art. Those features, in combination with the features stated in the preamble portion, serve to define the extent of protection of the invention or utility model.

Where the manner specified in the preceding paragraphs is not appropriate to be followed because of the nature of the invention or utility model, an independent claim may be presented in a different manner.

An invention or utility model shall have only one independent claim, which shall precede all the dependent claims relating to the same invention or utility model.

Rule 22 Any dependent claim of an invention or utility model shall contain a reference portion and a characterizing portion, and be presented in the following manner:

(1) a reference portion: indicating the serial number(s) of the claim(s) referred to, and the title of the subject matter;
(2) a characterizing portion: stating the additional technical features of the invention or utility model.

Any dependent claim shall only refer to the preceding claim or claims. Any multiple dependent claims, which refers to two or more claims, shall refer to the preceding claims in the alternative only, and shall not serve as a basis for any other multiple dependent claims.

§6.02 INTERPRETATION OF THE ARTICLES OF LAWS

Article 5 of *Judicial Interpretation II* specifies that the technical features recited in the preamble portion and characterizing portion of an independent claim and the reference portion and characterizing portion of a dependent claim shall all have the defining effect on the protection scope of the patent right. Such provision fully reflects the respect for the publicity of the claims and requires patent document drafters to pay enough attention to the expression of the above features at the patent application stage.

Rule 21 of the *Implementing Regulations of the Chinese Patent Law* specifies that an independent claim shall include a preamble portion and a characterizing portion; the preamble portion shall indicate the title of the claimed subject matter of the technical solution and technical features which are necessary for the definition of the claimed subject matter but which, in combination, are part of the most related prior art, the characterizing portion shall state the technical features which distinguish the invention from the most related prior art, and those features, in combination with the features stated in the preamble portion, serve to define the extent of protection of the invention. Rule 22 of the *Implementing Regulations of the Chinese Patent Law* specifies that a dependent claim shall include a reference portion and a characterizing portion, the reference portion shall indicate the serial number(s) of the claim(s) referred to, and the title of the subject matter, and the characterizing portion shall state the additional technical features of the invention or utility model.

Although the question of determining whether the above technical features pertain to the essential technical features of the patent should be solved at the patent granting and confirmation stages and it is inappropriate for the people's court which hears the dispute over infringement of patent right to discriminate such question again, the determination that both the preamble portion and the reference portion have the defining effect at the infringement judgment stage is actually in line with the *Implementing Regulations of the Chinese Patent Law*.

§6.03 ISSUES/DISPUTES ARISING IN THE LAW APPLICATION

[A] Any Technical Feature Incorporated into the Claim Has a Defining Effect on the Protection Scope

Case 1: In a dispute over infringement of a patent right between Dalian Renda New Wall Building Material Factory and Dalian Xinyi Building Material Company Limited ((2015) Min San Ti No. 1), Xinyi Company asserted in the retrial that the original court (High People's Court of Liaoning Province) mistakenly excluded the essential technical feature "barrel bottom wall layer structure" recited in the independent claim of the patent from the scope of infringement comparison on the grounds that "the barrel bottom only plays a secondary role" and reincorporated the feature "the barrel bottom does not contain a pure concrete single-layer structure of glass fiber clothes" which has been excluded from the protection scope by the patentee into the protection scope of the patent.

Renda Company argued that the barrel bottom wall layer structure is not an essential technical feature of the patent.

In this regard, the Supreme People's Court held in the retrial that from the perspective of the drafting requirements of the Claims, it should be determined that any technical feature that had been recited in the independent claim by the patentee was the essential technical feature, should not be omitted, and should be incorporated into the scope of the comparison of the technical feature. The Court did not favor the reckless application of the so-called "unessential technical feature designation principle." Second, from the perspective of the function of the Claims, the function of the Claims is to determine the protection scope of the patent right. That is, by the disclosure of all the technical features included in the technical solution of the invention or utility model to the public, the public can clearly know what kind of behavior will infringe the patent right, thus providing effective and reasonable protection for the patentee on the one hand and ensuring the public's freedom to use the technology on the other hand. Only by giving full and sufficient respect to all technical features recited in the Claims can the public not be at a loss due to unforeseen changes in the contents of the claims, thus ensuring the certainty of legal rights and fundamentally ensuring the normal operation and value realization of the patent system.

There is only one claim, i.e., an independent claim, in the Claims of the patent in this case. The independent claim clearly recites the structure of the barrel bottom and the wall layer of the barrel tube, respectively. Therefore, Renda Factory's assertion that the barrel bottom wall layer structure of the patent is not the essential technical feature cannot be established. "The barrel bottom is formed by stacking two layers of glass fiber clothes at least, the glass fiber clothes at each layer are pasted by one layer of sulfur aluminate or ferrite aluminate cement inorganic cement material, and bottom surfaces on both sides of the barrel bottom are respectively covered with one layer of sulfur aluminate or ferrite aluminate cement inorganic cement material," which is an essential technical feature of the patent of this case.

In this case, the Supreme People's Court clarified that any technical feature that had been recited in the Claims of the patent by the patentee is the essential technical feature and should be incorporated into the scope of the comparison of the technical feature. Henceforth the court which hears the infringement dispute will no longer discriminate whether a feature pertains to an essential technical feature.

[B] The Title of the Subject Matter Per Se Is Not a Specific Technical Feature, but It Can Be Compared Technically

Case 2: In a dispute over infringement of a patent right for invention between Shanghai Shangti Sports Development Co. Ltd. and Shanghai Yuanhang Medical Instrument Co. Ltd., and Shanghai Kangmeng Healthy Products Co. Ltd. ((2019) Zui Gao Fa Zhi Min Zhong No. 79), the title of the subject matter of Claim 1 of the patent involved is "a body-building training device that imitates qigong circulating vibration." The focus of the dispute lies in the following: can the content "imitates qigong circulating vibration" defined in the title of the subject matter be compared as the specific technical feature?

In this regard, the Intellectual Property Court of the Supreme People's Court believed that the title of the subject matter was a part of the preamble portion and had the defining effect on the determination of the protection scope. However, the title of the subject matter per se was not the specific technical feature but an abstract generalization of the technical solution composed of all technical features included in the claim and was the name of the technical solution of the patent. The basic function of the title of the subject matter of the patent lay in the patent granting management and classification retrieval. Therefore, such abstract and general relationship between the title of the subject matter and the technical solution constituted the degree of definition on the technical solution of the patent, which should be understood from the perspective of the persons of ordinary skill in the art within the function field and application field specified by the title of the subject matter.

For this case, paragraph [0012] of the Description of the patent involved explains the feature "imitates qigong circulating vibration." Persons of ordinary skill in the art can understand that the feature "imitates qigong circulating vibration" refers to the function to realize the technical effect of "making the whole body vibrate circularly" by the technical means of "the housing body producing up and down displacement of various frequency vibrations," ... The expression of "imitates qigong circulating vibration" in the title of the subject matter of the patent involved is a definition to the subject matter "body-building training device" according to the method of functional classification and is an abstract generalization of the technical effect that can be achieved by the technical solution of the present invention rather than a certain specific technical feature. In this case, although the title of the subject matter did not express that the sued infringing product named "cell rhythm device" has the function of "imitating qigong circulating vibration," it is also a body-building training device after examination, has the function of vertically vibrating up and down, and can provide a means for users located thereon to move up and down accordingly to obtain circular whole-body vibration and achieve a certain degree of exercise effect. It should be understood that the sued infringing product relates to the same technical subject matter as the patent involved, and technical comparison can be carried out.

In this case, the Supreme People's Court made it clear that the actual defining effect of the title of the subject matter on the protection scope of the claim depends on its influence on the subject matter per se to be protected by the claim. In this case, the title of the subject matter is expressed as the function of "imitating qigong circulating vibration." The alleged infringing product also has the technical means for achieving such function after examination, and thus it is determined that the alleged infringing product and the patent involved relates to the same technical subject matter and can be compared technically.

[C] The Actual Defining Effect of the Title of the Subject Matter Depends on Its Influence on the Subject Matter Per Se to Be Protected

There is no doubt that the essential technical feature recited in the preamble portion can define the protection scope of the claim. The title of the subject matter is a part of the preamble portion and is an overall generalization of the technical solution of the invention. In general, the title of the subject matter clearly indicates the type of the claim and adapts to the technical content of the claim. Whether the title of the subject matter has the defining effect should be analyzed from whether it reflects a specific technical feature and whether it is related to a technical feature to a certain extent. If persons of ordinary skill in the art deem that the title of the subject matter also indicates the specific technical feature after reviewing the claim, or that they will consider the title of the subject matter together when implementing the invention, the title of the subject matter should have a defining effect.

Case 3: In a dispute over infringement of a patent right for invention between Harbin Institute of Technology Galaxy Industry Co. Ltd. and Jiangsu Runde Pipes Industry Co. Ltd. ((2013) Min Shen Zi No. 790[1]), the retrial petitioner Harbin Institute of Technology Galaxy Industry Co. Ltd. asserted that *Interpretation of the Supreme People's Court on Several Issues concerning the Application of Law in the Trial of Patent Infringement Dispute Cases* (Fa Shi [2009] No. 21) and the *Implementing Regulations of the Chinese Patent Law* clearly distinguished the title of the subject matter from the technical feature with different legal terms, and emphasized that the protection scope of the patent right was defined by the technical features. Therefore, the determination "the title of the subject matter, as the necessary content of the claim, has a defining effect on the protection scope of the claim" made by the second-instance judgment had no legal basis.

In this regard, the Supreme People's Court held that in general, when the determination is made to the protection scope of the claim, the title of the subject matter recited in the claim should be considered, and the actual defining effect should depend on the influence of the title of the subject matter on the subject matter per se to be protected by the claim. In this case, when the determination is made to the protection scopes of Claims 2 and 6, consideration should be given to the actual defining effect of the title of the subject matter on the subject matter per se claimed.

The title of the subject matter of Claim 2 of the patent involved is "the method for making plastic drainage pipeline reinforced by steel strips according to claim 1," and the title of the subject matter of Claim 6 is "the apparatus for making a drainage pipe reinforced by steel strips according to the method of Claim 2." The author holds that the drainage pipe defined in Claim 1 and the manufacturing method defined in Claim 2 indicate the specific technical features, respectively, and conform to the definition of technical features. Therefore, such titles of the subject matters constitute definitions to the protection scope of Claim 2 or 6.

[D] How to Determine the Actual Defining Effect of the Title of the Subject Matter

The title of the subject matter is actually an abstract name for the whole technical solution of the invention and is different from the technical features in expression due to its generalization and abstraction. The title of the subject matter is generally closely related to the technical feature, and the technical solution composed of technical features is difficult to exist independently from the technical field determined by the title of the subject matter. Therefore, the title of the subject matter should be regarded as having the defining effect on the protection scope of the technical solution in general, but such definition should be an all-inclusive definition of the technical solution, which belongs to the definition of the scope of the applicable technical field

1. Case 2 of 2013 Annual Report on Intellectual Property Rights of the Supreme People's Court

of the technical solution and does not belong to the defining effect of the technical feature.

Case 4: In a dispute over infringement of a patent right for invention between HU Tao and Mobike (Beijing) Information Technology Co. Ltd., the disputes between both parties were: what the actual defining effect of "electromobile" recited in the title of the subject matter "an electromobile control system[2]" of independent Claim 1 of the patent involved is and whether the patent involved can be protected by the Chinese Patent Law in the technical field of the bicycle.

In this regard, Shanghai intellectual property court held in the first instance ((2017) Hu 73 Min Chu No. 278) that when the determination was made to the protection scope of the claim, the title of the subject matter recited in the claim should be considered, and the actual defining effect thereof depended on the influence of the title of the subject matter on the object to be protected by the claim. For this case, the "electromobile" was an integral part of the title of the subject matter of the patent involved, and described the usage of the patent involved and had a defining effect on the protection scope of the patent right involved. However, the actual defining effect should be determined in combination with the influence of the "electromobile" on the patent involved. First, "an electromobile control system" involved was a product patent of a lock device, and the "electromobile" was not an integral part of the lock device. Second, the "electromobile" was not the premise and foundation of the technical solution of the patent involved, and the technical solution of the patent involved could be implemented completely and separately from the electromobile. Third, it was not a reason for the novelty or inventive step of the patent involved that the patent involved was limited to the technical field of electromobile when be filed. Finally, the patent text involved listed a patent application for an invention in the technical field of the bicycle as a reference document. Therefore, as far as the application mode of the patent involved is concerned, it was conceivable for persons of ordinary skill in the art to apply the patent involved to the technical field of bicycle, which did not need any creative work. The defenses made by the Mobike Company that the alleged infringing product mobike and the electromobile protected by the patent involved belonged to different technical fields and that the infringement was not constituted were not accepted by the original court.

Shanghai High People's Court held in the second instance ((2017) Hu Min Zhong No. 369) that title of the subject matter of Claim 1 of the patent involved was "an electromobile control system," which specified that the application filed of the invention was the electromobile and explained that the invention involved the

2. **Claim 1 of the patent involved is:** an electromobile control system, characterized in that: a miniature camera, a graph decoder, a memory and a two-dimension code comparator form a two-dimension code recognizer, the miniature camera is electrically connected with the graph decoder, the graph decoder and the memory are both electrically connected with the two-dimension code comparator, two-dimension code data stored by the memory and image data photographed by the miniature camera and decoded by the graph decoder are compared by the two-dimension code comparator and sent to a controller, if comparison signals are uniform, the controller controls starting or/and multimedia playing of an electromobile, and if the comparison signals are nonuniform, the controller controls an anti-theft alarm to alarm.

improvement of the "control system" of the electromobile. According to the technical solution recited in Claim 1 of the patent, particularly the feature "if comparison signals are uniform, the controller controls starting or/and multimedia playing of an electromobile" recited in the characterizing portion, in combination with the contents "the purpose of the invention is to provide an electromobile control system and an operating method thereof. A user can align a two-dimension code image stored in a mobile phone with a camera, so that the electromobile can be completely unlocked. The anti-theft performance is improved, and the trouble that the user needs to carry a key to start the electromobile is avoided" and "if comparison signals are uniform, the controller controls the electromobile starting or/and multimedia playing signals, and the controller is turned on and off to unlock the electromobile," persons of ordinary skill in the art could clearly and unambiguously determine that the title of the subject matter was an abstraction and generalization of the technical solution of electromobile starting and unlocking to which the invention relates, and not merely an illustration of the possible use of the invention. On the other hand, the abstract and general relationship between the title of the subject matter and the technical solution, in turn, constituted a definition to the technical solution of the invention, that is, "an electromobile control system" was the starting and unlocking system of an electrically driven vehicle.

In this case, if not belonging to the application field and technical subject matter specified by the title of the subject matter of the patent, the alleged infringing technical solution would naturally not fall within the protection scope of the specific technical solution recited in the characterizing portion of the claim of the patent. Although "an electromobile control system" also had the function of locking the electromobile and could be called the "lock device" only in this sense, "an electromobile control system" further referred to the starting of the electrically driven system. In this sense, it was not complete and accurate enough for the original court to regard it as the "lock device." On this basis, it cannot be considered that the technical solution of Claim 1 of the patent involved can be completely implemented without "electromobile." Therefore, the court believed that the title of the subject matter "an electromobile control system" recited in the Claim 1 of the patent involved had a defining effect on determining the protection scope of the patent right and should be considered in infringement comparison.

The Supreme People's Court held in the retrial ((2018) Zui Gao Fa Min Shen No. 2954) that the title of the subject matter of Claim 1 of the patent involved was "an electromobile control system," which made it clear that the invention belonged to the technical field of electromobile. Moreover, with reference to the background art and the contents of the invention disclosed in the Description of the patent, in order to overcome the problems of insufficient anti-theft performance caused by the key starting mode of the electromobile, the purpose of the patent is to "provide an electromobile control system and an operating method thereof. A user can align a two-dimension code image stored in a mobile phone with a camera, so that the electromobile can be completely unlocked. The anti-theft performance is improved, and the trouble that the user needs to carry a key to start the electromobile is avoided" and "if comparison signals are uniform, the controller controls the electromobile starting or/and multimedia playing." *Persons of ordinary skill in the art can clearly and unambiguously determine that the title of the subject matter of Claim 1 is an abstraction and generalization of the technical solution of electromobile starting and unlocking to which the invention relates, and not merely an illustration of the possible use of the invention. At the same time, the title of the subject matter in Claim 1 in turn constitutes a definition to the technical solution of the invention*, that is, "an electromobile control system" is the starting and unlocking system of an electrically driven vehicle. Therefore, the title of the subject matter in Claim 1, in this case, has a defining effect on the protection scope of Claim 1 and should be considered in infringement determination. The alleged infringing product of Mobike Company is used in the bicycle product. Although there is a "lock device" function, there is no function of "control of the electromobile starting," which does not belong to the application field and technical subject matter specified in the title of the subject matter of the patent.

As can be seen, the actual defining effect of the title of the subject matter of the claim is that it specifies a specific application field and technical subject matter. If the alleged infringing product does not belong to the specified application field, it can be considered that it does not fall within the protection scope of the claim.

§6.04 CONCLUSION

A technical feature recited in the claim, whether in the preamble portion and characterizing portion of the independent claim or in the reference portion and characterizing portion of the dependent claim, has a defining effect on the protection scope of the patent right. The division of technical features is the basis of infringement comparison, and different divisions often lead to completely different comparison results. The definition of the technical feature provides a basis for making division.

At present, there are still many disputes in litigation about whether the title of the subject matter has a defining effect and what kind of defining effect it has. Although most rulings/judgments of the Supreme People's Court hold that the title of the subject matter, as the preamble portion of the independent claim, has a defining effect on the protection scope of the claim. However, whether the title of the subject matter has a defining effect should be analyzed from whether it reflects a specific technical feature and whether it is related to a technical feature to a certain extent. If persons of ordinary skill in the art consider that the title of the subject matter reflects a specific application field and technical subject matter after reading the claim, the title of the subject matter has a defining effect. If not indicating the specific technical feature, the title of the subject matter does not have a defining effect.

CHAPTER 7

Correction of Ambiguity in the Claims in Accordance With a Unique Understanding: Report on Law Interpretation and Case Study Related to Patent Infringement

Zhang Qiulin & Ge Xiaomei

Due to the natural limitation of literal expression, literalism should be avoided while the publicity of the claims is emphasized so as to make interpretation of the claims flexible. Regarding the ambiguity of expression in the patent documents, it should be allowed to correct the ambiguity according to a unique understanding of persons of ordinary skill in the art so as to make the patents with real technical contributions obtain relatively comprehensive protection. In addition, an analysis of judicial precedents shows that an obvious error in the claims is corrected according to the chapter discussed herein. This report includes six judicial precedents. Your attention is appreciated.

§7.01 BASIC PROVISIONS OF LAWS

***Interpretation (II) of the Supreme People's Court on Several Issues concerning the Application of Law in the Trial of Patent Infringement Dispute Cases* (hereinafter referred to as "*Judicial Interpretation II*") (hereinafter the "Article")**

Article 4 Where any grammar, word, punctuation, graphic or symbol, among others, in the Claims, the Description or the Drawings are ambiguous, but persons of ordinary skill in the art can obtain a unique understanding by reading the Claims, the Description and the Drawings, the people's court shall make determination according to the unique understanding.

§7.02 INTERPRETATION OF THE PROVISIONS

A claim is the publicity of protection scope thereof in the form of words, and the protection scope defined by the words thereof shall prevail. In view of the natural limitation of literal expression, the Article provides the issue of understanding ambiguous expressions in the patent documents.

According to the Article, in the case where any grammar, word, punctuation, graphic or symbol, among others, in the patent documents, are ambiguous: (1) the subject of understanding the ambiguities is persons of ordinary skill in the art; (2) the way of understanding the ambiguities is to determine the true meaning of the ambiguities by reading the Claims, the Description and the Drawings, that is, limited to the patent documents per se; (3) where a unique understanding can be obtained, the determination shall be made according to such understanding; and (4) where a unique understanding cannot be obtained, the protection scope shall be determined through the invalidation procedure or according to the reciting of the Claims of the patent.

In addition, the correction of an obvious error in the claim is also determined with reference to the Article; that is if an error belongs to the obvious errors that persons of ordinary skill in this art can immediately find out in the words of the claim by reading the Claims, the Description and the Drawings of the patent, the people's court can make correction according to the law. The "obvious error" can be defined by referring to the following provisions of the *Guidelines for Patent Examination*: the incorrect content can be clearly judged from the context of the original Description and Claims with no possibility of other interpretation or amendment to be made, and the amendment to the error must be the unique correct answer that can be seen by those skilled in the relevant art from the whole text and the context of the Description.

§7.03 ISSUES/DIFFICULTIES ARISING IN THE APPLICATION OF LAW

[A] The Ambiguity in the Claims Shall Be Determined According to the Unique Understanding from Reading the Text of the Patent

Case 1: In an infringement dispute over a patent for invention between Jiangsu Hompe Technology Co. Ltd and Changzhou Youon Public Bicycle System Co. Ltd. ((2016) Hu Min Zhong Zi No. 512), the patent involved relates to a management system for parking/picking-up/renting/returning a non-motorized vehicle and a control and identification method thereof. In view of the fact that the alleged infringement product in this case only has a renting/returning management function for a public bicycle of a bicycle-renting member and does not have a parking/picking-up management function for the bicycle owned by a bicycle-parking member. One of the main points of dispute between the two parties is whether the bicycle "parking/picking-up" and the bicycle "renting/returning" of the patent involved are in parallel or selective relationship, which can be further summarized as the understanding of the meaning of the symbol "/" between the bicycle "parking/picking-up" and the bicycle "renting/returning."

Regarding this issue, Shanghai Intellectual Property Court held in the first instance that the "parking/picking-up" and "renting/returning" in Claim 1.(3) and Claim 1.(4) of the preamble portion and characterizing portion of the patent involved are in parallel relationship, rather than in "or" relationship. The reasons are as follows: (1) the content in the Claims clearly recites the technical features of the terminal management and control unit in realizing parking management and vehicle renting management; (2) as seen from the content of the Description, the main technical problem to be solved by the patent involved is to identify the vehicle identity for parking management. In addition, the contents of the specific embodiments and of the Drawings both relate to the two functions of "parking/picking-up" and "renting/returning," with no content indicating that the system only has one set of functions of "parking/picking-up" or "renting/returning"; (3) the patent confirmation judgment document determines that the system disclosed in the Description of the patent can realize both the management functions of "picking-up" and "parking" and the management functions of "renting" and "returning"; and (4) from the perspective of persons of ordinary skill in the art, the use of the symbol "/" between "parking" and "picking-up," as well as "renting" and "returning" both indicates a parallel relationship, and thus the symbol "/" used between "parking/picking-up" and "renting/returning" should also be presumed to be parallel.

Shanghai High Court supported the above judgment of first instance in the trial of second instance, pointing out as follows: in this case, in view of the dispute between the two parties on the understanding of the "parking/picking-up/renting/returning" in the patent involved, that is, there is uncertainty in the technical extension of the patent involved. Even if the appellant subjectively has the corresponding intention in drafting the claim as stated, where it can be determined that "parking/picking-up" and the "renting/returning" are in parallel relationship objectively according to the cognition of persons of ordinary skill in the art, the resulting corresponding legal consequences should be borne by the appellant.

In this case, Shanghai High Court emphasized the patent applicant's duty of due diligence in writing patent documents. Except that the obvious errors, which can be found easily and understood uniquely and obviously, can be understood correctively, the patentee should be liable for the adverse legal consequences caused by the defects in his drafting. Specifically, regarding the ambiguity caused by a punctuation mark in the claims, the Courts of First Instance and Second Instance, from the perspective of persons of ordinary skill in the art, demonstrated that the unique understanding of the slash mark "/" should be parallel relationship rather than a selective relationship from the aspects of literal interpretation, logical interpretation, systematic interpretation and examination of the full content of the Description.

It is worth mentioning that before the introduction of the *Judicial Interpretation II*, in an infringement dispute over a patent for utility model between Guangzhou Xinlv Flame Retardant Decoration Material Co. Ltd, FU Zhihong and Taishan Xianqu Building Materials Co. Ltd ((2010) Min Shen Zi No. 871) in the annual report on cases of the Supreme People's Court in 2010, regarding the ambiguity in understanding the relationship among "bamboo, wood and plant fiber" in the claims, the protection scope of the claims is also interpreted in a clarified manner by those skilled in the art in combination with the Description and the Drawings.

[B] The Clear Wording in the Claims Shall Not Be Denied by the Content Disclosed in the Description

Case 2: In an infringement dispute over a patent for invention between Xi'an Qinbang Telecommunication Materials Co. Ltd. and Wuxi Longsheng Cable Material Factory, Shanghai Xisheng Cable Material Co. Ltd. and Furukawa Electric (Xi'an) Optical Communication Co. Ltd. ((2012) Min Ti Zi No. 3), the determination opinion held that in the feature "making the surface of the plastic film form an uneven and rough surface with a thickness of 0.04-0.09 mm" recited in Claim 1, the thickness should be interpreted as that of the plastic film itself.

In this regard, the Supreme People's Court held in the retrial that: first, the meaning of "making the surface of the plastic film form an uneven and rough surface with a thickness of 0.04-0.09 mm" in Claim 1 of the patent, in this case, is clear and complete, which means that the thickness of the uneven and rough surface of the plastic film is 0.04-0.09 mm. Second, according to the general principle of text interpretation, it should be considered that the same term used in the claims has the same meaning, and different terms have different meanings. The expression "making the surface of the plastic film form an uneven and rough surface with a thickness of 0.04-0.09 mm" used in Claim 1 is different from the expression about the thickness of the plastic film used in the embodiment, and thus the two expressions should be deemed to have different meanings. Third, in the process of invalidation declaration procedure, the patentee explicitly denies the disclosure of the Description that "the plastic film is kept 0.04-0.09 mm thick," indicating that the patentee himself does not believe that the term means "the thickness of the plastic film is 0.04-0.09 mm" either. Fourth, the limits of the interpretation of the claims. The Description of the patent, in this case, describes the technical solution too simply. It neither gives a detailed description for "making the surface of the plastic film form an uneven and rough surface with a thickness of 0.04-0.09mm," nor defines and explains the thickness of the plastic film. Instead, it only mentions that the thickness of the plastic film is 0.04 mm, 0.09 mm and 0.07 mm, respectively, in the embodiments. In this case, after reading the Claims and the Description, it is difficult for persons of ordinary skill in the art to form the understanding that the expression "making the surface of the plastic film form an uneven and rough surface with a thickness of 0.04-0.09 mm" in Claim 1 actually should be "the thickness of the plastic film is 0.04-0.09 mm." Although the numerical range of "0.04-0.09 mm" in the expression of "making the surface of the plastic film form an uneven and rough surface with a thickness of 0.04-0.09 mm" is close to and overlaps with the numerical values of the thickness of the plastic film in the embodiments, it still lacks sufficient evidence to deem that there is an obvious error in the expression such that the thickness of the uneven and rough surface of the plastic film is corrected to the thickness of the plastic film, simply based on the above.

This case is a typical one in the annual report of the Supreme People's Court in 2012. In this case, the Supreme People's Court clarified that when the meaning of the relevant expression can be clearly determined by those skilled in the art, and the Description does not specifically define the meaning of the term in the claims, the understanding of those skilled in the art on the content of the claim itself shall prevail, and the reciting of the claims shall not be denied by the content disclosed in the Description. However, if there is an obvious error in the expression of a specific term in the claims and persons of ordinary skill in the art can clearly, directly and unambiguously correct the meaning of the specific term in the claims according to the corresponding disclosure in the Description and the Drawings, the specific term shall be interpreted according to the meaning after correction.

[C] The Article Shall Be Applied for Correction of an Obvious Error in the Patent Document

Case 3: In an infringement dispute over a patent for utility model between Shenzhen DJ Innovation Technology Co. Ltd. and Guangzhou Walkera Technology Co. Ltd., CAO Ruifen ((2016) Yue Min Zhong No. 1115), DJI claimed that the expression "the lower arm shell and the lower arm shell are integrally molded or fixedly connected" in the technical features of the patent is a clerical error and that the patent involved should disclose that the lower arm shell and the lower shell are integrally molded or fixedly connected.

Guangdong High Court held in the second instance that, first, from the disclosure of the Description of the patent involved, the Description of the patent involved discloses in detail the arrangement of the product shell and the arm shell in two positions, which are both described as "the lower arm shell and the lower shell are integrally molded or fixedly connected." Second, from the common sense of design of the product involved, each arm is designed independently from others, and the lower arm shell and the lower shell should be integrally molded or fixedly connected. To sum up, on the premise of fully considering the characteristics of the technical field to which the patent pertains, judging from the cognitive level of those skilled in the art, the clerical error in the Claims of the patent involved is obvious, and those skilled in the relevant field, by comprehensively reading the Claims, the Description and the Drawings of the patent, can directly and unambiguously deduce that the content "the lower arm shell and the lower arm shell are integrally molded or fixedly connected" recited in the claims of the patent involved should be corrected to "the lower arm shell and the lower shell are integrally molded or fixedly connected."

In this case, Guangdong High Court corrected the clerical error in the Claims from the cognitive level of those skilled in the art based on the relevant disclosure of the features in dispute in the Description of the patent involved and the common sense of design of the product involved.

In addition, Guangdong High Court also clarified in this case that the following factors should be taken into consideration when the provision of Article 3 or Article 4 of the *Judicial Interpretation II* is applied to determining the defect in the claims.

(1) The technical contribution of invention-creation is fully taken into consideration, and the rights obtained by the patentee should correspond thereto. Considering the objective limitations of drafting patent documents, the effectiveness of the invention-creation, indeed involving an inventive step, shall be ensured at best within the scope of disclosure of patent application documents. Meanwhile, the technical contribution and technical value of the invention-creation shall also be comprehensively considered so that the rights obtained by the patentee match with the technical contribution thereof to maximally enhance the capability of judicial protection of intellectual property in driving innovative development.

(2) The technical solutions disclosed in the Claims, the Description and the Drawings are interpreted from the perspective of those skilled in the relevant art. There are significant differences in conventional terms, common knowledge and logical reasoning in different technical fields. Therefore, in determining whether the defects in the claims pertain to "ambiguity" provided in the above *Judicial Interpretation*, the characteristics of the technical field of the patent shall be fully considered, and the cognitive level of those skilled in the art should not be neglected.

(3) After reading through all patent documents such as the Claims, the Description and the Drawings of the patent, those skilled in the relevant art have a general ability to understand and implement the technical solutions disclosed by the patent and an ability to identify and judge the errors existing in the patent documents. Article 59 of the *Patent Law of the People's Republic of China* provides: the extent of protection of the patent right for invention or utility model shall be determined by the terms of the claims. The Description and the Drawings may be used to interpret the content of the claims. From this point of view, the content that can be directly and unambiguously deduced by those skilled in the relevant art after comprehensively reading the Claims, the Description and the Drawings of the patent shall also be used to interpret the content of the claims.

(4) The obviousness degree of the defect in the claims from the perspective of those skilled in the relevant art. If the defect is obvious information that is not profound and hidden to those skilled in the relevant art, and those skilled in the art can obtain the unique definite correction conclusion after completely reading the patent documents, the provision of Article 4 of the above *Judicial Interpretation* shall apply.

(5) The interests of the patentee and the public should be balanced. The publicity of the claims of the patent requires that it should enable the public to accurately and completely understand the technical solution and protection scope of the claims. The patentee is allowed to correct the defects in the claims of the patent. However, it cannot damage the publicity and delimitation effect of the claims on the protection scope of the patent, which may make the interpretation of the claims in the patent infringement action an additional opportunity for the patentee to amend the claims.

On this basis, when the defect in the claims complies with the provision of Article 4 of the *Interpretation (II) of the Supreme People's Court on Several Issues concerning the Application of Law in the Trial of Patent Infringement Dispute Cases*, it should be interpreted according to the corrected meaning. At this time, although the claims of the patent have defects, the protection scope thereof is clear. Therefore, the protection scope of the claims of the patent should be further clarified through correction in the judicial procedure. However, if the above conditions are not met, the protection scope shall be determined through the invalidation procedure or according to the reciting of the Claims of the patent. This method not only balances the interests of the patentee and the public but also promotes the substantive settlement of the dispute.

In an infringement dispute over a patent for utility model between Chuangqun Machinery Co. Ltd. and Dongguan Dianzhen Machinery Co. Ltd. ((2014) Yue Gao Fa Min San Zhong Zi No. 1212), Guangdong High Court discussed the above five factors again.

[D] The Condition for Correcting an Obvious Error Is to Be Able to Recognize and Solve the Error according to the Unique Understanding of the Patent Documents

Case 4: In an infringement dispute over a patent for utility model between Wuxi Guowei Ceramic Electrical Appliance Co. Ltd., JIANG Guoping and Changshu Linzhi Electric Heating Device Co. Ltd., Suning.Com Group Co. Ltd. ((2018) Zui Gao Fa Min Zai No. 111), Guowei Company and JIANG Guoping claimed that the expression "the left and right sides" in the feature "the heat-radiating aluminum strip (11) is pasted on the left and right sides of a heat-conducting aluminum tube (1) in a heat-generating core (10)" in Claim 2, in this case, is a clerical error and should be understood as "the upper and lower surfaces."

In this regard, the Supreme People's Court clarified that, with reference to the provision of Article 4 of the *Judicial Interpretation II*, the obvious error that can be corrected is required to meet two conditions: *first, persons of ordinary skill in the art can realize that there is an ambiguity or error in the disclosure or the Drawings of the patent application documents; and second, persons of ordinary skill in the art can obtain the unique understanding by reading the Claims, the Description and the Drawings to solve this ambiguity or error.*

First of all, according to the technical solution recited in Claim 2, after the heat-conducting aluminum tube is pressed, on the left and right sides thereof, semicircular grooves are formed, but a plane cannot be formed. Since the function of the heat-radiating aluminum strip is to conduct the heat out of the heat-generating core, even if the heat-radiating aluminum strip can be pasted in a semicircular groove, such a paste manner obviously neither complies with the basic principle of heat radiating and conduction nor can achieve the heat radiating function well. Therefore, *persons of ordinary skill in the art can realize that there is an error in pasting the heat-radiating aluminum strip on the left and right sides of the heat-conducting aluminum tube. Secondly, the disclosure in paragraph 0008 of the Description of the patent involved further highlights this error and gives a prompt to solve the error.* This disclosure not only prompts that there is an error in the pasting position of the heat-radiating aluminum strip in Claim 2 but also provides a prompt for a correct solution. *Finally, paragraph 0021 of the Description and the Drawings of the patent involved further provides the only answer to solve the error.* Meanwhile, FIG. 4 and FIG. 6 show that the heat-radiating aluminum strip is pasted on the upper and lower surfaces of the heat-conducting aluminum tube in the heat-generating core.

Therefore, the heat-radiating aluminum strip obviously should be pasted on the upper and lower surfaces of the heat-conducting aluminum tube instead of the left and right sides thereof. The "left and right sides" in the feature "the heat-radiating aluminum strip (11) is pasted on the left and right sides of a heat-conducting aluminum tube (1) in a heating core (10)" in Claim 2 of the patent involved is indeed a clerical error of "the upper and lower surfaces," which pertains to an obvious error that can be corrected.

In this case, the Supreme People's Court clarified that the provision of Article 4 of the *Judicial Interpretation II* can be applied for correction of an obvious error, and clarified that the error that can be corrected is required to meet two conditions: first, persons of ordinary skill in the art can realize that there is an ambiguity or error; and second, the unique understanding can be obtained by reading the patent application documents to solve this ambiguity or error.

Case 5: In an infringement dispute over a patent for invention between Nantong Qizhong Lubrication Equipment Co. Ltd. and Qidong Dele Lubrication Equipment Co. Ltd. ((2019) Zui Gao Fa Min Shen No. 565), the Supreme People's Court first quoted the second instance judgment as follows: "although the technical feature of Claim 1 of the patent involved that 'the oil outlet A and the oil outlet B are communicated with a central left part and a central right part in a main piston cavity respectively, the oil outlet A is further communicated with the left end of a control piston cavity, and the oil outlet B is further communicated with the right end of the control piston cavity' clearly expresses the connection relationship, this connection relationship cannot realize the basic function of this invention, that is, automatic direction reversion of the oil passage. Moreover, according to the corresponding disclosure of the Description and the Drawings, persons of ordinary skill in the art can clearly, directly and unambiguously determine that there is an obvious expression error in the connection relationship between the oil outlets and the main piston cavity and the control piston on the same side in Claim 1, which should actually be cross-connection relationship and should be corrected as 'the oil outlet A is further communicated with the right end of a control piston cavity, and the oil outlet B is further communicated with the left end of the control piston cavity'."

Then, the Supreme People's Court pointed out that during the inquiry of this case, Dele Company also admitted that persons of ordinary skill in the art, by reading the Description and the Drawings before the amendment, could realize that the technical solution defined in Claim 1 of the patent involved could not work normally and that only after amendment, could the function thereof be realized. In this case, Dele Company did not provide evidence to prove that the function of the patent involved can be realized by other correction methods.

In this case, the Supreme People's Court held that the obvious error in the claims from the perspective that the technical solution can achieve the basic function of the invention.

[E] The Claim Having Wrong Wording That Is Not Easy to Identify or from Which a Unique Understanding Cannot Be Obtained Cannot Be Corrected in Accordance with the Article

Case 6: In the above infringement dispute over a patent for utility model between Chuangqun Machinery Co. Ltd. and Dongguan Dianzhen Machinery Co. Ltd. ((2014) Yue Gao Fa Min San Zhong Zi No. 1212), Chuangqun Company claimed as follows: the paddle rod in the above technical feature was a clerical error, in the patent involved, it should be the wedge block that pushes the clamping claws to move close to or apart from each other, and the "paddle rod" in the above claim should be replaced with the "wedge block." In this regard, Guangdong High Court held in the second instance that:

(1) From the perspective of those skilled in the art, Claim 2 of the patent involved defines the features of the wire clamping mechanism of the patent involved. In combination with the reciting of the Claim and the Drawings, the wire clamping mechanism is provided with a "wedge block," and the wedge block performs the function of pushing the clamping claws to move apart from and close to each other. However, the "paddle rod" is a common component in the art, and it is recited in Claim 2 and Claim 9, respectively, and is one of the components of the patent product involved. Accordingly, those skilled in the art cannot very easily realize from the literal expression of Claim 2 that the "paddle rod" will lead to ambiguity. Moreover, even if those skilled in the art find out the contradiction between the Claims and the Drawings of the Description, it is impossible for them to determine whether the "paddle rod" is connected with the clamping claws in a manner not recited in the claims, so as to achieve the technical object of "pushing the clamping claws to move close to or apart from each other" in Claim 2. Therefore, those skilled in the art cannot easily find and finally determine that the "paddle rod" recited in Claim 2 pertains to ambiguity.
(2) Since the patent involved is defined by a plurality of technical features including the wire clamping mechanism, the cutter mechanism and the push-pull mechanism, and the "paddle rod" is also a common component in the art, even if those skilled in the art find a defect in the Claims by reading the patent documents, they cannot unambiguously determine that the defect exists in the wire clamping mechanism, the cutter mechanism or the push-pull mechanism. In other words, those skilled in the art cannot accurately determine the position of the defect.
(3) Those skilled in the art cannot obtain the unique understanding to correct the defect by reading the Claims, the Description and the Drawings. Even if those skilled in the art can accurately locate the defect to the "paddle pod" in Claim

> 2, the correction of the defect in this position can be realized by replacing the "paddle rod" with the "wedge block," by clarifying the relationship between the "paddle rod" and the clamping claws, or by setting the connection relationship between the "paddle rod" and the "wedge block." Moreover, all the above correction manners conform to the cognitive level of those skilled in the art, which fully proves that replacing the "paddle rod" with the "wedge block" is not the unique reasonable interpretation to correct the defect.

In this case, through an analysis of the technical solution in the text of the patent, Guangdong High Court held that regarding the clerical error claimed by the patentee, it is not very easy for those skilled in the art to realize that this wording will lead to ambiguity. Furthermore, even if the defect can be found, the position thereof cannot be accurately determined. Moreover, the correction manner claimed by the patentee is not a unique reasonable interpretation. Therefore, the claim of the patentee about the clerical error is not supported.

[F] For the Correction of an Obvious Error, Due Diligence Should Be Paid to Whether the Premise Is the Content Not Explicitly Recited in the Claims

Case 4: In the above infringement dispute over a patent for utility model between Wuxi Guowei Ceramic Electrical Appliance Co. Ltd., JIANG Guoping and Changshu Linzhi Electric Heating Device Co. Ltd., Suning.Com Group Co. Ltd. ((2018) Zui Gao Fa Min Zai No. 111), Jiangsu High Court held in the second instance that: The premise for the literal description "the left and right sides" of the pasting position of the heat-radiating aluminum strip in Claim 2 of the patent involved to be determined as a clerical error of "the upper and lower surfaces" is that a groove is required to be provided on the upper and lower surfaces of the heat-conducting aluminum tube in Claim 2 and that the groove functions to ensure that the width of the upper and lower surfaces is consistent with that of the heat-radiating aluminum strip. Therefore, the premise should be regarded as the implicit technical feature of Claim 2, which has a defining effect on the protection scope of Claim 2.

In this regard, the Supreme People's Court held in the retrial that the so-called implicit technical feature in the second instance judgment is actually a content that is not clearly recited in the claims and is used as the premise for correction when interpreting the meaning of the technical feature of the claims. Since the introduction of the content not clearly recited in the claims usually will further define and narrow the protection scope of the claims, it should be particularly cautious to introduce the content not clearly recited in the claims in the process of claim interpretation. Specifically in this case, first of all, based on the above discussion that the expression that the heat-radiating aluminum strip is pasted on the "left and right sides" of the heat-conducting aluminum tube in the heating core in Claim 2 of the patent involved pertains to an obvious error that can be corrected, the identification and correction of the obvious error do not take the presence of grooves on the upper and lower surfaces of the heat-conducting aluminum tube in Claim 2 of the patent as a premise. Second, the grooves on the upper and lower surfaces of the heat-conducting aluminum tube in Claim 1 of the patent involved have different functions from the semicircular grooves formed on the left and right sides of the heat-conducting aluminum tube after being pressed in Claim 2, and the above two grooves are not directly related. Finally, when correcting the obvious error in Claim 2, Decision No. 24085 does not take the presence of grooves on the upper and lower surfaces of the heat-conducting aluminum tube as a premise. Therefore, there lacks factual basis for the second instance judgment to determine that Claim 2 of the patent involved implicitly includes the technical feature that "a groove is required to be provided on the upper and lower surfaces of the heat-conducting aluminum tube and that the groove functions to ensure that the width of the upper and lower surfaces is consistent with that of the heat-radiating aluminum strip."

This case emphasizes that when an obvious error is corrected, attention should be paid to whether the premise that is not clearly recited in the claims is introduced. If there is no premise for error correction, this premise should not be regarded as an implicit technical feature to limit the protection scope of the claims. In this case, the Supreme People's Court denied the presence of the premise of error correction from the analysis of the disclosure of the Description, the interpretation of the technical solution and the consideration of the invalidation decision, and then overruled the determination of the Court of Second Instance.

§7.04 CONCLUSION

The application object of the Article is the ambiguity or obvious error in the claims, etc., and the judgment subject is persons of ordinary skill in the art. Moreover, the application of the Article requires reading the patent documents only, on the one hand and requires obtaining the unique understanding only, on the other hand. The above four application requirements should be strictly followed in order to ensure the proper and accurate application of Article 4 of the *Judicial Interpretation II*.

CHAPTER 8

The Interpretation Function of Files: A Report Series on Law Interpretation and Case Study Related to Patent Infringement

Dang Li & Ge Xiaomei

The patent examination files, as the internal evidence for interpreting the claims, have the same interpretative effect as the Description and the Drawings and the relevant claim in the Claims. In judicial practice, the claim may be interpreted by an attempt to using any other patent which has the divisional application relationship, priority right relationship, and even has the same applicant at the same time period with the patent involved. In addition, it should be noted that the interpretation effect of the observations to the claim of the patent may be different in the granting and confirmation procedures and the patent infringement procedure. This chapter includes five judicial cases in total.

§8.01 BASIC PROVISIONS OF LAWS

***Interpretation (II) of the Supreme People's Court on Several Issues concerning the Application of Law in the Trial of Patent Infringement Dispute Cases* (hereinafter referred to as "*Judicial Interpretation II*")**

Article 6 A people's court may interpret the claim of the patent involved by using any other patent which has the divisional application relationship with the patent involved and its patent examination files and the effective patent granting and confirmation judgments.

Patent examination files include the written materials submitted by the patent applicant or patentee in the patent examination, reexamination and invalidation procedures, the Office Action, meeting records, oral hearing records, effective Decision of Examination upon Request for Reexamination, and Examination Decision on the Request for Invalidation of Patent Right, and the like made by the patent administrative organ of the State Council and its Patent Reexamination Board.

Interpretation of the Supreme People's Court on Several Issues concerning the Application of Law in the Trial of Patent Infringement Dispute Cases (hereinafter referred to as "Judicial Interpretation I")

Article 3 The people's court may interpret a claim based on the Description and Drawings, relevant claim in the Claims, and patent examination files. If the Description defines any particular wording of a claim, such particular definition shall apply.

If the meaning of a claim cannot be clarified even by the approaches above, the claim may be interpreted according to reference books, textbooks and other public literatures and the common understanding on the part by persons of ordinary skill in the art.

§8.02 INTERPRETATION OF THE ARTICLE OF LAW

In the civil patent infringement procedure, in order to determine whether the sued infringement solution falls within the protection scope of the patent, it is necessary to clarify the meaning and protection scope of the claim by the claim interpretation.

Patent examination files are legal documents formed in the process of patent granting and confirmation. In judicial interpretation, patent examination files are taken as an important basis for interpreting and defining the protection scope of a claim. Article 3 of Judicial Interpretation I clarifies the interpretative function of the examination files of the patent involved per se. Article 6 of Judicial Interpretation II clarifies the interpretative function of any other patent which has a divisional application relationship with the patents involved and its examination files and further clarifies that the examination files include the observations and effective examination decisions in patent examination, reexamination, and invalidation procedures. Moreover, effective judgments in administrative proceedings against reexamination and invalidation can also be used to interpret the claim.

§8.03 ISSUES/DISPUTES ARISING IN THE LAW APPLICATION

[A] Any Other Patent Which Has a Divisional Application Relationship with the Patent Involved and Its Examination Files May Be Used to Interpret the Claim

Case 1: In a dispute over infringement of a patent right for invention between QIU Zeyou and Shandong Luban Construction Group General Company ((2011) Min Shen Zi No. 1309), the focus of the dispute of the case is whether the assembly of the top box and the side frame plate in the alleged infringing product is the same as or identical to the technical feature "the casing is assembled by splicing at least two block casing panels" of the patent for invention involved, which involves the interpretation of the block casing panel. The retrial petitioner QIU Zeyou asserted that the block casing panel can be any block, and the simple upper bottom or the sidewall can also be a block casing panel.

In this regard, the Supreme Court held in the retrial that the interpretation of QIU Zeyou regarding the block casing panel could not be established for the following reasons: 1. The meaning of the independently named term in the claim should be determined by the description for the specific term in the Description of the patent, other claims, and patent examination files. The Description had given a clear definition to "block casing panel," that is, "a block casing panel is a molded part comprising a part of the upper bottom and a part of the side wall connected thereto." 2. According to the general understanding of Claim 1 per se of the patent for invention involved, it can also be concluded that a block casing panel is a molded part comprising a part of the upper bottom and a part of the sidewall connected thereto. 3. The contents of paragraphs 5-7 of the Description of the patent for invention involved are not disclosed in the published Description of the parent application of the patent for invention involved. QIU Zeyou asserted that the block casing panel can be simply composed of an upper bottom or a sidewall on the basis of the undisclosed contents, which is not supported by the court. While protecting the interests of the patent applicant, the system of divisional application requires that the divisional application shall not go beyond the scope of disclosure contained in the parent application documents in order to balance the interests of the public, that is, no new contents that are not disclosed in the parent application documents shall be supplemented into the divisional application, so as to prevent the patent applicant from preempting the prior application date for invention-creations completed after the application date through the divisional application. Therefore, the divisional application shall be subject to the parent application documents. In this sense, for the divisional application, the parent application constitutes the special patent examination files of the divisional application, and the contents that are not disclosed in the parent application cannot be used as the basis for the right claim made by the patentee based on the divisional application. In this case, the patent for invention involved is a divisional application, and the contents of paragraphs 5-7 on page 2 of the Description of the patent for invention involved are not disclosed in the published Description of the parent patent application. According to the contents of the published Description of the parent patent application, the conclusion that the block casing panel can be simply composed of an upper bottom or a sidewall cannot be drawn. QIU Zeyou asserted that the block casing panel can be simply composed of an upper bottom or a side wall based on the contents that are not disclosed in the published Description of the parent patent application, which could not be established.

In the case, the Supreme Court first discusses the essential attribute of the system of divisional application: the divisional application is a special type of patent application, and the system of divisional application is a system that allows the patent applicant to file a separate patent application for invention-creation that has been disclosed in the parent application documents filed on the application date but cannot be protected in the parent application due to reasons such as lack of unity, while retaining the original application date in order to ensure the legitimate interests of the patent applicant from being damaged; and then clarifies the interpretation function of any other patent which has a divisional application relationship with the patent involved on the claim: the parent application constitutes special patent examination files of the divisional application, and the contents going beyond the scope of disclosure contained in the parent application should not serve as the basis for interpreting the claim of the granted patent of the divisional application in the determination of the protection scope of the claim of the granted patent of the divisional application.

[B] Any Other Patent Which Enjoys a Common Priority Right and Its Examination Files May Be Used to Interpret the Claim

Article 6 of the Judicial Interpretation II explicitly specifies that any other patent which has a divisional application relationship with the patent involved may be used to interpret the claim. In other words, the divisional application should be subject to the parent application documents, and the parent application constitutes the special patent examination files of the divisional application. It is only clarified in the scholarly papers that Article 6 of the Judicial Interpretation II can directly apply to the patent has a divisional application relationship. In judicial practice, the above provisions can be referred to for the patent, which has a priority right relationship with the patent involved, which can serve as the internal evidence for claim interpretation.

Case 2: In a dispute over infringement of a patent right for invention between Dyson Technology Limited and Suzhou Su-Vac Electric Motor Co., Ltd. ((2017) Zui Gao Fa Min Shen No. 1461 civil rulings for retrial review and trial supervision), one of the main disputes is that the Dyson Company believed that the second-instance judgment misinterpreted the "power source" and "power lead" of the patents involved, while Su-Vac Company had provided a related patent (200780027217.X), which is based on the same UK priority right patent (GB0614235.0) with the patent involved. It is explicitly determined in the observations of the related patent that the "power lead" is not the "power source."

Regarding the above dispute, first, the Supreme Court discussed in the retrial whether the specific observations regarding "power source" in the above-related patent can be used to interpret the claim of the patent involved, and held that the relationship between the subsequent application and the priority right application is substantially the same as the relationship between the divisional application and the parent application, and the subsequent application cannot likewise go beyond the scope of disclosure contained in the priority right application. The subsequent application that enjoys the priority right should have the same subject matter as the priority right application, which obviously has a closer internal relationship over the nonunity relationship between the divisional application and parent application. Therefore, the specific observations regarding the "power source" of the related patent in response to the Office Action can be used to interpret the claim of the patent involved.

In this case, the Supreme Court explicitly pointed out that in the determination of the meaning of the term of the claim, in the case that the same patent applicant or patentee had already made clear observations to the meaning of the same term in the granting and confirmation procedures of any other patent that has the same priority right with the patent involved, reference can be made to the above observations.

[C] Any Other Patent Applied by the Same Applicant in the Same Time Period and Its Examination Files May Be Used to Interpret the Claim

In judicial practice, referring to the above provisions, any other patent applied by the same applicant in the same time period may be used as internal evidence for claim interpretation.

Case 3: In a dispute over infringement of a patent right for invention between Hunan Qiuzeyouzhuanlizhanlve Planning Co., Ltd. and Shijiazhuang Donghai Rongfa Real Estate Development Co., Ltd. ((2018) Zui Gao Fa Min No. 5191), the focus issue is that the feature "overlapping layer" was not defined in the patent involved, and the patentee did not submit evidence to prove that the name "overlapping layer" is a generic name in the relevant industry. Hebei High Court of Second Instance introduced the patent for invention applied by QIU Zeyou, an associated applicant of the patentee, with patent No. ZL200710004620.2 and the name "Form component." The description of the production process of the patented product hollow form component in the Description explains the technical feature of the "overlapping layer."

In view of the above focus issue, the Supreme Court held in the retrial that the feature "overlapping layer" was not defined in the patent involved, the patentee failed to submit evidence to prove that the name "overlapping layer" is a generic name in the relevant industry, and the feature "overlapping layer" in the claim could be interpreted in combination with the Description and Drawings of the patent involved. Moreover, the patentee and its associated subject had applied for several patents in the same time period, and all of them involve the technical feature that the form component comprises an overlapping layer. Although the description of the overlapping layer in different patents is different in detail, there is no essential contradiction. With reference to the provisions of Article 6 of the Judicial Interpretation II, the overlapping layer can be defined in combination with the disclosure regarding the overlapping layer contained in other similar patents applied by the patentee.

As can be known from the above judicial practice, in addition to any other patent which has a divisional application relationship with the patents involved, as clearly specified in Article 6 of Judicial Interpretation II, the patent family of the patent involved, the priority right patent of the patent involved and the similar patents applied by the patentee can also be used as internal evidence to interpret the claim of the patent involved.

[D] A Restrictive Interpretation Cannot Be Made According to the Determination in the Noneffective Judgments for Patent Granting and Confirmation or the Examination Decision on the Announcement for Invalidation

In the second paragraph of Article 6 of judicial interpretation II, the scope of patent examination files as internal evidence is clarified. The files include written materials submitted by the patent applicant or patentee in the patent examination, reexamination and invalidation procedures, the Office Action, meeting records, oral hearing records, effective Decision of Examination upon Request for Patent Reexamination, and Examination Decision on the Request for Invalidation of Patent Right, and the like made by the patent administrative organ of the State Council and its Patent Reexamination Board. The examination decision involved in the confirmation and granting procedures should be an effective decision.

Case 4: In the second-instance civil judgment of a dispute over a patent right for invention between Royal KPN N.V. and Xiaomi Inc., one of the disputes is whether the patent involved includes the technical solution "buffering first and then compressing." KPN Company believed that the realization of the purpose of the invention of the patent involved did not depend on the sequence of compressing and buffering steps and proposed that the view was supported in the determination made by the Patent Reexamination Board in the Decision of Invalidation No. 32386. The decision contains the following content: "the collegiate panel held that claim 23 has defined that when data from the data fields of the first series are subjected to a compression process and then are accommodated in the data fields of the second series, the data to be accommodated in a data field of the second series are buffered."

In this regard, the Beijing Intellectual Property Court held in the first instance that the overall understanding of the claim made by those skilled in the art after reading the Description and Drawings should be further considered for the judgment of this issue. Although the sequence of compressing and buffering steps was not recited in the Claims, under the condition that other parts of the Description of the patent involved do not have any contrary disclosure, those skilled in the art would draw the conclusion that the patent involved performs compression first and then buffer after reading the above contents. In addition, since there is no effective conclusion on the case involved in the Decision of Invalidation No.28562, the prosecution history estoppel cannot be applied according to the above determination.

The Beijing High Court held in the second instance that according to Article 6 of Judicial Interpretation II, considering that the above determination was not the observations of KPN Company and the decision did not take effect, a corresponding restrictive interpretation of the patent involved cannot be made according to the determination in the decision.

In this case, the Beijing High Court has made it clear that if the determination is not the observations of the patent applicant/patentee, and the Examination Decision for Patent Invalidation has not yet taken effect, a restrictive interpretation cannot be made to the claim of the patent involved according to the determination in the decision.

[E] The Function of the Observations for Interpreting the Claim Is Different in the Granting and Confirmation Procedures and the Civil Infringement Procedure

Case 5: In the case of an administrative action against patent invalidation between ZHENG Yali VS Seiko Epson Corporation, the Patent Reexamination Board of the China National Intellectual Property Administration, Foshan Kaideli Office Products Co., Ltd. and Shenzhen Yicai Industrial Development Co., Ltd. (Supreme People's Court (2010) Zhi Xing Zi No. 53 Administrative Ruling), one of the main focuses of the case is how to understand the interpretation of Seiko Epson Corporation for "storage device" in the observations.

Regarding the technical feature "storage device," Seiko Epson pointed out in the observations in response to the First Office Action issued by the China National Intellectual Property Administration that "Claim 23 relates to FIG. 6 and FIG. 7, and the applicant explains that the 'storage device' refers to the 'semiconductor storage device 61' shown in FIG. 7 (b)." That is, Seiko Epson tries to make a restrictive interpretation to "storage device" by the observations.

In this regard, the Supreme Court held in the retrial that:

> First, regarding the function of the Observations, generally, the observations of the applicant in the examination files can be used as a reference for understanding the meaning of the Description and the Claims, and the reference value depends on the specific content of the observations and its relationship with the Description and the Claims.
>
> Second, regarding the characteristics of the interpretation for "storage device" in the Observations made by Seiko Epson, from the perspective of the contents of the interpretation, Seiko Epson interprets the generic term "storage device" as the specific term "semiconductor storage device" in combination with the Drawings. When a generic term is interpreted as a specific term which is included in the generic term, there may exist two understandings: first, this interpretation is only an example, that is, it means that the specific term belongs to the generic term; second, this interpretation is a specific reference, that is, the generic term is equivalent to the specific term. Therefore, the meaning of the interpretation for "storage device" in the Observations made by Seiko Epson still needs to be comprehensively judged in combination with the reasons of the interpretation, the amendment process, the originally published Description of the present patent, etc. Third, regarding the reason why Seiko Epson makes the interpretation to the "storage device" in the Observations, in the Observations, Seiko Epson amended the original Claim 23 into a new Claim 1. The original Claim 23 did not recite the feature "storage device,", which is introduced into the new Claim 1 in the amendment process, and Seiko Epson should make an explanation to the amendment to illustrate the reasons. From this aspect, it is unlikely for Seiko Epson to make a specific definition of the term "storage device" through the observations.
>
> Fourth, regarding the amendment process of Seiko Epson for the term "storage device,", in the originally published documents of the present patent, except the term "storage device," which is used independently once in the Description, the term of the semiconductor storage device is used throughout the Claims and remaining parts of the Description. The term "semiconductor storage device" appears more than 10 times in the Claims of the originally

> published documents. In the amended new Claims, the term is correspondingly amended into "storage device" and used up to 8 times. Obviously, this intentional amendment shows that Seiko Epson itself believes that "storage device" and "semiconductor storage device" have different meanings.
> Finally, regarding the use of the term "storage device" in the originally published Description of the present patent, as mentioned above, there is a usage of "storage device" as a generic term in the originally published Description of the present patent. It is unconvincing to make the understanding, that is, the "storage device" specifically refers to the semiconductor storage device, just based on the interpretation of Seiko Epson in the observations.

Therefore, the interpretation of "storage device" in the Observations made by Seiko Epson should be understood as the generic term, which includes the semiconductor storage device rather than the specific term of the semiconductor storage device.

In this case, the Supreme Court explicitly pointed out that: the interpretation method of the patent claim shows a certain difference in special occasions in the patent granting and confirmation procedures and civil infringement procedure. This difference is prominently reflected in the function of the observations of the party. In the patent granting and confirmation procedures, the applicant's observations in the examination files can only be used as a reference for understanding the meaning of the Description and the Claims rather than as a decisive basis in general. When the protection scope of the claim is interpreted in the civil patent infringement procedure, as long as the party abandons a certain technical solution through the observations in the patent application or granting procedures, the protection scope of the patent should be interpreted restrictively based on the party's observations in general.

§8.04 CONCLUSION

Based on the above discussion, in judicial practice involving file interpretation, the following points can be noted.

The consideration of the scope of internal evidence may not be limited to the patent involved per se in Article 3 of the Judicial Interpretation I and the divisional application patent in Article 6 of the Judicial Interpretation II. More broadly, referring to the divisional application patent in Article 6 of the Judicial Interpretation II, the patent family of the patent involved, the priority right patent of the patent involved, and other similar patents of the patentee may also be considered as the internal evidence for interpreting the claim of the patent involved.

In the case that the claim is interpreted based on the viewpoints in the examination decisions or judgments, the doubt can be made from the effectiveness of the decisions or judgments.

In addition, special attention should also be paid to the difference of the patent examination files, especially the observations of the party, for the interpretation of the patent claim in the patent granting and confirmation procedures and the civil infringement procedures.

CHAPTER 9

Interpretation on Claims Defined by Preparation Methods: A Report Series on Law Interpretation and Case Study Related to Patent Infringement

Dang Li & Ge Xiaomei

In the infringement judgment on product claims defined by preparation methods (Product-by-process), do the technical features of preparation methods function to define the protection scope of the patent? The answer is YES! However, the controversy still surrounds how to consider the process technical features of such claims in the course of the judgment of novelty and inventive step.

§9.01 BASIC PROVISIONS OF LAWS

***Interpretation (II) of the Supreme People's Court on Several Issues concerning the Application of Law in the Trial of Patent Infringement Dispute Cases* (hereinafter referred to as "*Judicial Interpretation II*")**

Article 10 Where the technical features of any product are defined through the preparation method in the claims, and the preparation method for the alleged infringing product is neither identical with nor equivalent to that of said product, the people's court shall affirm that the alleged infringing technical solution does not fall within the scope of protection of the patent right.

§9.02 INTERPRETATION OF THE PROVISIONS

According to their nature, claims are divided into two basic kinds, namely, process claims and product claims. The "product-by-process" claims will arise when the technical features in the product claims are defined by virtue of features of the process.

In the judicial practice, each country holds a different opinion on the definition of the protection scope of a "product-by-process" claim, including the "same product" rule, the "same process" rule, and the "actual impact" rule. In particular, according to the "same product" rule, the structure features, such as structure, composition and performance of the product recited in the claim, are taken into account, exclusive of any process features; according to the "same process" rule, the process feature is deemed to have the identical definitive effect with the structure feature; according to the "actual impact" rule, the process feature should be taken into account, and the key factor is whether the process feature imposes any influence on the subject matter of the invention. In the judicial practice of China, the "same process" rule is mainly adopted based on the principle that all the features in the claim shall be taken into account.

Article 10 of *Judicial Interpretation II* also explicitly provides that the preparation method in the product claim has a definitive effect on the protection scope of the patent right, thus identifying the definitive effect of the process in the "product-by-process" claim. The judicial interpretation further has an implication that it is a problem to be properly solved in the patent right granting and confirmation phase whether the technical feature of the product defined by the preparation method serves as an essential technical feature, and it is inappropriate for the people's court liable for the trial of the patent infringement dispute case to perform any discrimination. That is, the drafter of patent documents should pay enough attention to the above features and the expressions thereof in the patent application phase. The judicial interpretation enhances the public notice function of the claims, and in some sense, promotes the improvement on the drafting quality of patent application documents.

§9.03 POTENTIAL ISSUES/DISPUTES ARISING IN THE LAW APPLICATION

[A] Forms of "Product-by-Process" Claims

The "product-by-process" claim may be in the form of a claim with partial process features, in which one or more technical features are defined by process features. For example, an X device comprising structure A, structure B and structure C, wherein structure A is obtained by process D.

The "product-by-process" claim may be in another form of a claim with full process features, in which only the subject matter is a product and all technical features are preparation methods. For example, an X product characterized in that the product is obtained by steps A, B and C.

Besides the two forms above, there further exists a special form in which a product claim refers to a process claim and meanwhile further defines the specific structure of the product. For example, a product prepared by the method of Claim 1 and characterized in that the product comprises structure A, structure B and structure C.

[B] Definitive Effect of the Preparation Method Feature on the Protection Scope of the Claim

For the above "product-by-process" claim either partially or fully containing process features, the process features serve as a definition of technical features of the product or as full technical features of the claim, and in accordance with the principle that all the features in the claim shall be taken into account in the judicial practice and the provision of Article 10 of *Judicial Interpretation II*, the technical features therein have a definitive effect on the protection scope of the claim.

Case 1: In the patent right dispute case between Royal KPN and Xiaomi Technology Co. Ltd. ((2018) Jing Min Zhong No. 531 Civil Judgment issued by the Beijing Higher People's Court), the Beijing Higher People's Court affirms in the second instance that Claim 23 of the patent involved is a product claim, but the features "compressing," "buffering" and the like therein are involved in specific operation steps. According to the provision of Article 10 of *Judicial Interpretation II*, the sequence of the above steps "compressing," "buffering," and the like is apparently an essential consideration factor for determining the protection scope of Claim 23 of the patent involved.

Case 2: In the case of infringement dispute over a patent for invention between Chengdu Youta Pharmaceutical Co. Ltd. and Jiangsu Vanguard Pharmaceutical Co. Ltd. ((2010) Min Ti Zi No. 158 Civil Judgment issued by the Supreme People's Court), the claims of the patent involved seek to protect a soft capsule preparation of Lamiophlomis Rotata (Benth.)Kudo. In summary, the claims define the composition of raw materials and further define the method for extraction of one of the raw materials. In the retrial judgment, the Supreme People's Court has performed the infringement comparison based on the principle "for the judgment of whether the alleged infringing product falls within the protection scope of the patent right, the technical features of the alleged infringing product shall be compared with all technical features recited in the claims of the patent," actually acknowledging the definitive effect by the preparation method feature.

Case 3: In the case of infringement dispute over a patent for invention between Milliken and Changzhou Nanbo Compound Materials Co. Ltd. ((2017) Su Min Zhong No. 301 Civil Judgment), Claim 1 of the patent involved seeks to protect an apparatus for dividing a longitudinally extending conduit into compartments comprising a longitudinally extending insert, said insert being formed of at least two layers of a pliant material, said layers having lateral edges and being attached to each other near said lateral edges to form at least one compartment between said layers. The alleged infringing product comprises three O-pipes sewed together longitudinally, each O-pipe being formed of a pliant material. Milliken has claimed that the alleged infringing product is formed of six layers of a pliant material, said layers having lateral edges and being sewed to each other with threads near said lateral edges. Nanbo has defended that each pipe of the alleged infringing product is an independent O-pipe, which has no lateral edge and can be sewed in any position. Meanwhile, in the patent involved, the compartments are formed from the sewing of layered structures, while the alleged infringing product has no seam between pipes and comprises several independent pipes sewed together. The compartments exist with or without sewing. The dispute focuses on if there is any difference between layers and O-pipes and on the identification of compartments.

The Changzhou Intermediate People's Court has held in the first instance that: O-pipes of Nanbo may be construed as being formed from two layers of a pliant material attached seamlessly, in which the attachment leaves no clearly distinguishable traces. O-pipes may also be formed in such a manner. Consequently, O-pipes of the alleged infringing product likewise have "layers" and "lateral edges." The lateral edges of layers of a pliant material of the alleged infringing product are attached in a manner that every two layers of a pliant material are directly woven into an integrated part when they are manufactured, and then the three compartments formed by six layers of a pliant material are sewed again on the same sides. That is, the alleged infringing product has the technical features of "being attached to each other near lateral edges of layers" and "lateral edges of six layers of a pliant material being sewed to each other."

The Higher People's Court of Jiangsu Province has first determined in the second instance that: "lateral edge" is an edge defined by two ends of a straight line or a curve (an unclosed curve with endpoints) that can be shown on the transversal section of a pliant material, and "layer" can be construed as a pliant material used for space division. The layer of the alleged infringing product is an annular layer, which is formed of walls of the seamless textile sub-pipes and per se has no lateral edge. Based on the above, the technical feature "being attached to each other near said lateral edges (of said layers) to form at least one compartment between said layers" is deemed to define the position of the compartment (between layers), and more importantly, define the forming process (method) of the compartment. Consequently, the technical feature has the nature of a process feature and thus has a definitive effect on the protection scopes of product claims. The court has further held that the compartment of the alleged infringing product is enclosed by the wall of the single seamless textile sub-pipe; that is, the compartment already exists before the sewing. However, the compartment of the corresponding technical features in the claims is formed after the attachment of lateral edges. Therefore, the compartment of the alleged infringing product and that of the claims have a remarkable difference in the forming process. Accordingly, the technical feature is deemed as a distinguishing technical feature.

In the above cases, the definitive effect on the claims imposed by the process technical features serving as partial technical features is taken into account in the product claims. As to the preceding special form of the "product-by-process" claim, the process claim to which the claim refers defines the subject matter of the product, while the product per se is still defined by the specific structure features. It remains inconclusive whether the definition of the subject matter through the preparation method can be considered as "the technical features of any product defined through the preparation method" in Article 10 of *Judicial Interpretation II*.

Case 4: In the dispute over intellectual property between Guangdong Dongpeng Ceramics Co. Ltd. and Foshan Jiajun Ceramics Co. Ltd., Guangzhou Tianhe Jiayuan Building Materials Co. Ltd. and MA Jiehua ((2011) Yue Gao Fa Min San Zhong Zi No. 373 Civil Judgment issued by the Higher People's Court of Guangdong Province), the plaintiff claims to protect Claims 6 and 7. Claim 6 claims a flat ceramic tile with solid pores as decoration produced by the preparation method of claim 1, comprising: a base layer; a facing layer formed on one surface of the base layer; and a bottom layer formed on the other surface of the base layer; wherein the facing layer of the ceramic tile is provided with pores; the bottom layer is provided with a texture structure for meshing; and the base layer is made of porcelain, stoneware, or ceramic. Claim 1 claims a preparation method of a ceramic tile with solid pores as decoration, including the specific steps of preparing a fine material, forming, drying and the like. Both parties confirm that the technical features of the involved patent and the alleged product are identical other than the technical features in the preparation method of Claim 1.

The Guangzhou Intermediate People's Court has held in the first instance that the ceramic tile of Claim 6 is a new product, thereby presuming that the preparation method recited in Claim 1 is a manufacture process for a new product. The defendant fails to present the evidence of manufacturing the alleged product by a process different from the process under the patent involved in the case, assuming the litigation consequence of failing to produce evidence. Accordingly, it is presumed that the alleged product has all the essential technical features of Claims 1, 6 and 7 of the patent involved and thus falls within the protection scope of the patent.

The Higher People's Court of Guangdong Province has held in the second instance that: in the determination of protection scope for such an independent claim referring to another claim, all the features of the claim referred to shall be taken into account, and their actual definitive effect shall depend on what final impact they may impose on the claimed subject matter of the independent claim. As to the product and the production process specific to the product, they are technically associated, but it does not mean that the product cannot be manufactured by other processes. In this case, Claim 6 refers to Claim 1, but it does not further define the method of Claim 1. Likewise, the method of Claim 1 does not further define the product structure of Claim 6. Accordingly, the comparison focus of this case is still on the product structure and shape in Claim 6. Consequently, the trial result by the Court of First Instance is upheld.

Case 5: In the infringement dispute over a patent for invention between Harbin Institute of Technology Xinghe Industry Co. Ltd. and Jiangsu Runde Pipe Industry Co. Ltd. ((2013) Min Shen Zi No. 790 Retrial Civil Judgment), Claim 1 seeks to protect a plastic drainage pipeline reinforced by steel strips, independent Claim 2 seeks to protect a method for making the plastic drainage pipeline reinforced by steel strips according to Claim 1, and independent Claim 6 seeks to protect an apparatus for making a plastic drainage pipe reinforced by steel strips by the method according to Claim 2. One of the focus issues of this case is as follows: when a parallel independent claim refers to a preceding independent claim, how to determine the definitive effect on the protection scope of the independent claim imposed by the preceding independent claim.

The Supreme People's Court has held in the retrial that, in general cases, in the determination of the protection scope of a claim, the title of the subject matter recited in the claim shall be taken into account, and the actual definitive effect shall depend on the impact the title of subject matter imposes on the claimed subject matter per se. In this case, in the determination of the protection scopes of Claims 2 and 6, the actual definitive effect the titles of the subject matter thereof impose on the claimed subject matters per se shall be taken into account. And based on the disclosure contained in the claims and the description of the patent involved, it can be seen that the technical features recited in Claim 1 impose substantial effects on Claims 2 and 6, thus having the definitive effect.

In Cases 4 and 5, the process claim to which the claim refers defines the subject matter of the product, and the actual definitive effect shall depend on the impact the title of subject matter imposes on the claimed subject matter per se.

[C] Distribution of the Burden of Producing Evidence for "Product-by-Process" Claims

[1] Plaintiffs Produce Evidence

For the "product-by-process" claims, the definitive effect of the preparation method on the technical feature shall be taken into account, and the preparation method and other technical features jointly define the protection scope of the claim. As a result, Plaintiffs shall undertake the burden of producing evidence for the infringement claim. When producing evidence, plaintiffs need to consider both the product structure and the technical features of the preparation method.

Case 6: In the dispute over patent infringement between QIAO Changlin and Jinan Changlin Airbag Container Factory Co. Ltd. and SUN Juxiang ((2011) Min Shen Zi No. 1047 Civil Ruling Paper issued by the Supreme People's Court), Claim 1 of the patent involved seeks to protect a high-strength nylon airbag container, characterized in that it is formed by vulcanization of various cord threads coated with raw rubber and fabrics thereof or mixed fabrics of cord threads and steel wires after winding. The Supreme People's Court has held in the retrial that, from the photograph of the alleged infringing airbag product as presented by QIAO Changlin, only the appearance and shape of the alleged infringing product can be seen, but the specific preparation method cannot be known. Given that the airbag container is not a new product, QIAO Changlin, as the patentee claiming the infringement, should present the evidence that features of the manufacture process for the alleged infringing airbag product are identical with or equivalent to the process features recited in the involved patented technology. The manufacture process for the alleged infringing airbag product cannot be determined based on the existing evidence, resulting in that it is impossible to determine if the alleged infringing airbag product falls within the protection scope of the patent involved. Due to the failure to perform the burden of producing evidence, QIAO Changlin should assume the adverse consequences in this respect.

Case 7: In the case of an infringement dispute over a patent for invention between Beijing Wangzu Purifying Technology Development Co. Ltd. and Shaanxi Siwei Gaoke Filtration Materials Co. Ltd., etc. ((2006) Yi Zhong Min Chu Zi No. 9998 of the Beijing First Intermediate People's Court), Claim 1 of the patent involved seeks to protect a full-flow deep lubricating oil purifier filter element for the purification of gasoline and diesel engine lubricating oil, characterized in that it is made of wood chips (9 to 36 meshes), plant fibers (8 to 12 mm) and auxiliary materials thereof, the proportions being as follows (part by weight): wood chips of 100; plant fibers of 60 to 70; and auxiliary materials of 3.35 to 6.5. As shown in the authentication report provided by the plaintiff, the dimensions of wood chips and plant fibers of the two alleged infringing products are identical to those of the patent involved, but the contents of wood chips and plant fibers of the alleged infringing products are significantly different from those of the patent.

The Beijing First Intermediate People's Court has affirmed in the first instance that Claim 1 is drafted in a product-by-process manner, and the characterizing portion actually defines the raw materials for the preparation of the product and the proportions thereof. However, merely based on the existing evidence, it cannot be determined if the raw materials for the preparation of the product and the proportions thereof are exactly matched with the materials of the final product and the proportions thereof. That is, the plaintiff fails to produce evidence that the two alleged infringing products are manufactured as per the raw materials and the proportions thereof as defined in Claim 1 of the patent.

In case 7, the process defining the product is the proportions of raw materials, and the proportions of raw materials are not necessarily matched with the proportions of raw materials of the final product. If considering the two proportions identical, the plaintiff needs to undertake the corresponding obligation of producing evidence. Otherwise, the plaintiff may assume the adverse consequence of failing to produce evidence.

[2] Inversion of the Burden of Producing Evidence

Article 61.1 of the Patent Law provides that: where any infringement dispute relates to a patent for invention for a process for the manufacture of a new product, any entity or individual manufacturing the identical product shall furnish proof to show that the process used in the manufacture of its or his product is different from the patented process. Then, here comes an issue if the provision of Article 61 applies to the "product-by-process" claim. That is, under the rule of inversion of the burden of producing evidence, the alleged infringer is required to undertake the burden of producing evidence.

Case 8: In the appellate case of dispute over patent infringement between CIRS SPA and Changzhou Wujin Jiahua Chemical Engineering Co. Ltd. ((2006) Su Min San Zhong Zi No. 0025 of the Higher People's Court of Jiangsu Province), independent Claim 1 of the patent involved seeks to protect an anti-scaler for coating the polymerizing reactors for monomers, of the liquid types, obtained by means of the naphthols condensation with an aldehydic cross-linking product, characterized by that: for obtaining the condensate a reaction of combining hydrosulfite and a formaldehyde compound with 1-naphthol is performed in an alkaline environment; the anti-scaler contains hydrosulfite and/or radical bisulfites and/or bisulfite; the anti-scaler is in the form of a liquid of clear transparent color; and the anti-scaler is stored without oxygen. The accrediting body has issued a *Testing Report* showing that the anti-scaler product has other features of the claim involved than the process and stated in the cross-examination that only the components or composition of the product could be tested, while the reaction process could not be inferred backward based on the components of the product.

The Court of First Instance has affirmed that the patent involved protects a product, and the product under patent protection should be deemed as a new product. The process features in the claim of the patent involved are used to define the protection scope. The plaintiff fails to present the evidence of the production process adopted by the defendant and cannot infer backward the manufacture process based on the finished chemical product, but as provided by law, in the patent infringement litigation arising from a patent for invention for a process for the manufacture of a new product, the entity or individual manufacturing the identical product shall undertake the burden of producing evidence to show that the process used in the manufacture of its or his product is different from the patented process. Moreover, from the perspective of judicial economy, it is more convenient that the defendant presents the evidence of the process used in the manufacture of its product. Consequently, the Court of First Instance has ordered Jiahua Company to provide its process used in the manufacture of the alleged infringing product. However, the production process provided by the defendant is different from the process features of the patent involved in terms of reaction initiators, reaction steps and the like, and thus does not constitute the literal infringement or the infringement under the doctrine of equivalents.

In the second instance, the Higher People's Court of Jiangsu Province has firstly expounded if the production process provided by the defendant could serve as the factual basis for affirming the case. According to the identification conclusion, it is affirmed that the production process provided by the defendant is not the process actually used in the manufacture of the product involved. During the affirmation of whether the production process for the alleged infringing product is identical with the production process in the patent involved, the product under the patent involved of the plaintiff is deemed as a new product since it is allowed as a patent for invention. The defendant has argued that the patent involved relates to an old product. However, the defendant's argument is not supported due to the failure of the defendant to present the corresponding evidence. According to the provision of the Chinese Patent Law, where any infringement dispute relates to a patent for invention for a process for the manufacture of a new product, any entity or individual manufacturing the identical product shall furnish proof to show that the process used in the manufacture of its or his product is different from the patented process. In this case, the patent involved of the plaintiff is a patent for a new product, and thus the defendant shall present the evidence to show that its production process for the production of the alleged infringing product is different from the process of the patent involved. However, the identification conclusion has shown that the production process provided by the defendant is not the process actually used for the production of the alleged infringing product involved in the case, and thus the defendant shall assume the legal consequence of failing to produce evidence as prescribed by laws. Accordingly, it shall be affirmed that the defendant adopts the process identical to that of the patent involved for the production of the alleged infringing product.

In this case, the courts of both first instance and second instance held that the laws relating to a patent for invention for a process for the manufacture of a new product directly apply to the "product-by-process" claims and adopt the rule of inversion of the burden of producing evidence, that is, the alleged infringer is required to undertake the burden of producing evidence.

§9.04 CONCLUSION

Article 10 of *Judicial Interpretation II* explicitly provides that the preparation method in the product claim has a definitive effect on the protection scope of the patent right. In judicial practice, the definitive effect the preparation method imposes on the product claim needs to be taken into account. Like the claims of manufacture process, the manufacture process defined therein is also confronted with the issue of difficulties in producing evidence.

CHAPTER 10

Limitation by Numerical Features: A Report on Law Interpretation and Case Study Related to Patent Infringement

Dang Li & Ge Xiaomei

A determination of whether a numerical feature is an equivalent feature is an issue. It can be figured out through the interpretation of legal provisions herein and the judicial precedents that the infringement under the doctrine of equivalents generally does not apply if the emphasis is laid on the effect or the limitation role of numerical features and that there is a range of the application for the infringement under the doctrine of equivalents if the emphasis is not laid on the highlighting role of numerical features. This chapter includes a discussion of six typical judicial decisions.

§10.01 BASIC PROVISIONS OF LAWS

Interpretation (II) of the Supreme People's Court on Several Issues concerning the Application of Law in the Trial of Patent Infringement Dispute Cases **(hereinafter referred to as "*Judicial Interpretation II*")**

Article 12 Where the claim adopts such terms as "at least" or "no more than" to limit the numerical feature, and upon reading claims, description and drawings, a person with ordinary skills in the art deems that the technical solution of the patent particularly emphasizes the limitation role of such terms on the feature, the allegation of the right holder that a different numerical feature constitutes an equivalent feature shall not be supported by the people's court.

§10.02 INTERPRETATION OF THE PROVISIONS

In the description of claims, the numerical values can be used to define the technical features. Compared with other technical features defined by structure, process and the like, numerical features deliver a clear limitation in terms of the form of manifestation. As to the issue of whether the doctrine of equivalents applies to the technical feature of numerical range with such a clear limitation, the *Judicial Interpretation II* describes the circumstance where the application of the doctrine of equivalents to the technical features defined by numerical ranges is explicitly excluded, that is, if a person with ordinary skills in the art upon reading the application documents can deem that the technical solution of the patent particularly emphasizes the limitation role of numerical features, the allegation that a different numerical feature acts as an equivalent feature shall not be supported.

Besides the above provisions of the *Judicial Interpretation II*, Article 57 of *Guidelines for Patent Infringement Determination (2017)*, Beijing High People's Court further provides that: "in respect of a claim containing a numerical range feature, the allegation of the right holder that a different numerical feature constitutes an equivalent feature generally shall not be supported. In respect of a claim of a utility model having a numerical feature, the allegation of the right holder that a corresponding numerical feature in an accused infringing technical solution constitutes an equivalent feature shall not be supported, except that the different numerical feature belongs to the technical content appearing after the filing date." As can be seen, in the guidelines for infringement determination provided by the Beijing High People's Court, extremely strict requirements are established for the determination of infringement by the numerical features and the numerical range features under the doctrine of equivalents. The allegation of equivalent features is generally not supported.

§10.03 POTENTIAL ISSUES/DISPUTES ARISING IN THE LAW APPLICATION

[A] Exclusion of the Application of the Doctrine of Equivalents in Determination of a Numerical Feature

[1] The Numerical Range with Clear Limitation Shall Not Be Broken Through, and the Application of the Doctrine of Equivalents Is Excluded

Case 1: In the case of infringement dispute over a patent for invention between Yangquan City Dongfeng Refractories Co. Ltd. and Yixing City Lianzhu Refractories Factory Co. Ltd. ((2011) Min Shen Zi No. 263), Dongfeng Company has alleged the infringement based on Claim 5 of the patent involved. Claim 5 is described as follows: a mullite casting nozzle brick prepared according to the method of Claim 1 or 2, characterized in that the main crystal phase of a crystal phase structure of the mullite casting nozzle brick is mullite, the rest is a corundum phase and a small amount of cristobalite, and the Al_2O_3 content is 70 to 75% or above, the C content is 3 to 6%, and the apparent porosity is not more than 10%. The disputed technical feature lies in that the apparent porosity of the alleged infringing product is 12.9%, while the apparent porosity in the claim of the patent involved is not more than 10%.

The Beijing First Intermediate People's Court has held in the first instance that Dongfeng Company fails to prove the manufacture process for the alleged infringing product and that the alleged infringing product has an apparent porosity somewhat different from the apparent porosity in Claim 5. The Beijing High People's Court has held in the second instance that it is impossible to prove the equivalence between the technical feature "the apparent porosity is not more than 10%" in Claim 5 and the technical feature of the alleged infringing product that the apparent porosity is 12.9%. Dongfeng Company has alleged that compared with the technical feature, "the apparent porosity is not more than 10%" in Claim 5 of the patent involved, the technical feature of the alleged infringing product that the apparent porosity is 12.9% constitutes technical inferiority, and thus equivalence exists between such two technical features.

In this regard, the Supreme Court has held in the retrial that: in the claims of the patent involved, the apparent porosity is defined, in the description thereof, by the numerical range with a very clear limitation of "not more than 10%," and according to the disclosure of the description, it should be deemed that the technical effect disclosed in the patent involved can be achieved only by the mullite casting nozzle brick with an apparent porosity of not more than 10%. This definite range limitation shall not be broken through during the interpretation of the claim. Moreover, other evidence further shows the remarkably different technical effects achieved by the mullite casting nozzle brick with an apparent porosity of not more than 10% and by the mullite casting nozzle brick with an apparent porosity of 12.9%. Consequently, the two technical features cannot be deemed equivalent.

In Case 1, it is deemed that the limitation of a numerical range is very clear, and this definite range limitation shall not be broken through during the interpretation of the claim. Meanwhile, according to the disclosure of the description, it is clear that the technical effect of the patent involved cannot be achieved without the numerical feature limitation and that the numerical feature of the alleged infringing product achieves a different effect. Accordingly, the doctrine of equivalents cannot apply to the numerical feature in the patent involved.

[2] The Application of the Doctrine of Equivalents Is Excluded When the Numerical Features Have the Function of Emphasis

Case 2: In the case of infringement dispute over a patent for invention between Kingclean Electric Co. Ltd. and Xiaogou Electric Appliance (Beijing) Co. Ltd. ((2016) Su Min Zhong No. 639), Kingclean has claimed to protect Claim 1, which contains the technical feature "the air intake channel has a cross-sectional area of less than 150 mm^2, and the air intake channel has a height H of less than 5 mm." For the technical feature "the air inlet has a cross-sectional area of 285 mm^2 and a height of 7.5 mm, and the air outlet has a cross-sectional area of 118.5 mm^2 and a height of 3.1 mm" in the alleged infringing product, Kingclean has alleged that the alleged infringing product has the corresponding technical feature of the patent involved as long as its air intake channel has any cross-sectional area of less than 150 mm^2 and any height of less than 5 mm. The Suzhou Intermediate People's Court has held in the first instance that the technical feature of the claim should be limited to all cross-sectional areas and heights and affirmed that, as to the air inlet of the alleged infringing product, the cross-sectional area of 285 mm^2 and the height of 7.5 mm are both larger than the dimensions defined in the claim, and thus the alleged infringing product does not fall within the protection scope of the patent involved according to law.

In this regard, the Higher People's Court of Jiangsu Province has first affirmed in the second instance, based on the disclosure of the description and the general principles of fluid mechanics, that the technical features "cross-sectional area of air intake channel" and "height of air intake channel" in the claim of the patent involved should be construed as the cross-sectional area and the height at the air inlet. Further, on this basis, the technical feature "the air intake channel has a cross-sectional area of less than 150 mm^2, and the air intake channel has a height H of less than 5 mm" in Claim 1 has been compared with the technical feature "the air inlet has a cross-sectional area of 285 mm^2 and a height of 7.5 mm" of the alleged infringing product. In accordance with the disclosure of the description of the patent involved, it has been affirmed that the limitation by the two numerical features on the cross-sectional area and the height at the air inlet is the key to realize the purpose of the patent for the invention involved. However, the numerical ranges of the alleged infringing product do not fall within the defined numerical ranges. Therefore, the technical feature of the alleged infringing product has not constituted an equivalent feature of the corresponding technical feature of the patent involved.

Case 3: In the case of dispute over patent infringement between Dalian Renda New Wall Building Materials Plant and Dalian Xinyi Building Material Company Limited ((2005) Min San Ti Zi No. 1), Dalian Renda has claimed to protect Claim 1, which contains the technical feature "the bottom of the cylinder consists of at least two superimposed layers of glass fiber cloth." Compared with the patent involved, the alleged infringing product of Xinyi Company is short of one layer of glass fiber cloth at the cylinder duct portion and has no glass fiber cloth at the cylinder bottom portion. The Dalian Intermediate People's Court has held in the first instance that: it is only the numerical difference between one layer and two layers, and such difference does not cause any qualitative change; consequently, the alleged infringing product and the patent involved have substantially identical means and achieve identical functions and effects, and an infringement under the doctrine of equivalents is constituted. The Liaoning High People's Court has held in the second instance that, different from the limitation of a numerical range for compounds, compositions and the like, this kind of difference just relates to the numerical replacement and does not cause any change to the essence of the product. The Liaoning High People's Court supports the order awarded by the Court of First Instance.

In this regard, the Supreme Court deems that: the claim explicitly contains the restrictive statement with a very clear limitation of "at least two layers," and the description also discloses that the glass fiber cloth cylinder can consist of "as few as two superimposed layers only." Consequently, this definite restrictive condition shall not be broken through during the interpretation of the claim. Moreover, the difference in the number of glass fiber cloth layers in the patent involved cannot be simply considered as a numerical difference. Instead, such difference performs different functions in the sense of physical mechanics on the anti-pressure capability of cylinder member, the volume of the inner cavity, and the floor weight. The glass fiber cloth in "one layer" only cannot achieve the effect substantially identical with that achieved by the glass fiber cloth in "at least two layers." Therefore, the technical feature of the alleged infringing product that a layer of glass fiber cloth is inserted in the cement inorganic binding material in the cylinder duct portion is not equivalent to the corresponding technical feature of the patent, let alone identical with it.

In Cases 2 and 3, based on the disclosure of the Description, whether the numerical features contribute to solving the technical problem of the patent and achieving the corresponding technical effect is determined, that is, whether the numerical features are necessary for the achievement of the technical effect. On this basis, it has been concluded that the numerical features are of particular emphasis function on the technical solution of the patent, and thus the application of the doctrine of equivalents is excluded.

[3] The Application of the Doctrine of Equivalents Is Excluded When the Combination of Multiple Numerical Features Can Be Deemed Necessary for the Achievement of the Technical Effect

Case 4: In the civil dispute of the second instance regarding an infringement dispute over a patent for invention between American Membrane (Nantong) Co. Ltd. and Hangzhou Cobetter Filtration Equipment Co. Ltd. ((2017) Zhe Min Zhong No. 559), American Membrane has claimed to protect Claim 1 as follows: 1. A method for producing a porous semi-permeable filter membrane, characterized in that the method includes the following steps in sequence: (1) at the equilibrium point of water vapor absorption, dissolving a polymer solid material with water vapor absorption capacity of 2% to 4% in a highly polar organic solvent, and adding a water-soluble polymer additive that is compatible with the polymer solid material to prepare an uniform solution in which the polymer solid material accounts for 10% to 30% of the total parts by weight, the organic solvent accounts for 15% to 30% of the total parts by weight, and the water-soluble polymer additive accounts for 40% to 75% of the total parts by weight; (2) after adjusting the temperature of the above solution to 10 to 50° C, lying the solution on a continuously rotating roller or conveyor belt, having the solution contacted with air with relative humidity of 40% to 95%, dry-bulb temperature of 10 to 50°C and dew-point temperature of 10 to 50°C after the adjustment, putting a formation on the roller or conveyor belt into a water bath of 5°C to 50°C for final molding, and then peeling off a formed filter membrane from the roller or conveyor belt; and (3) final treatment: stretching the filter membrane at a variable or constant speed, washing the filter membrane with a cleaning agent, and drying the filter membrane at a temperature of 25°C to 80°C to obtain a product.

After comparison, the technical solution of Cobetter is distinguished from Claim 1 in the following: the relative humidity is different from the relative humidity of 40% to 95% after adjustment as defined in Step (2) (the court has measured the relative humidity of 24.5% and temperature of 22°C for the air); and the filter membrane is not stretched, and the drying temperature is different from the temperature of 25°C to 80°C as defined in Step (3) of Claim 1 of the patent (the court has measured that the drying temperature is 95°C to 99°C). The Hangzhou Intermediate People's Court has held in the first instance that: American Membrane fails to present any evidence of achieving the identical technical effect in a case where such significant numerical difference exists between the relative humidity of 24.5% and the relative humidity of 40% to 95% defined in the patent, and thus the factual basis for identifying the technical features to be equivalent is absent; on the other hand, since in the patent, a plurality of parameters is set in one technical step, creating a definite limitation on numerical ranges, it shall be deemed that the combination of parameters conforming to each parameter range is indispensable for achieving the functions of the patented technology, and the protection scope of the patent, as prescribed by laws, is defined by a variety of parameter ranges. The definite limitation of the claims shall not be broken through during the interpretation of the claims. Otherwise, the protection scope of the patent will be expanded groundlessly. Based on Article 12 of *Judicial Interpretation II*, it has been affirmed that the alleged technical solution contains no features identical with or equivalent to the corresponding technical features of the patent involved. In the second instance, the Higher People's Court of Zhejiang Province has upheld in the second instance the judgment made by the Court of First Instance.

In Case 4, the steps of the claim contain a plurality of parameters with clearly defined numerical ranges. Thus, these parameters shall be deemed necessary for the achievement of the technical effect. The application of the doctrine of equivalents is excluded when the technical solution of the alleged infringing product contains the distinguishing technical feature defined by one or more parameters.

[B] Application of the Doctrine of Equivalents in Determination of a Numerical Feature

[1] The Doctrine of Equivalents Applies to the Numerical Range Features

Case 5: In the case of infringement dispute over a patent for invention between Hangzhou Grascent Co. Ltd. and Hangzhou Youbang Flavor & Fragrance Co. Ltd. [(2014) Zhe Zhi Zhong Zi No. 17], Hangzhou Grascent has alleged the infringement based on Claim 1 of the patent involved, which is described as follows: a method for preparing epoxy pinane by using sodium percarbonate as a reagent, characterized in that after mixing pinene and sodium percarbonate with a solvent, adding acetic anhydride gradually under stirring, wherein an additive amount molar ratio of pinene to sodium percarbonate = 1: (1.1-3.0) and sodium percarbonate to acetic anhydride =

1: (0.5-2.0), a reaction temperature is room temperatur-65°C, and the reaction time is 1-24 hours. The distinction has been affirmed in the *Judicial Appraisal Opinion* as follows: it is recited in Claim 1 of the patent involved that the molar ratio of pinene to sodium percarbonate is 1: (1.1-3.0) (hereinafter referred to as "Feature B"), while it is recited in the technical feature of the alleged infringing process that the molar ratio of pinene to sodium percarbonate is 1:1.011 (hereinafter referred to as "Feature b"). The Hangzhou Intermediate People's Court has held in the first instance that Claim 1 of the patent involved clearly defines the composition and proportions of reactants. Despite the allegation of technical equivalence since Feature b in the alleged infringing process is completely identical with Feature B in the technical features of the patent in terms of the technical means adopted and the function and technical effect realized, Hangzhou Grascent fails to present any valid evidence, and thus the allegation is not supported by the Hangzhou Intermediate People's Court.

In this regard, the Higher People's Court of Zhejiang Province has held in the second instance that: the protection scope of the patent shall be determined on the basis of the scopes defined by the technical features clearly stated in the Claims, including the scopes determined by the features equivalent to the stated technical features. The determination of whether the technical features are equivalent shall be performed in terms of means, function and effect, and the technical features shall be examined in accordance with the knowledge criteria of a person with ordinary skills in the art. On the basis that the means are substantially identical, the function is identical, and the effect is identical, it has been affirmed that Feature b in the alleged infringing process is completely identical with Feature B in the technical features of the patent thereby constituting technical equivalence.

In Case 5, based on the determination according to the doctrine of equivalents, the numerical range features have been examined in terms of means, function and effect in accordance with the knowledge criteria of a person with ordinary skills in the art. As compared with the corresponding technical feature of the patent involved, the technical feature of the alleged infringing process has been deemed to adopt the substantially identical means and achieve the identical function and effect, and thus it has been affirmed that the doctrine of equivalents applies to the numerical feature in the patent involved.

[2] The Doctrine of Equivalents Can Apply When the Numerical Features Have No Function of Emphasis

Case 6: In the first instance of a civil dispute regarding an infringement dispute over a patent for invention between YU Zuotao and Shanghai Qizhi Trading Company and Zhejiang Taobao Network Co. Ltd. [(2018) Zhe 01 Min Chu No. 879], YU Zuotao has claimed to protect Claim 1 as follows: a playing card automatic dealing apparatus, characterized in that: four sets of bin gates (28, 32, 35, 38) controlled by electromagnets (11, 8, 5, 3) are uniformly arranged below a transmission belt (2); the front of each bin gate is provided with a photoswitch (16, 13, 10, 7); opening and closing of each bin gate are regularly controlled by a microcomputer according to information which is collected by the photoswitch; five card storage bins (29, 33, 36, 39, 42) under the bin gates are used to store dealt cards; a dealing limiting plate (17) arranged on the front of the transmission belt is a front arm of a card inlet bin; and two dealing limiting pieces (45) on the bottom are inclined forward with 35°, which is favorable for a dealing rubber roller (24) below the card inlet bin to push forward cards. Qizhi Trading Company has argued that the angle of the "dealing limiting pieces" of the alleged infringing product cannot be 35°, and thus a feature identical with or equivalent to the corresponding technical feature of the patent involved cannot be constituted. Consequently, the alleged infringing product does not fall within the protection scope of the patent involved.

With the actual measurement by the Hangzhou Intermediate People's Court, the angle of the "dealing limiting pieces" of the alleged infringing product is approximately 35.5°. Moreover, the Hangzhou Intermediate People's Court has held that: first, the errors necessarily exist in processing and measurement, and the numerical values measured by the court may be deemed to fall within the error range, and the numerical feature within the error range shall be considered as an identical feature; second, even if the minor deviation in angle exists indeed, as compared with the corresponding technical feature of the patent involved, in the "dealing limiting pieces" of the alleged infringing product, the two angle values produce no significant difference in terms of technical means, function and achievable effect. The feature of the angle of 35.5° can be envisaged by a person with ordinary skills in the art without the exercise of any creative work, thereby constituting an equivalent feature of the corresponding technical feature of the patent involved. Further, a person with ordinary skills in the art, upon reviewing the patent involved, will not deem that the limitation role of such angle is particularly emphasized in the technical solution of the patent involved. It is hence affirmed that the doctrine of equivalents can apply to the feature and that the alleged infringing product has the preceding numerical technical feature.

In Case 6, the disputed focus is on the numerical technical feature. Compared with the patent involved, the alleged infringing product shows a minor difference in the numerical technical feature and produces no significant difference in terms of technical means, function and achievable effect. And the Description and the Claims do not emphasize the limitation role of the numerical technical feature. Consequently, it is affirmed that the doctrine of equivalents can apply to the feature.

§10.04 CONCLUSION

Article 12 of *Judicial Interpretation II* identifies the circumstance where the application of the doctrine of equivalents to the technical features defined by numerical ranges is excluded, which also sets the tone for the infringement judgment of numerical features. Generally, the doctrine of equivalents in principle cannot apply to the technical features defined by numerical ranges, and the application is an exception. Without convincing reasons, it is difficult for the allegation of equivalence to be recognized.

In addition, the judicial interpretation is beneficial to the enhancement of the public notice function of the claims, strengthens the definiteness in the protection scope of the patent, provides the definite legal basis for the social public, and in some sense promotes the improvement on the drafting quality of patent application documents.

CHAPTER 11
A Defining Effect of a Sequence of Steps of a Process Claim

Zhang Junjie & Ge Xiaomei

In the case that the sequence of steps is clearly defined in the process claim, the steps per se and the sequence thereof certainly have a defining effect on the protection scope of the claim. What if the sequence is not clearly defined? Can it be interpreted as the steps being implemented in any sequence? It is incorrect!

The chapter will unlock the interpretation rules of the process claim in the case that the sequence of steps is not clearly defined in combination with the judicial practice, and your attention is appreciated.

§11.01 BASIC PROVISIONS OF LAWS

***Interpretation II of the Supreme People's Court on Several Issues concerning the Application of Law in the Trial of Patent Infringement Dispute Cases* (hereinafter referred to as "*Judicial Interpretation II*")**

Article 11 In the case that a process claim does not clearly recite a sequence of technical steps while persons of ordinary skill in the art determine directly and clearly that the technical steps should be performed in a specific sequence after reading the Claims, the Description and the Drawings, the People's Court shall determine that the sequence of the steps has a defining effect on the protection scope of the patent right.

§11.02 INTERPRETATION OF THE ARTICLE OF LAW

The process patent protects any activity that includes elements of time or process, such as the product manufacturing processes, methods of use, and methods of communication. In general, the purpose to be achieved by the process invention is generally achieved by the combination of the process steps and a specific sequence of steps. On the one hand, for process invention, which has a specific sequence of steps, both of the steps per se and the sequence of steps pertain to the essential technical features of the process patent and should perform the defining effect on the protection scope of the patent right. The protection scope of the patent right shall not be understood as the steps being implemented in any sequence. On the other hand, for the process invention with a specific sequence of steps not recited in the claim, it is inappropriate to regard the recited sequence of steps as the sequence of implementation, and it is not appropriate to use the sequence of the words in the claim as the basis for defining the protection scope of the patent right.

Article 11 of the *Judicial Interpretation II* prescribes that the sequence of steps that is not explicitly recited in the process claim can constitute the technical feature of the patent under a certain condition. That is, in the case that persons of ordinary skill in the art determine directly and clearly that there exists a specific sequence after reading the claims, the Description, and the Drawings, the sequence of steps has a defining effect. This chapter substantially compensates for the negligence in drafting patent documents to a certain extent. While emphasizing the basic orientation of the publicity of the claims, the interpretation of claims needs to maintain a certain degree of flexibility and avoid literalism so that patents with genuine technical contributions can obtain more comprehensive protection.[1]

According to the above provisions, the conditions for applying the provision of "ruling to dismiss the action and initiating a separate action" are as follows:

> The interpretation of the process claim which does not clearly define a sequence of steps: if the claim includes the expressly defining expressions such as "in turn," "orderly," "sequentially," "step by step," it can be considered that the claim clearly recites the sequence, and this chapter does not apply, that is, both the steps per se and the sequence of steps perform the defining effect on the protection scope of the claim. On the contrary, if the claim does not recite the expressly defining expression, even if the claim is drafted as "a method comprises the following steps," this chapter should apply, namely, persons of ordinary skill in the art can determine directly and clearly that there is a specific sequence after reading the claims, the Description and the Drawings.

1. SONG Xiaoming, WANG Chuang, LI Jian, Understanding and Application of *Interpretation (II) on Several Issues concerning the Application of Law in the Trial of Patent Infringement Dispute Cases* [J], People's Judicature (Application), 2016(10): 30-31.

§11.03 ISSUES/DISPUTES ARISING IN THE LAW APPLICATION

[A] In the Case That There Is No Definition on the Sequence of Steps, Whether There Is a Specific Sequence Should Be Determined in Combination with the Patent Documents

In a dispute over infringement of patent right for invention between OBE-WERK OHNMACHT & BAUMGÄERTNER GMBH & CO. KG and Zhejiang Kanghua Glasses Co. Ltd. ((2008) Min Shen Zi No. 980), the patent relates to a method of manufacturing spring hinges used for eyeglass legs, Claim 1 in the announcement text for grant of patent right is as follows "1. A method of manufacturing a spring hinge including at least a housing, a hinge member, and a spring, characterized in that the method comprises the following steps: providing a metal strap for forming the hinge member; cutting free a region substantially corresponding to a shape of the hinge member; impressing a rounded portion in order to form an elongate extension to the hinge element; and stamping out a hinge hole of the hinge member." The focus of the dispute, in this case, is whether the above steps should be implemented sequentially according to the sequence recited in the claim.

The retrial petitioner OBE Company held that Claim 1 only described the steps of the method of the patent and did not define the sequence of steps; the steps per se rather than the sequence of steps in Claim 1 were the key to the technical problem and the protection scope of Claim 1 covered combinations of various sequences of the steps.

In this regard, the Supreme Court held in the retrial that for the process invention which has a sequence of steps, both of the steps per se and the sequence of the steps should perform the defining effect on the protection scope of the patent right. Since the current laws did not prescribe whether the implementation sequence of steps should be defined in the process claim, in the case that the implementation sequence of steps was not defined in the claim, the patent administrative organ of the State Council generally examined the claims according to the sequence of the steps recited in the claim in the patent granting and confirmation procedures and did not interpret the protection scope of the claim as implementing the steps in any sequence. Therefore, in the infringement litigation, where a claim does not define the sequence of steps, this shall not serve as an excuse for not taking into account the defining effect that the sequence of steps has on the claim, and the determination shall be made as to whether the steps shall be carried out in a specific sequence from the perspective of persons of ordinary skill in the art by referring to the Description, the Drawings, the examination files, the entire technical solution presented in the claim, and the logic relationship between steps.

According to the four steps recited in Claim 1, first, the function of the step for providing materials is to provide processing materials for other steps. Therefore, the step for providing materials must be implemented before the other steps. Second, the function of the cutting step is to cut free a region from the metal strap substantially corresponding to the shape of the hinge member. According to the Description and the Drawings, the region includes "a basic profile for forming the elongate extension 9" and "at least a portion of a region 497." Since the impressing step is to impress "the basic profile for forming the elongate extension 9" made by the cutting step, and the stamping step is to make a hinge hole in the "region 497" made by the cutting step. Moreover, the Description neither discloses the technical contents of implementing the stamping step or the impressing step before the cutting step nor gives any relevant technical enlightenment. It is difficult for persons of ordinary skill in the art to expect that the invention purpose of the patent involved can also be achieved, and the same technical effect can be produced by implementing the stamping step or the impressing step before the cutting step. Therefore, the cutting step in Claim 1 should be implemented before the impressing step and stamping step.

(Note: the Beijing No.1 Intermediate Court held in the first instance that the processing steps of Kanghua Company are four. Although the sequence of die forging and drilling was adjustable after the hinge member was punched down from the metal strap, the adjustment of the sequence of steps did not produce any new effect. Therefore, the sued method was equivalent to the method of Claim 1 involved and fell within the protection scope.

The Beijing High Court held in the second instance that the technical solution of the patent involved was achieved on the basis that the hinge was not separated from the metal strap and the steps were performed successively. The alleged infringement method first separated the hinge from the metal strap and then used the punching, forging, and punching equipment in the traditional machining process in sequence, wherein the sequence of rounding and punching can be adjusted. As can be seen, the alleged method was different from the method of the solution of the patent in which the hinge member was not separated from the metal strap, and the steps were performed successively. Therefore, the alleged method was neither the same nor equivalent to the patent involved and did not fall into the protection scope.)

The judgment of this case was made by the Supreme People's Court in 2009, and it is also the first judgment made by the Supreme Court concerning the sequence of steps of the process patent. In this case, the Supreme Court put forward the principle of how to determine the protection scope of a patent when the sequence of steps is not defined in the process patent claim: in the case that the sequence of steps is not defined in the claim, it cannot be considered that the protection scope of the claim includes combinations of the various sequences of the steps, and the specific sequence for implementing the steps should be understood from the perspective of persons of ordinary skill in the art in combination with the relevant materials in the patent documents. Until 2016, the *Judicial Interpretation II* of the Supreme Court made clear provisions on the issue.

[B] Whether There Is a Specific Sequence Should Be Judged According to the Understanding of Those Skilled in the Art after Reading the Patent Documents

Although the claim does not clearly define the sequence of steps, in the case that those skilled in the art determine that there is a logical sequence of each step after reading the Claims, the Description, and the Drawings, it should be determined that the sequence of steps has a defining effect on the protection scope of the claim, that is, only when the alleged infringement solution is consistent with the sequence of the steps, will the alleged infringement solution fall within the protection scope of the claim. On the contrary, if there is no logical sequence of the steps, it should be determined that the sequence of the steps does not have a defining effect on the protection scope of the claim.

In a dispute over infringement of a patent right for invention between Guizhou ZhuoLin Technology Co. Ltd. and Shenzhen Huameilong Internet of Things Technology Co. Ltd., and Guizhou Runze Hengxin Technology Co. Ltd. ((2018) ZUI GAO FA MIN ZAI No. 63), the patent relates to a method for producing pair code of an anti-counterfeit bottle cap. Whether the various steps should be implemented sequentially according to the recited sequence is one of the focuses of the dispute in this case.

The retrial petitioner Huameilong Company held that there was a particular sequence among the steps in process Claim 1 of the patent involved. It was not stated in the patent involved that each step can be adjusted arbitrarily, and only one embodiment was disclosed in the Description and was implemented according to the specific steps of Claim 1. By the analysis of the technical solution claimed in Claim 1 and the logical relationship among the steps, it can be further determined that there is a specific implementation sequence among the steps, that is: checking a code lock- > grouping box- > manufacturing a code label- > pairing a code - > checking a code - > performing corresponding scanning.

The Respondent ZhuoLin Company held that Claim 1 of the patent involved did not clearly define the sequence of steps of checking a code lock, manufacturing a code label, and threading a tag. Moreover, according to the disclosure of the Description of the patent involved, for those skilled in the art, the sequence of checking a code lock, manufacturing a code label, and threading tag can be adjusted according to the subjective will of a person, and such adjustment only related to the adjustment of the production management method and did not perform a defining effect on the protection scope of the patent right.

In this regard, the Supreme Court believed that whether the steps were implemented in a specific sequence should be judged according to the understanding of persons of ordinary skill in the art after reading the Claims, Description and Drawings. According to the expression of Claim 1, step (1) was checking a code lock, and step (2) was disturbing and grouping the code lock; that is, the checked multi-box lock bodies were arranged neatly, and one lock body was picked up from each box in the arranged box and placed in the grouping box. It can be seen that there was a sequencing requirement between steps (1) and (2); step (3) was manufacturing a code label, and step (4) was threading tag, that is, the code label and the Chinese tag and the English tag of the code lock bottle cap were threaded to the lock body together. It can be seen that the sequence between steps (3) and (4) was also clear. Therefore, Zhuolin Company's claim that there was no definition that the patent involved should be implemented in a specific sequence cannot be established. The original judgment did not take the defining effect of the implementation sequence of steps on the protection scope of the patent involved into consideration, and the conclusion that the sued infringement technical solution is determined to fall within the protection scope of the patent involved was incorrect. Therefore, all claims of Zhuolin Company were dismissed in the retrial.

As can be seen, in this case, the Supreme Court believed that there was a logical sequence among steps (1) and (2) and steps (3) and (4) according to the understanding of persons of ordinary skill in the art after reading the Claims, Description and Drawings, and thus determined that the sequence of steps had a defining effect on the protection scope of the patent involved. That is, the defining effect of the sequence of steps can be obtained on the basis of the understanding of the logical sequence of each step by persons of ordinary skill in the art after reading the Claims, Description and Drawings.

[C] Whether There Is a Specific Sequence Can Be Determined According to the Difference of Technical Effects Brought by Step Interchange

If the interchange of each step does not produce any substantial difference in technical function and technical effect, it can be considered that the sequence of steps does not have a defining effect on the protection scope of the claim; if the interchange of each step produces a substantial difference in technical function and technical effect, it can be considered that the sequence of steps has a defining effect on the protection scope of the claim.

In a dispute over infringement of a patent right for invention between CHEN Shundi and Zhejiang LeXueEr Household Articles Co. Ltd. and HE Jianhua and a third party WEN Shidan ((2013) Min Ti Zi No. 225), the patent relates to a processing method of a cloth-plastic hot-water bag. The claim of the patent is as follows:

> 1. A processing method of a cloth-plastic hot-water bag, ... characterized in that: ... step 6: installing the threaded plug seat with a composite layer in the bag mouth, contacting with the inner layer, and thermally bonding the hot-water bag mouth and the threaded plug seat composite layer by a high-frequency heat sealing machine; step 7: trimming the bag body of the hot-water bag; step 8: using plastic materials to make a threaded plug cover; ... step 10: assembling the sealing gasket and the threaded plug cover into each other and screwing them into the threaded plug seat; step 11: inflation pressure test, filling compressed air into the hot-water bag for pressure-tight test; step 12: packaging. Whether the above steps should be implemented sequentially according to the recited sequence is the focus of the dispute in this case.

In this regard, the Supreme Court believed that whether the sequence of steps of process patent performed a defining effect to restrict the application of the doctrine of equivalents in step interchange depended on whether these steps must be implemented in a specific sequence and whether such interchange would bring about substantial differences in technical function or technical effect. Specifically, in this case, the implementation of step 6 and step 7 did not have a unique sequence correspondence, performing trimming first or performing thermal bonding first had no substantial influence on the realization of the whole technical solution, and the interchange of these two steps did not produce any substantial difference in technical function and technical effect, so the interchanged steps of the sued infringement process pertained to the same technical feature as the step 6 and step 7 of Claim 1 of the patent involved. However, after the interchange of step 10 and step 11, the technical effects of reducing operation links, saving time, and improving efficiency, as asserted by LeXueEr Company, were indeed produced. Therefore, the difference in technical effects caused by such step interchange is substantial, and the interchanged steps and step 10 and step 11 of Claim 1 of the patent involved did not constitute equivalent technical features.

[D] Whether There Is a Specific Sequence of Steps Has a Significant Influence on the Determination of the Protection Scope of the Claim

(1) If the sequence of steps disclosed in the Description is different from that recited in the claim, the sequence of steps in the claim may be interpreted as including a plurality of sequences of steps listed in the Description according to the understanding of those skilled in the art to the Description, that is, the protection scope of the claim includes the sequence of steps in the Description.

In the above case of a dispute over infringement of a patent right for invention between OBE-WERK OHNMACHT & BAUMGÄERTNER GMBH & CO. KG and Zhejiang Kanghua Glasses Co. Ltd. ((2008) Min Shen Zi No. 980), two embodiments in the Description adopt different sequences of steps, respectively. On this basis, the retrial petitioner asserted that each step in the claim can be performed according to different sequences and further asserted that the protection scope of Claim 1 included the combination of various sequences of the steps.

In this regard, the Supreme Court held in the retrial that according to the disclosure contained in the Description, although the sequence of the impressing step and the stamping step can be interchanged, once the sequence of the two was determined in the actual processing process, the sequence of the two can only be performed in sequence. In conclusion, the four steps in Claim 1 should be carried out in the sequence of the step for providing materials, the cutting step, the impressing step, or the stamping step, and there was a specific sequence for the implementation among the steps.

(2) If the sequence of steps disclosed in the Description is not consistent with the sequence of steps recited in the claim, in the case that the sequence of steps in the claim is interpreted as having the defining effect, the solution which has a different sequence of steps in the Description can apply to the principle of donation and is not protected.

In the above case of a dispute over infringement of a patent right for invention between CHEN Shundi and Zhejiang LeXueEr Household Articles Co. Ltd. and HE Jianhua and a third party WEN Shidan ((2013) Min Ti Zi No. 225), LeXueEr Company further asserted that since the patent involved sought to protect a processing method of a product, both the steps per se and the sequence of steps of the process claim should perform a defining effect on the protection scope of the patent right. Moreover, since the interchange of step 10 and step 11 was disclosed in the Description of the patent involved, and the other sequence of steps disclosed in the Description should not be included in the protection scope of the patent involved according to the principle of donation, the change in steps of the alleged infringing method did not fall within the protection scope of the patent involved.

In this regard, the Supreme People's Court held that the Description of the patent involved clearly disclosed on page 3 that the sequence of step 10 and step 11 can be interchanged. However, the interchanged steps were not reflected in the claim, and thus the interchanged steps cannot be included in the protection scope of the patent right involved. The assertion of LeXueEr Company that the solution of the interchanged steps 10 and 11 should apply to the principle of donation had a legal basis and was supported by the court.

§11.04 CONCLUSION

If the contribution point of the invention-creation lies in the improvement of the sequence of steps or the strict sequence requirements for the steps, the sequence of steps should be clearly recited in the claim so as to obtain a stable patent right in the right confirmation procedure.

If different sequences of steps of the invention-creation have different beneficial effects, such different solutions should be defined in the claim, and different embodiments are described in the Description simultaneously. The solutions of different sequences can be protected by drafting different embodiments.

If it is considered that the sequence of steps of the invention-creation can be adjusted, the corresponding explanation should be made in the Description so as to assert that the solution which has a different sequence of steps from the sequence of steps recited in the claim also falls into the protection scope of the patent.

For a process patent that does not have a clear sequence of steps, the resolution principle of the US court's in related cases is that unless the process claim recites the sequence of steps, it is usually interpreted as these steps not requiring a specific sequence. However, if a specific sequence is required logically or grammatically in the expression of the claim or a sequence is directly or indirectly required in the Description, it is considered that these steps should be carried out in the specific sequence. In the process of hearing cases, the US courts adopt a two-step test method:

The first step, whether the steps must be implemented in the drafted sequence, is determined by analyzing the expression of the claim grammatically or logically. If the answer is no, turning to the second step, that is, whether such narrow interpretation is required directly or indirectly, is determined by the Description. If the answer is also no, it is not required to implement the steps in the drafted sequence.[2]

2. The defining function of the sequence of steps in process patent to the protection scope, YAN Wenjun, published in June 2019, China Invention & Patent.

CHAPTER 12

Interpretation of a Close-Ended Claim for a Composition

He Yibo & Gu Runfeng

Generally, a close-ended claim should be interpreted as not containing any structural components or steps (except impurities) other than those recited in the claim. This interpretation rule has been generally recognized and accepted in the industry. Moreover, it is unnecessary to consider whether the added features have a substantial effect to determine if there is an infringement or not, which highlights the respect for the publicity of the claims and the trust of the public in the protection scope of the patent.

§12.01 BASIC PROVISIONS OF LAWS

***Interpretation (II) of the Supreme People's Court on Several Issues concerning the Application of Law in the Trial of Patent Infringement Dispute Cases* (hereinafter referred to as "*Judicial Interpretation II*")**

Article 7 Where any alleged infringement technical solution is supplemented with other technical features on the basis of including all technical features of the close-ended claim for a composition, the people's court shall determine the alleged infringement technical solution does not fall within the protection scope of the patent, except when the added technical features pertain to the conventional quantity of inevitable impurities.

The close-ended claim for a composition as mentioned in the preceding paragraph generally excludes the claim for a traditional Chinese medicine composition.

The Guidelines for Patent Examination (amended in 2010) **(hereinafter referred to as "*the Guidelines*")**

Part II, Chapter 10, 4.2.1 Open-Ended Mode, Close-Ended Mode and Their Application Requirements

The claim for a composition shall be characterized by the features of the composition, such as the components, or the components and the contents thereof. There are two modes of presentation for the claim for a composition: open-ended and close-ended. The open-ended mode means that the composition does not exclude those components that are not mentioned in the claim. The close-ended mode means that any of the other components that are not mentioned in the claim shall be excluded. The commonly used wording for open-ended mode and close-ended mode is as follows:

(1) open-ended mode: wording such as "comprising," "including," "containing," "essentially comprising," "substantially comprising," "mainly consisting of," "be mainly composed of," "substantially consist of," "be substantially composed of," etc. All of them indicate that some components which are not indicated in the claim may be further included in the composition, though the components not indicated may take quite a great proportion in content;
(2) close-ended mode: wording such as "consisting of ...," "be composed of ...," "be balanced with ...," etc. All of them indicate that the composition claimed is composed of the indicated components only, without any other components to be included in. However, there may be impurities, and the impurities may take only normal proportion in content.

§12.02 INTERPRETATION OF THE PROVISIONS

Article 7 of *the Judicial Interpretation II* clarifies the rules of interpreting the close-ended claims for a composition that have been controversial for a long time in practice, and also highlights the respect for the publicity of the claims and the maintenance of the trust of the public in the protection scope of the patent. Since the *Guidelines for Patent Examination* of each version stipulates the same provisions for the close-ended claim for a composition, that is, the composition should not contain components other than the features recited in the claim, except a constant quantity of inevitable impurities. Through long-term patent practice, this drafting manner and the interpretation rules have been generally accepted in the industry, and the interpretation rules stipulated in Article 7.1 of the *Judicial Interpretation II* are consistent with those in the *Guidelines*.

The close-ended claim for a traditional Chinese medicine composition provided in Article 7.2 of the *Judicial Interpretation II* is an exception to Article 7.1 of the same. The composition in the field of traditional Chinese medicine is fundamentally different from chemical drugs in the aspects of modes of action, production processes, physical and chemical parameters, etc., so that it is not suitable to simply apply the interpretation rules of Article 7.1 of the *Judicial Interpretation II*. Moreover, China has a unique advantage in the field of traditional Chinese medicine. Hence, it complies with the actual development of the traditional Chinese medicine industry to adopt claim interpretation rules different from those of the chemical drug composition, which is beneficial to the protection of innovation in the field of traditional Chinese medicine and to the promotion of the development of the industry. Therefore, the provision of Article 7.1 is, in principle, not applicable to the interpretation method of a claim for a traditional Chinese medicine composition mainly drafted in the mode of "be made of" and the like, and examination should be conducted on whether the added technical features of the alleged infringement product have a substantial effect on the solution of the technical problem. If there is no substantial effect, it is generally considered that the alleged infringement product falls within the protection scope of the patent.

§12.03 ISSUES/DISPUTES ARISING IN THE APPLICATION OF LAW

[A] A Close-Ended Claim for a Composition Is Determined According to Symbolic Wording

A claim for a composition can generally be identified through symbolic wording of close-ended modes, such as "consisting of ...," "be composed of ...," "be balanced with ...," etc., in the *Guidelines*.

Case 1: In an infringement dispute over a patent for invention between HU Xiaoquan and Shanxi Zhendong Taisheng Pharmaceutical Co. Ltd., the Pharmaceutical Branch of Shandong Telier Marketing and Planning Co. Ltd. (A Civil Judgment of the Supreme People's Court (2012) Min Ti Zi No. 10), the close-ended expression used is "consisting of ... ." The Supreme People's Court pointed out that Claim 2 of the patent involved explicitly adopts the close-ended expression provided in the *Guidelines* and pertains to a close-ended claim, the protection scope of which should be determined according to the general interpretation of a close-ended claim.

In addition, according to the judicial precedents of the Supreme People's Court, "be composed of ..." and "be balanced with ..." can also be used as symbolic wording.

Case 2: In an infringement dispute over a patent for invention between Hebei Xinyu Co. and Yichang Monkey King Co. (A Civil Decision of the Supreme People's Court (2013) Min Shen Zi No. 1201), the close-ended expressions used are "be composed of.." and "be balanced with iron and inevitable impurities thereof." The Supreme People's Court pointed out that Claim 1 of the patent involved adopts wording such as "be composed of ..." and "be balanced with iron and inevitable impurities thereof," which indicates that the patentee has listed exhaustively the components of the "gas shielded welding wire for high strength structural steel" claimed in Claim 1 with a clear expression of meaning, and thus Claim 1 pertains to a close-ended claim.

[B] When There Is No Symbolic Wording, It Is Necessary to Comprehensively Determine the Close-Ended Claim for a Composition in Combination with Other Claims and the Description

Case 3: In an infringement dispute over a patent for invention between Hubei Wushi Pharmaceutical Co. Ltd. and Aonuo (China) Pharmaceutical Co. Ltd. (A Civil Judgment of the Supreme People's Court (2009) Min Ti Zi No. 20), Claim 1 is a claim for a composition, and adopts the expression manner of "a medical formulation prepared by raw materials with the following weight ratios." The Supreme People's Court pointed out that such an expressive manner of Claim 1 does not pertain to the forms of the wording of the close-ended mode, such as "consisting of ..." and "be composed of..." listed in the *Guidelines*. In addition, from the perspective of the defining relationship between Claim 1 and Claim 2, Claim 1 does not adopt a close-ended expression manner. Therefore, Claim 1 should be understood as a claim with an open-ended expression manner.

When there is no symbolic wording, there are two situations for identifying whether it is a close-ended claim for a composition:

> First, if there are open-ended symbolic wording in the claim, such as "comprising," "including," "containing," "essentially comprising," "substantially comprising," "mainly consisting of," "be mainly composed of," "substantially consist of," "be substantially composed of," etc., it generally can be determined as an open-ended mode.
>
> Second, if there is no open-ended symbolic wording in the claim, it is necessary to make a comprehensive judgment in combination with other claims and the disclosure of the Description.

Case 4: In the administrative ruling between Clariant Products (Germany) Co. Ltd. and the Patent Reexamination Board of the China Intellectual Property Administration (A Second-Instance Administrative Ruling of Beijing High People's Court (2018) Jing Xing Zhong No. 4836), Claim 1 does not adopt an obvious close-ended or open-ended expression manner. Beijing High People's Court pointed out: according to the reciting of Claim 1 of the present patent, the chemical product claimed by the patent further contains 0.01 to 6 wt% of telomer in addition to diethyl phosphinate and does not explicitly exclude the presence of other chemical substances including acetic acid. Moreover, dependent Claims 6 and 7 further define that the residual moisture content is 0.01 wt% to 10 wt% and 0.1 wt% to 1 wt%. This indicates that Claim 1 does not define by a close-ended mode that only two ingredients, i.e., diethyl phosphinate and telomer, are comprised, without any other components (including acetic acid). Therefore, the protection scope of Claim 1 of the present patent should be understood as a chemical product that may further contain other components in addition to diethyl phosphinate and 0.01 to 6 wt% of telomer.

[C] The Components of the Alleged Infringement Product Are Identified According to the Description and the Product Instruction of the Product Involved Issued by the Relevant National Department

Case 1: In an infringement dispute over a patent for invention between HU Xiaoquan and Shanxi Zhendong Taisheng Pharmaceutical Co. Ltd., the Pharmaceutical Branch of Shandong Telier Marketing and Planning Co. Ltd. (A Civil Judgment of the Supreme People's Court (2012) Min Ti Zi No. 10), the Supreme People's Court confirmed in the retrial that: according to the facts found out by the Court of First Instance, it was disclosed in the medicine instruction in the box of the alleged infringement product: "the names of all excipients are: sodium bicarbonate and arginine." Taisheng Company and the branch of Telier claimed in the retrial session of this court that the ingredients of the alleged infringement product include arginine in addition to adenosine disodium triphosphate and magnesium chloride, to which HU Xiaoquan has no objection.

In this case, the Supreme People's Court clearly pointed out that the components of the alleged infringement product can be identified according to the Description and the Product Instruction of the product involved issued by the relevant national department.

[D] Addition of Other Features (Including Excipients) on the Basis of the Close-Ended Claim for a Composition Does Not Constitute an Infringement

Case 1: In an infringement dispute over a patent for invention between HU Xiaoquan and Shanxi Zhendong Taisheng Pharmaceutical Co. Ltd., the Pharmaceutical Branch of Shandong Telier Marketing and Planning Co. Ltd. (A Civil Judgment of the Supreme People's Court (2012) Min Ti Zi No. 10), the Supreme People's Court pointed out that arginine as an excipient is added to the alleged infringement product. No matter whether this excipient is a known conventional excipient in the prior art, it is not a conventional impurity accompanying adenosine disodium triphosphate and magnesium chloride. The alleged infringement product contains arginine in addition to adenosine disodium triphosphate and magnesium chloride in Claim 2 of the patent involved. Therefore, the alleged infringement product does not fall within the protection scope of Claim 2 of the patent involved.

Case 2: In an infringement dispute over a patent for invention between Hebei Xinyu Co. and Yichang Monkey King Co. (A Civil Decision of the Supreme People's Court (2013) Min Shen Zi No. 1201), the decision pointed out that: when the principle of full coverage is applied, the protection scope of the claim should be determined first. The close-ended claim is a special type of claim, which, with specific wording or expressions, defines that the protection scope of the claim only includes the technical features and equivalents thereof clearly recited in the claim and excludes other components, structures or steps. Therefore, for a close-ended claim, if the alleged infringement product has other features in addition to the technical features clearly recited in the claim, the product should be identified as not falling within the protection scope of the claim.

[E] Excipients as Components of the Composition Do Not Pertain to the Conventional Quantity of Inevitable Impurities

Case 1: In an infringement dispute over a patent for invention between HU Xiaoquan and Shanxi Zhendong Taisheng Pharmaceutical Co. Ltd., the Pharmaceutical Branch of Shandong Telier Marketing and Planning Co. Ltd. (A Civil Judgment of the Supreme People's Court (2012) Min Ti Zi No. 10), the judgment pointed out that: the adenosine disodium triphosphate magnesium chloride freeze-dried powder injection for injection claimed in Claim 2 of the patent involved is only composed of adenosine disodium triphosphate and magnesium chloride, and there are no other components except a normal content of impurities. The excipients are not impurities and also fall within the scope of those excluded by Claim 2 of the patent involved.

§12.04 CONCLUSION

Article 7 of the *Judicial Interpretation II* clarifies the interpretation rules of the close-ended claim for a composition. The interpretation rules provided in Article 7.1 of the *Judicial Interpretation II* are consistent with those in the *Guidelines*. The close-ended claim for a traditional Chinese medicine composition provided in Article 7.2 is an exception to Article 7.1.

In a specific application, it is required to note the following points: (1) where the claim of the patent involved is a close-ended claim for a composition, it is only composed of the components (including excipients) pointed out, except for a conventional quantity of inevitable impurities; (2) when the alleged infringement technical solution is only composed of the components pointed out in the claim of the patent involved, it constitutes an infringement; however, when further containing other components except for a conventional quantity of inevitable impurities, it does not constitute an infringement; and (3) the above determination rules are generally not applicable to a claim for a traditional Chinese medicine composition.

Regarding the above, the key is to judge whether a claim for a composition is of close-ended mode and to make clear the components thereof as well as the components of the alleged infringement product. On this basis, the judgment on whether an infringement is constituted is made according to the Article discussed herein.

CHAPTER 13

Determination of Functional Features

Lu Weiting & Ge Xiaomei

Functional features (means plus function) are a kind of relatively special technical feature. Its literal meaning covers all the embodiments that can realize the function. However, in the infringement litigation, functional features are restrictively interpreted. Therefore, the determination, exclusion rule, and interpretation rule of functional features have an important impact on determining the protection scope of the patent right.

This chapter discusses twelve judicial precedents so as to conduct an in-depth analysis of the issues related to functional features in judicial practice.

§13.01 BASIC PROVISIONS OF LAWS

***Interpretation of the Supreme People's Court on Several Issues Concerning the Application of Law in the Trial of Patent Infringement Dispute Cases* (hereinafter referred to as "*Judicial Interpretation I*")**

Article 4 For technical features described by function or effect in a claim, the people's court shall determine the content of these technical features according to the specific embodiments of the functions or effects described in the Description and the Drawings or an equivalent embodiment.

***Interpretation (II) of the Supreme People's Court on Several Issues Concerning the Application of Law in the Trial of Patent Infringement Dispute Cases* (hereinafter referred to as "*Judicial Interpretation II*")**

Article 8 Functional features mean the technical features which define the structures, components, procedures, conditions or the mutual relationship thereof, among others, through their functions or effects in invention and creation, except when persons with ordinary skills in the art can directly and explicitly determine the specific embodiments for achieving the aforesaid functions or effects only by reading the claims.

Where, in comparison with the indispensable technical features for achieving the functions or effects as mentioned in the preceding paragraph as recorded in the Description and the Drawings, the corresponding technical features of the accused infringing technical solution realize basically the same functions and achieve basically the same results by basically the same means as the stated technical features, with which persons with ordinary skills in the art are able to associate without any creative activity when the accused infringing act occurs, the people's court shall determine the corresponding technical features are identical with or equivalent to the functional features.

§13.02 INTERPRETATION OF THE ARTICLES OF LAW

The determination of whether the disputed technical feature is a "functional feature" has an important impact on the protection scope of the patent right. Therefore, when interpreting the claims and determining the protection scope of the patent right, it is usually necessary to first determine whether the disputed technical feature is a "functional feature."

According to the above legal provisions, in combination with the combing and analysis of judicial precedents, *the restrictive interpretation of functional features lies in:*

- the content of functional features shall be determined according to the specific embodiments in the Description and the Drawings or an equivalent way;
- the content of functional features shall be defined as the indispensable technical features for achieving the functions or effects.

The exclusion rule for determining functional features is as follows:

(1) technical features defined solely by function or effect do not necessarily belong to functional features;
(2) the standard for exclusion of functional features is that persons with ordinary skills in the art can directly and explicitly determine the functional features only by reading the claims;
(3) the knowledge level and cognitive ability of persons with ordinary skills in the art depend on the evidence provided by the parties;
(4) the technical features defined by structure and function at the same time are not functional features;
(5) features that are generalized and defined by the relationship of structural parts or the relevance of parameters should generally not be determined as functional features;
(6) the determination of functional features requires the consideration of the technical solutions of the claims as a whole, which are not suitable to be divided mechanically; and

(7) the determination of functional features requires the consideration of whether the division of technical features is appropriate.

§13.03 ISSUES/DISPUTES ARISING IN THE LAW APPLICATION

Determining whether a technical feature is a functional feature is directly related to how to interpret the technical feature, further affecting the determination of the protection scope of the claim. Therefore, the determination of functional features has inevitably become the first problem that needs to be solved in judicial practice. In judicial practice, many technical features have the "form" of functional features, but they do not have the "essence" of functional features. This has led to controversy about the determination of functional features. In view of this, this article makes a preliminary exploration of the determination of functional features by combining the interpretation of functional features in our country's trial practice with the exception of functional features.

[A] The Determination of Functional Features Is a Matter of the Application of Law, Which the Court Can Examine Ex Officio

Case 1: In an infringement dispute over a patent right for invention between VALEO SYSTEMES D'ESSUYAGE and Xiamen Lucas Auto Parts Co. Ltd. (Lucas Company) et al. ((2019) Zui Gao Fa Zhi Min Zhong No. 2[1]), the focus of the dispute is whether the accused infringing product has the technical feature "a closed position in which it (the safety fastener) extends with regards to the securing element in order to prevent its elastic deformation and lock the connector."

The Shanghai Intellectual Property Court held in the first instance that the above technical feature only discloses the orientation relationship between the safety fastener and the securing element, that is, the elastic element. This orientation relationship is not sufficient to prevent the elastic deformation of the securing element. Persons with ordinary skills in the art cannot directly and explicitly determine the technical solution for achieving the function of "preventing the elastic deformation of the securing element and locking the connector" only by reading the claims, and thus the above technical feature is a functional feature.

The grounds for the appeal of Lucas Company and Fuke Company are substantial as follows: the above technical feature of Claim 1 of the patent involved is a functional feature, and the original judgment made an error regarding the determination of the indispensable technical features for achieving the function. The accused infringing product does not have the technical features identical with or equivalent to the above functional feature. That is, the appellants argued that there is no disagreement that the disputed technical feature is a functional feature.

1. Selected as Guiding Case No. 115 of the Supreme People's Court

In this regard, the Intellectual Property Court of the Supreme People's Court first explained that the essence of the disputed feature is still an orientation or structural feature, not a functional feature as mentioned in the aforementioned judicial interpretation. The court further pointed out that the interpretation of the claims is a legal issue, and there are obvious differences in infringement comparison methods between functional features and other types of technical features, which may affect the result of infringement determination. Therefore, even if the party does not raise an objection to the determination of functional features, it should still be examined and corrected.

In this case, the Supreme People's Court made it clear that the determination of functional features belongs to the scope of the court's examination ex officio. Even if both parties do not raise objections to the determination of functional features, the court should still examine and correct them.

[B] The Content of Functional Features Shall Be Determined According to the Specific Embodiments in the Description and the Drawings or an Equivalent Way

Case 2: In an infringement dispute over a patent right for invention between Philips Consumer Lifestyle B.V. and Foshan City Shunde Jutian Electric Appliance Co. Ltd. ((2017) Yue Min Zhong No. 1125[2]), Philips seeks for the protection of independent Claim 1 and dependent Claim 5. The focus of the dispute, in this case, is whether the accused product has the feature of "air guide member."

The related technical feature in Claim 1 is: the air guide member (11) is located on the outer wall (4) below the bottom wall (5), and the air guide member is provided for directing the airflow essentially upwards into food present in the food preparation chamber (2), and the related technical feature in Claim 5 is that the air guide member (11) comprises a frusto-conical upwardly tapering air guide part (16).

Philips alleged that "frusto-conical upwardly tapering" is a description of the shape and structure of the air guide member, and the air guide member constituted by "frusto-conical upwardly tapering" is not a functional feature. Philips also argued that the content "only provided with a frusto-conical upwardly tapering air guide part" in Embodiment 1 also belongs to the feature content and protection scope of the "air guide member."

In this regard, the Guangdong High People's Court held in the second instance that the content of the functional feature of the air guide member should be determined in conjunction with the specific embodiments disclosed in the Description and the Drawings. First of all, according to the relevant disclosure in the Claims and the Description, the function and effect achieved by the "air guide member" is to guide the radial component of the airflow essentially vertically upwards as much as possible and to prevent air from swirling as much as possible. This is an important basis and premise for determining the content of the technical feature "air guide member." Second, from

2. Selected in the fifty typical intellectual property cases of the Chinese courts in 2017, and the top ten intellectual property protection cases of Guangdong Province in 2017

the perspective of persons with ordinary skills in the art, it is difficult to effectively derive from Embodiment 1 an implementing mode in which the frusto-conical upwardly tapering air guide part provided is an "air guide member." Thirdly, the basic embodiments of the "air guide member" in the patent involved are to provide air guide ribs, and it is clearly disclosed that the function of the air guide ribs is to "promote the upward airflow, prevent a circular (swirling) airflow and create a pressure increase towards the central location." This is right consistent with the purpose of the patent involved in achieving "directing the airflow essentially upwards" and overcoming the defect "air swirling and inability to be directed upwards" in the background art.

In summary, it is untenable that Philips asserted to determine the content of the technical feature "air guide member" according to Embodiment 1. According to Claim 1, the Description and Embodiments 2, 3 and 4 of the patent involved, the indispensable technical feature of the "air guide member" that realizes the function of "directing the airflow essentially upwards" should include the following features: located on the outer wall (4) below the bottom wall (5), and provided with air guide ribs extending radially or curvedly and meeting at a central location.

The literal meaning of "functional feature" is very broad, covering all specific embodiments that can achieve the function and effect, regardless of whether the embodiments are existing before the filing date of the patent involved or newly discovered or invented after the filing date, or whether the right holder is aware of the embodiments on the filing date, or whether it is disclosed in the Description. In patent drafting and examination, many restrictive provisions have been made for such technical features, requiring "trying to avoid the use as much as possible."

Correspondingly, "functional features" are interpreted restrictively in infringement litigation, and the content of these technical features shall be determined according to the specific embodiments of the functions or effects described in the Description and the Drawings or an equivalent embodiment.

[C] The Content of Functional Features Shall Be Defined as the Indispensable Technical Features for Achieving the Functions or Effects

Case 3: In an infringement dispute over a patent right for invention between Wenzhou Ningtai Machinery Co. Ltd. and Wenzhou Qianfeng Technology Co. Ltd. ((2016) Zhe Min Zhong No. 506),[3] both parties have disputes over whether "an upper cutter mounting plate which can be lifted up and down" is a functional technical feature and its scope of protection.

In this regard, the Zhejiang High People's Court held in the second instance as follows: in this case, Claim 1 of the patent involved recites the structure of the upper cutter mounting plate and its relationship with the upper cutter, upper support portion, and support plate to a certain extent. However, no specific embodiment is given for how to realize the function of lifting up and down. In addition, in practice, there are

3. One of the fifty typical cases of intellectual property issued by the Supreme People's Court in 2017.

many ways to realize the function of lifting up and down. After reading the functional expression, persons with ordinary skills in the art cannot directly and explicitly determine the specific embodiments to realize the function of lifting up and down. Therefore, this court deems that the above-disputed feature is a functional technical feature.

When determining whether the functional technical features are identical or equivalent, the technical features indispensable for achieving the function should be correctly summarized from the disclosure of the Description and the Drawings and compared with the corresponding technical features of the accused infringing technical solution. Those technical contents that are not necessary to achieve the function shall not be included in the comparison of functional technical features.

According to the disclosure of the Description and the Drawings of the patent involved, the indispensable technical feature of the upper cutter mounting plate for achieving the function of lifting up and down is determined as follows: the piston rod of the vertical cylinder passes through the upper cutter mounting plate and is fixed to the upper end of the support connecting rod, which acts on the upper cutter through the support connecting rod. Regarding the vertical guide rod on the upper cutter mounting plate and the vertical guide sleeve matched with the vertical guide rod mentioned in the embodiment, although the longitudinal movement trajectory of the upper cutter mounting plate can be made more stable, the piston rod of the vertical cylinder itself can also realize lifting the upper cutter mounting plate up and down even without the vertical guide rod and the guide sleeve. Therefore, the vertical guide rod and the guide sleeve are not indispensable technical features for achieving lifting up and down.

In this case, the Zhejiang High People's Court pointed out that when determining the content of functional features, technical details that are not directly and necessarily related to the realization of the function or effect should be excluded, and after the indispensable technical features for achieving the function are extracted from the disclosure of the Description and the Drawings, the technical features shall be compared with the corresponding technical features of the accused infringing technical solution.

If all the technical details disclosed in the embodiments (including many technical details irrelevant to the realization of the functions) are directly used as the content of the functional features, the protection scope of the patent right will be greatly narrowed, and the accused infringer only needs to make slight changes so as to circumvent the liability of infringing on the patent right of others, leading to the futility of the protection of functional features.

Case 4: In an infringement dispute over a patent right for utility model between Guangzhou Tongming Solar Technology Co. Ltd. and Shenzhen Huaze Xingye Technology Co. Ltd. ((2018) Zui Gao Fa Min Shen No. 1018[4]), the parties have disputes over whether the "first heat dissipation area" and the "second heat dissipation area" in Claim 1 are functional features, and furthermore, whether it shall be understood to be

4. Selected as a typical case in the Annual Report of the Supreme People's Court on Intellectual Property Cases (2018).

provided with heat dissipation holes or equivalent embodiments according to the disclosure of the Description.

In this regard, upon retrial, the Supreme People's Court held that even if the "first heat dissipation area" and "second heat dissipation area" were interpreted as "functional features" as asserted by the applicant for the retrial, when "determining the content of these technical features according to the specific embodiments of the functions or effects disclosed in the Description and the Drawings or an equivalent embodiment," the specific circumstances in the relevant specific embodiments described in the Description should also be analyzed to determine the protection scope with the essential technical features for achieving the function of "heat dissipation," and not all the technical features related to "heat dissipation" disclosed in the Description can be used to determine the protection scope of the "first heat dissipation area" and "second heat dissipation area."

In this case, the Description of the patent involved discloses that the "first heat dissipation area" and "second heat dissipation area" have multiple specific embodiments for achieving heat dissipation, and the provision of heat dissipation holes is only a preferred embodiment disclosed in the Description of the patent involved. According to the Description of the patent involved, persons with ordinary skills in the art can understand that even if heat dissipation holes are not provided, heat dissipation can be achieved only by heat radiation in a specific area itself, that is, "providing heat dissipation holes" is not an indispensable technical feature for achieving "heat dissipation."

In this case, the Supreme People's Court explicitly pointed out that the interpretation of "functional features" should be based on the technical features "indispensable" for achieving the function disclosed in the Description and the Drawings, and it is not advisable to simply use all the technical features related to achieving the functions and effects of the "functional features" in the Description and the Drawings to define the protection scope of the "functional features."

As a result, it is helpful to encourage the right holder to disclose the technical contents related to the functions and effects of "functional features" on his own initiative, enrich the prior art, facilitate the public to better understand the patent technical solutions, and free the right holder from worrying that the protection scope of the "functional features" is unnecessarily restricted since the disclosed specific embodiments are too specific and detailed.

[D] The Exclusion Rule for Functional Features

[1] Technical Features Defined Solely by Function or Effect Do Not Necessarily Belong to Functional Features

Case 5: In an infringement dispute over a patent right for utility model between WANG Enguang and Fujian Meizhikou Household Goods Co. Ltd. as well as Zhejiang Tmall Network Co. Ltd. ((2016) Min Zhong No. 877), both parties have disputes over whether "the frame body includes a second end that matches with the drive assembly" defined in the technical feature D of Claim 1 is a functional feature.

In this regard, the Fuzhou Intermediate People's Court held in the first instance that the "drive assembly" only describes the function of the assembly but does not define the specific structure of the assembly and thus is a functional feature. The content and protection scope of the technical feature should be determined in conjunction with the Description and the Drawings.

The Fujian High People's Court held in the second instance as follows:

> Although the "drive" in the Claims is a functional term, it is combined with "assembly" to form a compound noun "drive assembly." In the above technical features of the patent involved, the "drive assembly" only refers to a specific part, rather than having a definitive effect on the technical feature in terms of the function or effect. Thus, the "drive assembly" should not be a functional feature in the sense of a patent. Therefore, the embodiments in the Description of the patent involved cannot be understood as defining the protection scope of the present patent, and it cannot be taken for granted that the preferred embodiments shall be understood as that the frame body and the drive assembly are directly connected or matched with each other. The drive assembly of the accused infringing product indirectly realizes the matching relationship between the drive assembly and the frame body through the gear set. For persons with ordinary skills in the art, it is common knowledge to drive through the gear or the gear set, and its ultimate function is still to drive the functional part via the gear set by the drive assembly. Therefore, this technical solution is consistent with the content recited in this feature.

It is not sufficient to determine a certain technical feature as a functional feature solely based on its use of functional description. In practice, many devices are named by means of the functions they perform, such as filters, transformers, brakes, pliers, etc. These technical terms have universally understandable meanings in the art, and persons with ordinary skills in the art can know the manner in which the function or effect is achieved, and thus the technical feature defined by function or effect cannot be equivalent to the functional feature.

[2] The Standard for Exclusion of Functional Features Is That Persons with Ordinary Skills in the Art Can Directly and Explicitly Determine the Functional Features Only by Reading the Claims

Case 6: In an infringement dispute over a patent right for utility model between Kangjia Plastic Hardware and Electronic (Dongguan) Co. Ltd. and Changzhou Keoke Kitchenware Co. Ltd. et al. ((2016) Yue Min Zhong No. 1804), both parties have disputes over whether "the frame body includes a second end that matches with the drive assembly" defined in the technical feature D of Claim 1 is a functional feature.

In this regard, the Guangzhou Intellectual Property Court held in the first instance that the drive assembly is a description of a certain technical feature by function, which belongs to the common knowledge. Those skilled in the art can understand how to realize the technology as referred to and how the basic structure thereof is like. Thus, it is a non-functional definition and should not be included as a functional technical feature. Not all technical features expressed in terms of the function or effect are functional features. The drive assembly describes the function of the assembly but does not define the specific structure of the assembly. It cannot be taken for granted that the preferred embodiments shall be understood as that the frame assembly and the drive assembly are directly connected or matched with each other, but should be understood as that the drive assembly can be located on the outside of the frame body in some way and transmit driving force into the frame body.

The Guangdong High People's Court held in the second instance that the "drive assembly" in Claim 1 is only expressed by a function of the feature in the juicer but does not specifically define the structure of the feature, and those skilled in the art cannot directly and explicitly determine the specific embodiments for achieving the functions only by reading the claims. Therefore, the feature is a functional feature.

Note: Case 5 and Case 6 are based on the same claims; that is, both relate to the interpretation of the same technical feature of the same patent right.

In the judgments of the above Case 5 and Case 6, regarding the determination of whether the same technical feature "driving assembly" of the same patent is a functional feature, the Fujian High People's Court in the second instance overturned the Fuzhou Intermediate People's Court's determination in the first instance, and the Guangdong High People's Court in the second instance overturned the Guangzhou Intellectual Property Court's determination in the first instance. Moreover, the determinations of the two binding judgments in the second instance are not consistent. Accordingly, it can be seen that the determination of functional features is quite controversial.

However, the common point of the above judgment documents is that they both recognize that persons with ordinary skills in the art can directly and explicitly determine the embodiments for achieving the functions or effects in combination with the common knowledge, and thus it is not a functional feature.

[3] The Knowledge Level and Cognitive Ability of Persons with Ordinary Skills in the Art Depend on the Evidence Provided by the Parties

Case 7: In an infringement dispute over a patent right for invention between SMC Corporation and Shenchi Pneumatic Co. Ltd. as well as Suzhou Shannaisi Pneumatic Co. Ltd. ((2016) Su Min Zhong No. 291[5]), the focus of the dispute between the two parties and the key issue of the court trial is whether the technical feature "the solenoid drives the valve core in the direction approaching or away from the valve seat" in the preamble portion of Claim 1 of the patent involved is a functional feature, and how to determine the content of the technical feature.

In this regard, the Suzhou Intermediate People's Court held in the first instance that the technical feature "the solenoid drives the valve core in the direction approaching or away from the valve seat" is a technical feature expressed in terms of achievable functions. The feature does not explicitly determine each part in the solenoid, and its

5. One of the top ten cases of judicial protection of intellectual property in Jiangsu courts in 2017.

interaction relationship with the valve core, and thus, is a functional feature. In this regard, the content of the technical feature shall be determined in combination with the specific embodiments of the functions or effects described in the Description and the Drawings or an equivalent embodiment.

The Jiangsu High People's Court held in the second instance that the technical information of the electromagnetic valve disclosed in the new evidence *China Electric Power Encyclopedia (Second Edition)* submitted by SMC Corporation in the second instance should serve as the knowledge mastered by persons with ordinary skills in the art during the interpretation of the patent claims in this case. Therefore, the interaction relationship between the valve core, valve seat and solenoid defined by the claims of the patent involved has already been the common knowledge of persons with ordinary skills in the art. When reading the Claims of the patent involved, persons with ordinary skills in the art can clearly understand how the feature "the solenoid drives the valve core in the direction approaching or away from the valve seat" is achieved, and there is no need to learn related technical information from the specific embodiments of the patent Description to learn its specific embodiments. Therefore, the appraisal opinion of the appraisal report No. 136-1 should not be accepted, and the feature "the solenoid drives the valve core in the direction approaching or away from the valve seat" of the patent involved should not be regarded as a functional feature, let alone define the structure of the technical feature to the specific embodiments of the patent Description and its equivalent embodiments.

Note: in another litigation based on the patent involved, the Shanghai No. 2 Intermediate People's Court has entrusted the Forensic Institution of the Ministry of Industry and Information Technology to issue a technical appraisal opinion (namely appraisal report No. 136-1). The report held that the feature A3, "the solenoid drives the valve core in the direction approaching or away from the valve seat," does not list each part of the solenoid one by one and its interaction relationship with the valve core, but only lists the function and effect of the solenoid as driving the valve core in the direction approaching or away from the above valve seat, and thus A3 is a functional technical feature.

In this case, the second-instance judgment was straight up about that the result of "different judgments for the same case" results from different evidence presented by the parties in each case: in the case of (2013) Hu Er Zhong Min Wu (Zhi) Chu Zi No. 51 and the first instance of this case, the parties did not submit the relevant evidence to prove the "solenoid" and its internal structure for achieving the function of "driving the above valve core" are generally known to persons with ordinary skills in the art and overturn the appraisal opinion of No. 136-1 appraisal report. The court that made the judgment on the case determined the feature "the solenoid drives the valve core in the direction approaching or away from the valve seat" of the patent involved as a functional feature based on the technical facts ascertained. However, in the second instance of the case, based on new evidence, it can be proved that persons with ordinary skills in the art can clearly understand the technical feature "the solenoid drives the valve core in the direction approaching or away from the valve seat" when reading the Claims of the patent involved. Therefore, the Court of Second Instance applied the relevant provisions of the *Judicial Interpretation II* on the basis of the newly ascertained facts and determined that the technical feature is not a functional feature.

It can be seen that the knowledge level and cognitive ability of persons with ordinary skills in the art will affect the determination of functional features. And *the cognitive level and ability of persons with ordinary skills in the art depend on the evidence provided by both parties*. Where the parties fail to provide sufficient evidence, the court determines at its discretion whether a certain technical feature is generally known to those skilled in the art. As a result, there may be different judgments in the same case.

Reminder: judging by the appearance, the technical content generally known to those skilled in the art can also be an explicit technical solution, which is not only limited to technical terms but also requires the parties to provide evidence or is more dependent on the evidence provided by the parties.

[E] The Technical Features Defined by Structure and Function at the Same Time Are Not Functional Features

Case 8: In an infringement dispute over a patent right for utility model between LU Jie and Linhai Linong Machinery Factory et al. (2017) Zui Gao Fa Min Shen No. 1804[6]), both parties have disputes over whether the "supporting rail" in Claim 1 is a functional feature.

In this regard, the Supreme People's Court, upon retrial, held that the technical features defined by both "structure" and "function or effect" at the same time are not "functional features." Although there is no evidence to prove that "supporting rail" is a technical term commonly used in the art, those skilled in the art can directly and explicitly determine that the "rail" in "supporting rail" is a structural feature only by reading the Claims, and that "supporting" further defines the function of "rail." Those skilled in the art are familiar with various conventional implementations of "rail," and under normal circumstances, the structural feature "rail" itself is sufficient to achieve the function of "supporting." Those skilled in the art can directly and explicitly determine the function of "supporting rail" achieved by using a "rail" with an appropriate structure according to the specific situation of the "supporting rail" in the technical solution of Claim 1. In summary, the "supporting rail" is a technical feature that is simultaneously defined by the product structure and its function and is not a functional feature.

In this case, the Supreme People's Court explicitly pointed out that if the technical features not only define the function or effect, but also define the structural features corresponding to the function or effect, and those skilled in the art can directly and explicitly determine the specific embodiments of the structural feature only by reading the Claims, and the specific embodiments can achieve the function or effect, such

6. Selected as a typical case in the Annual Report of the Supreme People's Court on Intellectual Property Cases (2018).

technical features defined by both "structure" and "function or effect" at the same time are not "functional features."

We believe that for the technical features defined by both structure and function at the same time, if the structural feature itself is sufficient to achieve the function defined by the functional feature according to the common knowledge, such technical features belong to the circumstance where persons with ordinary skills in the art can directly and explicitly determine the specific embodiments for achieving the above function or effect only by reading the claims and fall within the category excluded by the functional features.

Reminder: due to the characteristics of Chinese word formation, there are many technical features written in the form of "function + structure noun." If the technical features are not yet well-known in the art, the ideas of this case may be referred to so as to analyze the word formation of the disputed technical feature to distinguish the structural feature from the perspective of those skilled in the art and further demonstrate whether it is sufficient to determine the conventional embodiment of the structure, so as to correctly identify the functional feature.

In the preceding Case 1 of an infringement dispute over a patent right for invention between VALEO SYSTEMES D'ESSUYAGE and Lucas Company et al. ((2019) Zui Gao Fa Zhi Min Zhong No. 2[7]), the focus of the dispute is whether the accused infringing product has the technical feature "a closed position in which it (the safety fastener) extends with regards to the securing element in order to prevent its elastic deformation and lock the connector."

In this regard, the Intellectual Property Court of the Supreme People's Court held in the second instance that if a certain technical feature has defined or implied the specific structure, components, steps and conditions or the relationship therebetween, etc., of the technical features of the invention, it is not a functional feature as referred to in Article 8 of the *Judicial Interpretation II* in principle, even if the technical feature also defines the function or effect achieved thereby.

The disputed technical feature actually defines the orientation relation between the safety fastener and the securing element and implies a specific structure—"the safety fastener extends with regards to the securing element," the orientation and structure perform a function of "preventing the elastic deformation of the securing element and locking the connector." Based on the orientation and structural relation, in combination with the Description and the Drawings of the patent involved, persons with ordinary skills in the art can understand that the feature "the safety fastener extends with regards to the securing element" can achieve the effect of preventing the elastic deformation of the securing element and locking the connector in the case that the distance between the extension part and the outer surface of the securing element is sufficiently small. It can be seen that the aforementioned technical feature is characterized in that it not only defines the specific orientation and structure but also defines the function of the orientation and structure, and the specific content of the orientation and structure can be clearly determined only by combining the orientation

7. Selected as Guiding Case No. 115 of the Supreme People's Court.

and structure with the function that they perform. Although this technical feature of "orientation or structure + functional description" has a description of the function, it is essentially still an orientation or structural feature, not a functional feature in the sense of Article 8 of the *Judicial Interpretation II*.

In the infringement comparison of the technical feature, the Intellectual Property Court of the Supreme People's Court pointed out that the disputed feature defines the orientation and structural relationship between the safety fastener and the securing element and also describes the function that the safety fastener performs. The function has a definitive effect on determining the orientation and structural relationship between the safety fastener and the securing element. This technical feature is not a functional feature, and its definition by orientation and structural relationship and by function should all be considered when determining the infringement.

In this case, the Supreme People's Court once again declared that "the technical feature defined by structure and function at the same time" is not a functional feature. It is also pointed out that if a certain technical feature of the patent claim has defined or implied a specific structure, component, step, condition, their relationship between each other or the like, the technical feature is still not a functional feature as referred to in Article 8 of the *Interpretation (II) of the Supreme People's Court on Several Issues concerning the Application of Law in the Trial of Patent Infringement Dispute Cases*, even if this technical feature also defines the function or effect achieved thereby.

It should be noted that there is a difference in the judgment logic between this case and the aforementioned Case 8: for the technical feature defined by structure and function at the same time, the specific content of the feature can be clearly determined in this case only by combining the orientation and structure with the function it performs. The Supreme People's Court clarified that the technical feature of "orientation or structure + functional description" is still an orientation or structural feature in nature, not a functional feature.

We believe that the judgment logic of this case reflects the current trend of China's courts to strictly exert the restrictive interpretation of functional features, that is, to strictly exert the standard for determining functional features, and it is not appropriate to easily define the protection scope of the claims by the embodiments in the Description and the Drawings and equivalent embodiments.

[F] Features That Are Generalized and Defined by the Relationship of Structural Parts or the Relevance of Parameters Should Generally Not Be Determined as Functional Features

In practice, there are indeed technical features that cannot or should not be directly defined by structural features, such as features that summarize the relationship between structural parts or the relevance between their parameters in the machinery field. Although these features have the "form" of functional description, they still essentially define the specific features such as structure and should not be determined as functional features.

Case 9: In an infringement dispute over a patent right for invention between Changsha Shenxiang General Machine Co. Ltd. and Hunan Guangyi Technology Co. Ltd. et al. ((2013) Min Ti Zi No. 127[8]), both parties have disputes over whether the technical feature "there is an adjustable gap between the grinding surface of the grinding disc and the grinding roller to form a gap-type running-in surface" of Claim 1 is a functional feature.

In this regard, the Supreme People's Court brought the case to trial and held that the protection scope of the patent right is subject to the content of its claims, and generally, the specific embodiments disclosed in the examples of the Description should not be used to restrict the protection scope of the patent right. The patent involved belongs to the field of mechanical products, and the characteristics of this technical field objectively determine that when drafting the claims, the technical solution to be claimed can usually be defined according to the structure and its position or connection relationship. The features "there is a gap between the grinding disc and the grinding roller" and "form a gap-type running-in surface" in the feature "there is an adjustable gap between the grinding surface of the grinding disc and the grinding roller to form a gap-type running-in surface" as defined in Claim 1 of the patent involved have clearly defined the relative positional relationship and structural features between the grinding disc and the grinding roller. Regarding the understanding of "there is an adjustable gap," the Patent Reexamination Board has also conducted an examination during the examination procedure for invalidation of the patent involved. It is determined in Decision No. 7581 that the technical feature "there is an adjustable gap between the grinding surface of the grinding disc and the grinding roller" in Claim 1 is a generic generalization of the specific embodiment. In addition to including the use of an adjusting screw to adjust the gap, it also includes other adjusting manners commonly used in the art to adjust the gap between the grinding disc and the grinding roller. All of these adjusting manners can achieve the most basic objective of the present invention.

In this case, the Supreme People's Court held that the above technical feature "there is an adjustable gap between the grinding surface of the grinding disc and the grinding roller to form a gap-type running-in surface" is a generic generalization of the specific embodiment and is not a functional feature. The protection scope of this feature should not be limited to the case where the adjusting screw in the specific embodiment adjusts the gap.

Case 10: In an infringement dispute over a patent right for invention between Litens Automotive (Suzhou) Co. Ltd. (Litens Suzhou Company) and Gates Unitta Power Transmission (Shanghai) Co. Ltd. (Gates Shanghai Company), Chery Automobile Co. Ltd. et al. ((2015) Su Zhi Min Zhong Zi No. 00172[9]), the disputed technical features J and K are respectively as follows: J: "present a periodic fluctuating load torque ... the angular positions of the protruding and receding portions of the

8. The top case of appeal against patent infringement judgment by the Supreme People's Procuratorate.
9. Selected in the top ten cases of judicial protection of intellectual property in Jiangsu courts in 2018.

noncircular profile relative to the angular position of the second rotor," and K: "and the magnitude of the eccentricity of the noncircular profile, are such that the noncircular profile applies to the second rotor an opposing fluctuating corrective torque which reduces or substantially cancels the fluctuating load torque of the rotary load assembly."

In this regard, Litens Suzhou Company argued that the angular positions of the protruding and receding portions of the noncircular profile in the technical features J and K belong to the feature of the positional relationship, and the magnitude of the eccentricity belongs to the structural feature, and the periodic fluctuating load torque and the fluctuating corrective torque are physical quantity that can be actually measured and perceived, and belong to the feature in the class of product structure in a broad sense. Therefore, the scope of Claim 1 defined by the technical features J and K should be determined by the literal content of the two technical features themselves and should not merely be understood as the specific parameters and specific setting manners disclosed in the patent Description.

Gates Shanghai Company argued as follows: technical features J and K neither define the mutual positional relationship and connection relationship of each component in the synchronous drive system nor make specific definition on the structure or shape of the noncircular profile in the synchronous drive system, let alone define the angular position of the noncircular profile and the specific numerical value of the eccentricity as well as the specific methods and steps of setting the angular position and eccentricity of the noncircular profile. Instead, the angular position and eccentricity of the noncircular profile are defined by using words with uncertain meanings (such as relative, reduce, and substantially cancel) combined with the desired effect (that is, generating a corrective torque to reduce or substantially cancel the load torque). Accordingly, the technical features J and K of Claim 1 are functional features.

The Jiangsu High People's Court held in the second instance that the technical features J and K are not functional features for the following reasons:

> First of all, the features J and K are not the technical features that define the technical solution to be claimed by the patent merely by function, effect or abstract working principle. Technical features J and K define the relevance between the spatial position of the noncircular profile and the physical quantity (fluctuating load torque) that appears during the use of the patent product and periodically changes over time and do not define the claims only in terms of function or effect.
>
> Second, according to the prior determination of the procedure of confirming the right related to the patent involved, the technical features J and K of the patent involved have clearly informed persons with ordinary skills in the art of how to implement the patent involved, that is to say, based on the understanding of the technical features J and K, persons with ordinary skills in the art can know how these two technical features are implemented and can solve the technical problem to be solved by the patent involved.

According to the contents determined in the procedure of confirming the right of the above patent involved, the contribution of the patent involved to the prior art lies in the proposal of using the noncircular profile to generate a fluctuating corrective torque to cancel or reduce the fluctuating load torque to solve the problem of torsional vibration in the synchronous drive system. Moreover, persons with ordinary skills in the art can clearly know how to implement it from the claims, especially the information recited in the technical features J and K, namely: (1) the geometric characteristics of the noncircular profile (which has protruding and receding portions) can be used to generate a fluctuating corrective torque to be applied to the second rotor; and (2) the angular positions of the protruding and receding portions of the noncircular profile and the eccentricity of the noncircular profile are adjusted, such that the fluctuating corrective torque partially cancels (reducing the torsional vibration) or completely cancels (eliminating the torsional vibration) the periodic fluctuating load torque generated on the second rotor. As for how to adjust the angular position and eccentricity of the noncircular profile, it is not limited to the specific embodiments disclosed in the patent Description.

Reminder: When it comes to the determination of complicated technical features, on the one hand, textbooks, reference books and other technical materials may be referred to; and on the other hand, the prior determination of the procedure of confirming the right may be fully used to clearly and distinctly elaborate the content of the technical features and prevent the disputed technical features from being "misidentified" as functional features.

[G] The Determination of Functional Features Requires the Consideration of the Technical Solution of the Claims as a Whole, Which Are Not Suitable to Be Divided Mechanically

In the preceding Case 4 of an infringement dispute over a patent right for utility model between Guangzhou Tongming Solar Technology Co. Ltd. and Shenzhen Huaze Xingye Technology Co. Ltd. ((2018) Zui Gao Fa Min Shen No. 1018[10]), the parties have disputes over whether the "first heat dissipation area" and the "second heat dissipation area" in Claim 1 are functional features, and furthermore, whether it shall be understood to be provided with heat dissipation holes or equivalent embodiments according to the disclosure of the Description.

In this regard, upon retrial, the Supreme People's Court held as follows:

> In case of determining whether the disputed technical feature is a "functional feature," it is not only necessary to consider the literal meaning of the technical feature itself, but also necessary to incorporate the technical feature into the overall technical solution defined by the claim for understanding. For the technical features that contain specific functions and effects, where persons with ordinary skills in the art can directly and explicitly determine the specific embodiments for

10. Selected as a typical case in the Annual Report of the Supreme People's Court on Intellectual Property Cases (2018).

> achieving the function or effect only by reading the claims, the technical feature is not a "functional feature" as specified in Article 4 of the *Judicial Interpretation I.*

In this case, from the perspective of the definition on Claim 1, the "first heat dissipation area" and the "second heat dissipation area" are essentially the regional division of specific portions of the lamp body and lampshade of the product of the patent involved. According to the overall technical solution defined in Claim 1, in the space of the lampshade, the area sealed by the waterproof ring is the first waterproof area, and the area excluding the first waterproof area is the first heat dissipation area. In the space of the lamp body, the area sealed by the waterproof ring is the second waterproof area, and the area excluding the second waterproof area is the second heat dissipation area.

In summary, persons with ordinary skills in the art can directly and explicitly determine the specific embodiments of the feature in combination with the meanings of the first heat dissipation area and the second heat dissipation area themselves and the overall technical solution of Claim 1, and thus the feature is not a functional feature.

In this case, the Supreme People's Court emphasized the important impact of the determination of whether it is a "functional feature" on the protection scope of the patent right and pointed out that in case of determining whether the disputed technical feature is a "functional feature," it is not only necessary to consider the literal meaning of the technical feature itself, but also necessary to incorporate the technical feature into the overall technical solution defined by the claim for understanding. If the specific embodiments for achieving the function or effect can be directly and explicitly determined at this time, the technical feature is not a "functional feature."

Case 11: In a case of Patent Administration (Patent) between TPI COMPOSITES MEMBER (TAICANG) CO. LTD. and Intellectual Property Office of Suzhou City ((2019) Zui Gao Fa Xing Shen No. 2876), the Supreme People's Court held in the retrial as follows: in this case, the "frame" of the "web locking frame" is a description of a specific structural feature. In addition, in combination with the disclosure of Claim 1 of the patent involved (the web locking frame is located right below the hanger, and the position of the web positioning frame corresponds to the position of the web locking frame) and the disclosure of Claim 4 of the patent involved (the web locking frame includes a second vertical plate and a second connecting rod, wherein the second vertical plate is connected to the lower middle part of the hanger, and a locking member is provided on the second vertical plate; one end of the second connecting rod is connected to the second vertical plate, and the other end is connected to the positioning foot stand). Those skilled in the art can directly and explicitly determine the specific embodiments for achieving the web locking function only by reading the claims. Therefore, the web locking frame is not a functional feature.

From the judgment of this case, it can be seen that the provision "can directly and explicitly determine the specific embodiments for achieving the aforesaid functions or effects only by reading the claims" defined in Article 8 of the *Judicial Interpretation II* refers to reading the overall technical solution defined by the claims, even in combination with the claims related to the disputed technical feature, rather than merely the disputed technical feature itself.

[H] The Determination of Functional Features Requires the Consideration of Whether the Division of Technical Features Is Appropriate

Case 12: In an infringement dispute over a patent right for invention between Wuxi Fodoo Technology Co. Ltd. (Fodoo Company) and Wuxi Taiyuan Machinery Manufacturing Co. Ltd. (Taiyuan Company) et al. ((2019) Zui Gao Fa Zhi Min Zhong No. 578), the features disputed by both parties are concentrated in the feature "a lower spinning drive sprocket (15) and an upper spinning drive sprocket (8) are mounted at both ends of each spinning transmission shaft (11), and the lower spinning drive sprocket (15) is driven by the spinning drive mechanism" in Claim 1.

Specifically, Fodoo Company argued that as long as the mechanism can drive the rotation of the spinning transmission shaft, it belongs to the spinning drive mechanism. The geared motor in the accused product is a specific term of "spinning drive mechanism" and is equivalent to the disputed feature. Whereas, Taiyuan Company argued that the "spinning drive mechanism" should be determined as a functional feature, that its protection scope should be defined within the embodiments disclosed in the Description, and that the accused product does not have a spinning drive mechanism.

In this regard, the Intellectual Property Court of the Supreme People's Court held that, indeed, the term "spinning drive mechanism" only describes the "mechanism" with the function of "driving spinning." Only by reading the Claims of the patent involved, persons with ordinary skills in the art cannot know the specific structure and manner of the "spinning drive mechanism."

However, in case of further understanding the part "spinning drive mechanism," it is not appropriate to separate it from the related content in Claim 1 of the patent involved. With reference to the complete description of the contents of the claim related to the "spinning drive mechanism" in Claim 1 of the patent involved, it can be seen that the content of the above claim actually defines the position relationship, connection relationship, and power transmission orientation and structural relationship between the spinning transmission shaft and the rotary shaft, between the lower spinning drive sprocket and the spinning transmission shaft, especially between the spinning drive mechanism and the lower spinning drive sprocket. And it can be directly and explicitly determined that the spinning drive mechanism and the lower spinning drive sprocket at the lower end of the spinning transmission shaft adopt a specific structure of a chain meshing connection. It can be seen that the above content of the claim related to the "spinning drive mechanism," especially the defined content "the lower spinning drive sprocket (15) is driven by the spinning drive mechanism," constitutes a specific technical unit that can relatively independently achieve certain technical functions and produce relatively independent technical effects, and shall be determined as a technical feature.

The above analysis further shows that the meaning of the technical term "spinning drive mechanism" cannot be understood in isolation from the context of the foregoing content of the claims related to the "spinning drive mechanism" of Claim 1. Therefore, determining the "spinning drive mechanism" alone as a technical feature and further arguing whether the technical feature is a functional feature does not help to accurately understand the protection scope of the claims of the patent involved, nor does it contribute to the correct comparison of the accused infringing dispute technical feature with the corresponding technical feature in Claim 1 of the patent involved.

In this case, the Supreme People's Court pointed out that the division of technical features should be based on the standard of a minimum functional unit. It should not be too broad or too fine. If the division is not appropriate, it will sometimes even lead to a dispute concerning the unnecessary functional features, as in this case. Furthermore, it would affect the accurate definition of the protection scope of the claims.

Meanwhile, it should be noted that: consistent with the judgment logic of Case 4, the Supreme People's Court also pointed out in this case that the interpretation involving the disputed technical terms in the claims should take into consideration the technical solution of the claims as a whole, and the interpretation should not be separated from the context of the technical solution.

§13.04 CONCLUSION

Since the rule "embodiment + equivalent embodiment" is adopted for functional features to define their protection scope, in order to avoid "injury to the innocent," the determination of functional features is particularly important. It is true that at this stage, the relevant provisions on functional features have already been relatively detailed, and the author is also trying to find some "commonality" from the individual cases, but the determination of functional features has strong individuality in each individual case. The cognitive level and ability of those skilled in the art are also constantly changing. Technologies that have not yet been generally known to each other may have become well-known at this time. Even if both structure and function are used for definition at the same time, it may be complicated and indistinguishable. What can be explicitly determined only by reading the claims in one case may not be explicitly determined in another case, and thus specific analysis on specific circumstances is required. Behind the appearance of "different judgments for the same case," as attorneys, what we can do is to make reasonable use of the "rules" that are beneficial to our clients, present sufficient evidence, and win the "first chance" of such litigation through the determination of functional features.

CHAPTER 14

Definitive Effect of the Usage Environment Features

Zhang Junjie & Ge Xiaomei

There is no doubt that the usage environment features have a definitive effect on the protection scope of the claims, but the disagreement and dispute are concentrated in what kind of definitive effect the features have.

Article 9 of the Interpretation (II) of the Supreme People's Court on Several Issues Concerning the Application of Law in the Trial of Patent Infringement Dispute Cases *(hereinafter referred to as* Judicial Interpretation II*) only stipulates from the negative side the circumstances that do not constitute the possession of the usage environment features. The judicial precedents provide guidance on what kind of circumstances constitute the possession of the usage environment features from the positive side: under normal circumstances, it is only required that the claimed object may be used in the usage environment, and it is not required that the claimed object must be used in the usage environment.*

This chapter includes six judicial precedents in total.

§14.01 BASIC PROVISIONS OF LAW

***Interpretation (II) of the Supreme People's Court on Several Issues Concerning the Application of Law in the Trial of Patent Infringement Dispute Cases* (hereinafter referred to as "*Judicial Interpretation II*")**

Article 9 Where the accused infringing technical solution cannot apply to the usage environment defined by the usage environment features in the claims, the people's court shall determine the accused infringing technical solution does not fall within the scope of protection of the patent right.

§14.02 INTERPRETATION OF THE ARTICLES OF LAW

The provision of Article 9 of the *Judicial Interpretation II* aims to enhance the certainty of the protection scope of the patent right, to provide the public with clear legal expectations, and to promote the improvement of patent document drafting. This also takes into full consideration the current situation that China's patent quality as a whole at the present stage is still at a relatively low level, and the need for the implementation of the innovation-driven development strategy.

Article 9 of the *Judicial Interpretation II* is directed to the usage environment features and stipulates that the above features have definitive effects on the protection scope of the patent right, which fully reflects the respect for the publicity of the claims. As to whether the above features and terms are essential technical features of a patent, it is a problem that should be resolved at the stage of patent right granting and confirmation. People's court for the trial of patent infringement dispute cases should not make any further screening thereto. That is to say, the drafter of the patent document should pay enough attention to the expression of the above features and terms during the patent application stage. (SONG Xiaoming, WANG Chuang, LI Jian, *Comprehension and Application of "Interpretation (II) on Several Issues Concerning the Application of Law in the Trial of Patent Infringement Dispute Cases"* [J], People's Justice (Application), 2016(10): 30-31)

§14.03 ISSUES/DISPUTES ARISING IN THE LAW APPLICATION

[A] Determination of Usage Environment Features

Case 1: In an infringement dispute over a patent right for invention between Shimano Inc. and Ningbo Sunrun Industry & Trade Co. Ltd. ((2012) Min Ti Zi No. 1), the Supreme People's Court defined the usage environment features as follows: "the usage environment features refer to the technical features used in the claims to describe the background or conditions used for the invention." When features in the claims are not specific definition on the claimed subject matter, but on the environment used by the subject matter or the connection relationship between the component parts of the subject matter and external components, these features can be preliminarily determined as the usage environment features. For details, please refer to the following cases.

Case 2: In an infringement dispute over a patent right for invention between VALEO SYSTEMES D'ESSUYAGE and Xiamen Lucas Auto Parts Co. Ltd. as well as Xiamen Fuke Auto Parts Co. Ltd. ((2019) Zui Gao Fa Zhi Min Zhong No. 2), the claimed subject matter of the patent involved is "a connector of a wiper," including the feature "which is used for ensuring the connection and articulation between a wiper arm and a part of a wiper brush body." However, the above technical feature does not directly define the structure of the connector, but the connection relationship between the connector and other parts, such as a wiper arm, a brush body part, etc. The feature actually defines the environment in which the connector is used and belongs to the usage environment features.

Case 3: In an infringement dispute over a patent right for invention between Jiaxing Zhonghua Chemical Co. Ltd. and Ningbo Wanglong Tech Co. Ltd. as well as Jiaxing Shengyuan IMP. & EXP. Co. Ltd. ((2014) Zhe Zhi Zhong Zi No. 246), the independent claim claims the "solid-liquid separation method of the oxidation liquid in the synthesis of vanillin." The Jiaxing Intermediate People's Court held at first instance that the technical features of the independent claims of the patent involved include two categories: one is the usage environment feature, and the other is step feature, wherein the features defining the oxidation liquid and the oxidizing agent belong to the usage environment features.

Case 4: In an infringement dispute over the retrial of the application of a patent right between Huawei Technologies Co., Ltd. and ZTE Corporation ((2014) Min Shen Zi No. 148), the title of the subject matter of Claim 1 is "a device for implementing transmission by-pass in a chain networking E1." The technical solution claimed by Claim 1 of the patent, in this case, is a system with specific functions. At the same time, according to the disclosure of the patent Description of this case, it can be seen that "chain networking" is one of the networking methods between subsystems of the mobile communication system. Therefore, "chain networking" is a definition of the connection relationship between a base station controller and a base station and between a base station and a base station in the system and is not a definition of the usage environment or conditions of the system.

Case 5: In an infringement dispute over a patent right for invention between China International Marine Containers (Group) Ltd. and Qingdao CIMC Container Manufacture Co. Ltd. as well as Qingdao Taiping Container Co. Ltd. ((2014) Min Ti Zi No. 40), Claim 1 claims "a transporting platform," including the features "for stacking non-standard containers" and "each of the transverse beams comprises: at least one top fitting, arranged on the upper part of the transverse beam for fitting the bottom corner fitting of the non-standard container." The foregoing two features actually respectively describe the background or conditions used by the transporting platform and the specific corner fitting of the invention of this case and belong to the usage environment features.

[B] Usage Environment Features Having a Definitive Effect on the Claims

Case 1: In an infringement dispute over a patent right for invention between Shimano Inc. and Ningbo Sunrun Industry & Trade Co., Ltd. ((2012) Min Ti Zi No. 1), the Supreme People's Court held that: the usage environment features that have been written into the claims are essential technical features and have definitive effects on the protection scope of the claims. The extent to which the usage environment features define the protection scope of the claims needs to be specifically determined according to the individual circumstances. Generally speaking, it should be understood it is only required that the claimed subject matter may be used in this kind of usage environment. It is not required that the claimed subject matter must be used in this kind of usage environment, except when those generally skilled in the art can clearly and reasonably know that the claimed object must be used in this kind of usage environment upon reading the patent Claims, Description and patent examination dossiers. A detailed analysis in combination with the features of the patent, in this case, is as follows.

The claimed subject matter of the patent involved is "a rear derailleur bracket of a bicycle," and the claims include the features "the bicycle frame has a connection structure (14a) formed on a derailleur mounting extension (14) of the rear fork end (51) of the bicycle frame" (referred to as the usage environment feature 1) and "the rear derailleur has a bracket member (5), a support member (4) for supporting the chain guide (3), and a pair of connecting members (6, 7) for connecting the support member (4) and bracket member (5)" (referred to as the usage environment feature 2). The Supreme People's Court held in the retrial as follows: regarding the usage environment feature 1, it should be understood that the bicycle rear derailleur bracket claimed by the patent, in this case, must be used on the rear fork end of the bicycle frame with the usage environment feature 1; and the bicycle rear derailleur bracket claimed by the patent, in this case, must be used on the rear derailleur with the usage environment feature 2. In summary, the usage environment features of the patent in this case, have definitive effects on the protection scope, and the bicycle rear derailleur bracket claimed by the patent, in this case, must be used in this usage environment. Shimano Inc. argued that the usage environment features present in the patent claims, in this case, do not constitute the essential technical features of the patent in this case and do not affect the protection scope of the claims. His/her arguments for the application of reexamination are untenable and not supported.

[C] The Extent to Which the Usage Environment Features Define the Protection Scope

The definitive effect of the usage environment features depends on its substantial impact on the claimed technical solution itself and should be comprehensively defined in combination with the description of the patent solution, the comparison object and the like.

(1) Under normal circumstances, the accused solution falls within the protection scope in a case where it can be used in the usage environment.

Case 2: In an infringement dispute over a patent right for invention between VALEO SYSTEMES D'ESSUYAGE and Xiamen Lucas Auto Parts Co. Ltd. as well as Xiamen Fuke Auto Parts Co. Ltd. ((2019) Zui Gao Fa Zhi Min Zhong No. 2), the Supreme People's Court held as follows: the accused infringing product has the usage environment features as long as it can be used in the usage environment defined by the usage environment features in the patent claims. As to whether the accused infringing product can also be used in other usage environments, it will not affect the result of infringement judgment in principle. Therefore, when the accused infringing product can realize the connection and articulation between the wiper arm and the wiper brush body part, regardless of whether the accused infringing product can also be used to connect a non-standard wiper arm, the result of the infringement judgment, in this case, will not be affected substantially.

(2) When it is clearly defined to be used in the usage environment, the accused solution falls within the protection scope in a case where it can only be used in the usage environment.

(3) The accused solution cannot fall within the protection scope in a case where it cannot apply to the usage environment.

Case 6: In an infringement dispute over a patent right for utility model between Feitian Technologies Co. Ltd. (Feitian Company) and Beijing Infosec Technologies Co. Ltd. as well as Wuhan Luojia Xin'an Technology Co., Ltd. ((2018) Jing Min Zhong No. 533), the patent involved claims "a transmission device for data safety," including the feature "the device further comprises a communication protocol module for an embedded system platform and a security module, the communication protocol module used for completing the analysis of the communication protocol of each embedded system platform." The Beijing High People's Court held in the second instance as follows: since the infringing products involved cannot directly work in the embedded system platform environment, it can at least be determined that the infringing products involved are not developed based on the embedded system platform environment. Moreover, the transmission device for data safety claimed by Claim 1 of the patent involved is only directed to the environment feature of the embedded system platform, and the evidence in the case can prove this. And Feitian Company also recognizes that the technical solution of the infringing product involved is actually only applicable to the Windows operating system. Therefore, the technical solution of the infringing product involved does not fall within the protection scope of Claim 1 of the patent involved.

§14.04 CONCLUSION

(1) Usage environment features shall be used with caution in the drafting of the claims.

Since the product in actual use may not be used in the usage environment defined by the claims, it may be difficult to fix the evidence in infringement litigation. It is advised to use the usage environment features with caution when drafting the claims and try to use the features of the subject matter itself for definition.

(2) Dealing with circumstances that must include the usage environment features.

If the usage environment features are needed in the claims for defining, it is advised to generalize the usage environment features or make them generic or add a parallel solution with the usage environments.

CHAPTER 15

Application of the "All Elements Rule"

Wang Meng & Ge Xiaomei

The "All Elements Rule" is the basic theory for determining patent infringement. Although its scope and methods of application have aroused many discussions in the exploration of judicial practice, there is no dispute at present. This chapter discusses seven judicial precedents so as to conduct an in-depth analysis of the application basis, the scope application and specific application situations of this rule.

§15.01 BASIC PROVISIONS OF LAW

***Interpretation of the Supreme People's Court on Several Issues concerning the Application of Law in the Trial of Patent Infringement Dispute Cases* (hereinafter referred to as "*Judicial Interpretation I*")**

Article 7 When determining whether the accused infringing technical solution falls into the scope of protection of a patent, the people's court shall examine all the technical features described in the claim asserted by a right holder.

Where the accused infringing technical solution contains technical features identical or equivalent to all the technical features described in a claim, the people's court shall determine that it falls into the scope of protection of the patent; or where, compared with all the technical features described in a claim, the technical features of the accused infringing technical solution are lack of more than one technical feature as described in the claim or contain more than one technical feature which is neither identical nor equivalent to any technical feature as described in the claim, the people's court shall determine that it does not fall into the scope of protection of the patent.

§15.02 INTERPRETATION OF THE ARTICLES OF LAW

Article 7, paragraph 1 of the *Interpretation of the Supreme People's Court on Several Issues Concerning the Application of Law in the Trial of Patent Infringement Dispute Cases* relates to the primary principle of determining infringement in accordance with the Chinese Patent Law—the "All Elements Rule," which is expressly stipulated for the first time.

Legislative background: in the practice of patent trials, from the perspective of focusing on protecting the interests of patentees, the principle of superfluity establishing was created and used by the court. There are different views in the theoretical and practical fields, which easily prevents the public from clarifying the scope of protection of the claims. It is impossible to clearly know what kind of implemented behavior will not infringe the patent right.

Legislative intent: to deny the principle of superfluity establishing that is more controversial, to clarify all the interpretation features recited in the claims, and to determine the protection scope of a patent. In this way, by showing the public all the technical features included in the technical solution constituting the invention or utility model, the public can clearly know what kind of implemented behavior will not infringe on the patent right. Only when all the interpretation features recited in the claims are comprehensively and fully respected, the public will not be at loose ends due to unforeseen changes in the contents of the claims, thereby ensuring the certainty of legal rights.

According to the above provisions, the conditions for applying the "All Elements Rule" are as follows:

(1) determining all the technical features described in the claim asserted by a right holder;
(2) looking for the corresponding technical features in the accused infringing technical solution;
(3) determining whether the accused infringing technical solution contains technical features identical or equivalent to all the technical features described in a claim;
(4) if all the technical features are included, it should be determined to fall into the scope of protection of the patent; and
(5) if more than one technical feature is missing, or if more than one technical feature is neither the same nor equivalent, it shall be determined that it does not fall into the scope of protection of the patent.

§15.03 ISSUES/DISPUTES ARISING IN THE LAW APPLICATION

The "All Elements Rule" is the primary principle in the process of determining patent infringement. If this principle is not satisfied, a non-infringement determination can be made. It is no longer necessary to consider defense based on prior art, compensation calculations, willful infringements and other links. However, in the process of applying the "All Elements Rule," a comprehensive technical comparison is required, which involves difficulties such as Doctrine of Identical and Doctrine of Equivalents. Therefore, the actual application process of the "All Elements Rule" can be said to be extremely difficult.

[A] Appropriate Division of Technical Features Is the Basis for Applying the "All Elements Rule"

Appropriate division of technical features is the basis for determining the scope of protection of the claims, comparing infringement and comparing the openness of the patent invalidation. The standard for the division of technical features and the important impact on each procedure will be elaborated as follows.

[1] The Standard for Dividing Technical Features Lies in Whether Relatively Independent Technical Functions Can Be Achieved

Case 1: In the retrial of an infringement dispute over a patent right between ZHANG Qiang and Yantai Qixia Dayi Industry and Trade Co. Ltd. as well as WEI Eryou ((2012) Zui Gao Fa Min Shen No. 137[1]), one of the focus issues of the case is whether the five targets of the patent involved are equivalent to the nine targets in the corresponding technical features of the accused infringing product.

Claim 1 of the patent involved recites that "the trainer comprises five targets," and the Description discloses the content "there are five target positions arranged in the order of head, chest, and abdomen on the panel, and a target is installed in each target position." The corresponding technical features of the accused infringing product are nine targets, which are divided into "left head hitting position, right head hitting position, left arm hitting position, right arm hitting position, left rib hitting position, right rib hitting position, abdomen hitting position, left hip hitting position, right hip hitting position" according to the disclosure of the product description.

Although the number of targets of the patent involved and the accused infringing product is different, since each target of the patent involved performs a separate function upon hitting, the five targets cannot be considered as one technical feature and should be decomposed into head targets, abdomen targets and waist targets. The accused infringing product includes head targets and abdomen targets. The hip targets thereof are equivalent to the waist target of the patent involved in function and effect. Therefore, it should be determined that the accused infringing technical solution includes the technical features identical or equivalent to the five targets of the patent involved. The Court of First Instance held that the technical features "five targets" of the patent involved is nonequivalent to the technical features "nine targets" of the

1. This case is the Case 01 in the Intellectual Property Annual Report of the Supreme People's Court in 2012.

accused infringing product, and it pertains to an error in the application of law. It is also improper that the Court of Second Instance did not make any correction.

In this case, the Supreme People's Court clearly pointed out: when dividing the technical features of the claims, the technical unit that can achieve a relatively independent technical function should generally be regarded as one technical feature, and it is not appropriate to classify multiple technical units that achieve different technical functions as one technical feature.

[2] Appropriate Division of Technical Features Has an Important Impact on the Determination of the Protection Scope of the Claims

Appropriate division of technical features has an important impact on the protection scope of the patent claims. If the technical features are divided too finely, the protection scope of the patent will be inappropriately restricted; and if the technical features are divided too broadly, the protection scope of the patent will be inappropriately broadened.

Case 2: In an infringement dispute over a patent right for invention between Wuxi Fodoo Technology Co. Ltd. and Wuxi Taiyuan Machinery Manufacturing Co. Ltd. et al. ((2019) Zui Gao Fa Zhi Min Zhong No. 578), the Supreme People's Court also pointed out that technical features should be relatively small technical units that can relatively independently realize certain technical functions and produce relatively independent technical effects in the overall technical solution of the invention. The division of technical features of the claims should not be too broad or too fine. Otherwise, it will affect the precise definition of the protection scope of the patent right. Therefore, the interpretation related to the disputed technical terms in the claims cannot be separated from the context of the technical solution in which technical terms are located.

The complete expression of the content of claim related to the "spinning drive mechanism" in Claim 1 of the patent involved is: "two freely rotatable spinning transmission shafts (11) are centrally symmetrically provided in a revolving shaft (10), a lower spinning drive sprocket (15) and an upper spinning drive sprocket (8) are mounted at both ends of each spinning transmission shaft (11), and the lower spinning drive sprocket (15) is driven by the spinning drive mechanism." It can be seen that the combination of above position, connection, transmission orientation and structure can jointly achieve a relatively independent function, that is, "the spinning drive sprocket is driven by the spinning drive mechanism, such that the spinning transmission shaft is driven to spin in the revolving shaft." Accordingly, the above contents of the claims related to the "spinning drive mechanism," especially the defined content by "the lower spinning drive sprocket (15) is driven by the spinning drive mechanism," constitutes a specific technical unit that can relatively independently realize certain technical functions and produce relatively independent technical effects, and thus should be recognized as a technical feature. Therefore, solely determining the "spinning drive mechanism" as a technical feature, and thereby arguing whether the technical feature is a functional feature, does not help to accurately understand the protection scope of the claims of the patent involved, nor does it help correctly compare the technical features of the accused infringing dispute with the corresponding technical features in Claim 1 of the patent involved.

This case highlights the important impact of the appropriate division of technical features on the protection scope of the patent claims. If the division is improper, it is possible to fall into unnecessary arguments that do not contribute to the understanding of the protection scope of the claims.

[3] Appropriate Division of Technical Features Has an Important Impact on the Determination of Infringement

Appropriate division of technical features also has an important impact on the determination of infringement. If the technical features are divided too finely, in the infringement comparison, it is easy to mistakenly determine that the infringement is not found due to the lack of the technical features of the accused infringing technical solution; and if the technical features are divided too broadly, it is easy to ignore a certain essential technical feature in the infringement comparison and wrongly determine that the infringement is found.

Case 3: In the retrial of an infringement dispute over a patent right for utility model between LIU Zonggui and Taizhou Fenglilai Plastic Co., Ltd. ((2017) Zui Gao Fa Min Shen No. 3802[2]), the Supreme People's Court determined the focus issue of the retrial as: whether the accused infringing product contains technical features identical or equivalent to the feature "both ends thereof (adjusting rod) are respectively sleeved with a spring, and a sleeve body with an aperture smaller than the diameter of the spring is sleeved on the periphery of the spring" as recited in Claim 1 of the patent involved.

In the second-instance judgment of this case, the second-instance court (Zhejiang High People's Court) determined as follows: the adjusting rod of the patent involved is sleeved with a spring, and a sleeve body with an aperture smaller than the diameter of the spring is further sleeved outside the spring. However, the accused infringing product relates to the content that both ends of the spring are respectively hung on the adjusting rod and the chair body to achieve the purpose of adjusting the chair body. Due to the lack of the technical feature "sleeve body" recited in the claims, it should be determined that the accused infringing product does not fall into the protection scope of the patent involved.

Upon retrial, the Supreme People's Court held that the key to this case is to properly divide the technical features so that the technical features can be compared correctly. The division of technical features should be combined with the overall technical solution of the invention, and consideration should be given to smaller technical units that can relatively independently realize certain technical functions and produce relatively independent technical effects.

2. This case is the Case 03 in Intellectual Property Annual Report1 of the Supreme People's Court in 2017.

The feature "both ends thereof (adjusting rod) are respectively sleeved with a spring, and a sleeve body with an aperture smaller than the diameter of the spring is sleeved on the periphery of the spring" recited in Claim 1 of the patent involved can achieve the function that when the height of the chair body needs to be adjusted, a restoring force is generated on the adjusting rod, so that the pin body and the slot are fastened. It can be seen that although the "sleeve body" is a part, its function and effect must be achieved relying on the cooperation of the spring, and the two parts must cooperate with each other so as to perform a function in the overall technical solution. Therefore, in Claim 1 of the patent involved, the sleeve body itself cannot achieve a relatively independent function and should not be treated as an independent technical feature. When comparing the technical features of the claims of the patent involved with the corresponding technical features of the accused infringing product, the feature "both ends thereof are respectively sleeved with a spring, and a sleeve body with an aperture smaller than the diameter of the spring is sleeved on the periphery of the spring" should serve as an independent technical feature for comparison, instead of using the "sleeve body" as an independent technical feature for comparison.

The accused infringing product achieves the corresponding function by providing the hinge pin and hanging the spring at both ends of the adjusting rod, while the patent involved achieves the corresponding function by providing a sleeve body at both ends of the adjusting rod and outfitting the spring. Although the two do not belong to the same technical feature, whether the chair is adjusted by the tension principle of spring or the compression principle of spring, the basic nature of the spring's restoring force is both used, and the means are basically the same. The function of using the restoring force to fasten the pin body and the slot is achieved, and the effects that the two can achieve are basically the same.

It can be seen that the Zhejiang High People's Court determined that the "sleeve body" is an independent technical feature, while the Supreme People's Court deemed that the "sleeve body" itself does not have a relatively independent function and should not be treated as an independent technical feature. That is, the unreasonable division of technical features determined by the Court of Second Instance is the key to ordering the retrial in this case. The reason why the Supreme People's Court and the Zhejiang High People's Court have made different determinations on whether the same technical features are identical or equivalent is that the basis for the division of technical features is different. The Zhejiang High People's Court divided the "sleeve body" that does not have an independent function into an independent technical feature. As a result, the technical feature identical or equivalent to the "sleeve body" cannot be found in the accused infringing technical solution, and it is concluded that it does not fall into the protection scope of the claims. Therefore, how to reasonably divide the technical features is the first and important link in the infringement litigation. The following focuses on the analysis of how to nearly reasonably divide the technical features from the two stages of infringement litigation and invalidation procedure.

Reminder: in litigation practice, except for some technical solutions with particularly simple and clear technical features, the division by the two parties of technical features of Claim 1 is inconsistent in most cases. From the plaintiff's point of view, they usually split the technical features as broad as possible, such that it is easier to make the accused infringing technical solution close to the patent involved and fall into the scope of protection. Whereas, from the defendant's point of view, they usually split the technical features as finely as possible, such that it is easier for the accused infringing technical solution to keep off all the technical features of the patent involved and escape the risk of infringement. But in the end, what the judge has to determine is necessarily to determine which party's split is more reasonable and more coincident with the technical essence of the patent involved. Therefore, whether as a plaintiff or as a defendant, after proposing a technical split solution from the perspective of one's own perspective, it is also necessary to make a reasonable prediction and psychological precaution of the other party's technical split solution so as to find a solution. Furthermore, it is necessary from an objective perspective to effectively divide the technical features in accordance with the technical essence so as to predict in advance the division manner determined by the judge.

[4] Appropriate Division of Technical Features Has an Important Impact on the Public Comparison in the Patent Invalidation Procedure

The invalidation process also inevitably involves the division of technical features. From the perspective of the petitioner for invalidation, the more specific splitting of the claims makes it easier to search for good reference documents. For example, as for the part "sleeve body" in the above reference case, it is easy to find a document that discloses the sleeve body for being sleeved outside the spring in the prior art, but it would be difficult to find a document that discloses that the sleeve body is sleeved outside the spring and provided at both ends of the adjusting rod, and thus finally can be used to adjust the chair position. Therefore, in order to increase the probability of a patent being invalidated, the technical features of the technical solution cannot be divided too finely and improperly. In this way, although it is easy to find the reference documents to defeat the too small technical features one by one, the possibility of being recognized by the collegiate panel is not easy to determine. If the patentee's counter-attack is reasonable, it is more likely to be denied by the collegiate panel. From the perspective of the patentee, it will inevitably make judgments based on the invalidation request document of the petitioner for invalidation. At this time, it is necessary to screen out the split technical features that are inconsistent with the technical essence so as to make a response strategy that is beneficial to oneself and defend one's own patent.

Reminder: In order to prevent the claims from being improperly split in the stage of defending rights, effective preparations should be made from the drafting stage, the smaller technical unit that can perform a relatively independent function should be carefully considered, communication with the inventor should be made in detail, and the actual effect in the application documents should be determined, such that accurate and well-summarized technical terms or technical concepts can be determined. Careful analysis on whether there are specific associated relationships between multiple technical terms or technical concepts corresponding to the technological improvement of the invention and the extent to which these specific associated relationships are defined or described is particularly required. At the same time, these technical terms or technical concepts, as well as their associated relationships, should be elaborated or properly explained in the Description and/or Drawings. In this way, the relevant technical features in the claims can be explained at the stage of litigation.

[B] The Scope of the "All Elements Rule" Includes the Identical Infringement and the Equivalent Infringement

In the past judicial practice of our country, the "All Elements Rule" only applies to identical infringement, not to the doctrine of equivalents, and some cases are resolved with reference to this spirit. However, with the development of infringement theory and trial practice, the Supreme People's Court has repeatedly clarified that the "All Elements Rule" is applicable not only to the determination of the identical infringement but also to the determination of the equivalent infringement.

In the foregoing Case 2 of an infringement dispute over a patent right for invention between Wuxi Fodoo Technology Co. Ltd. and Wuxi Taiyuan Machinery Manufacturing Co. Ltd. et al. ((2019) Zui Gao Fa Zhi Min Zhong No. 578), the focus of the dispute lies in whether the technical features of the accused infringing product, that is, "a coupler is mounted at the lower end of each spinning transmission shaft, the coupler is connected to a geared motor downwards, the lower end of the geared motor is mounted with a slip ring, and the geared motor drives the spinning transmission shaft to spin by the coupler" constitute the features identical or equivalent to the corresponding technical features of Claim 1 of the patent involved, that is, "a lower spinning drive sprocket is mounted at the lower end of each spinning transmission shaft, and the lower spinning drive sprocket is driven by the spinning drive mechanism."

In this regard, the Supreme People's Court clearly pointed out that the "All Elements Rule" not only applies to the identical infringement (literal infringement) of constituting the identical features as the literal semantics of the technical features recited in the claims but also applies to the equivalent infringement of the equivalent features that exceed the literal and semantic boundary of the technical features recited in the claims but belong to the equivalent features that can be envisaged by a person with ordinary skills in the art without any creative work and formed by simply replacing or transforming the technical features.

Second, all parties, in this case, confirmed that the lower end of the spinning transmission shaft of the accused infringing product lacks a lower spinning drive sprocket. Therefore, the above distinguishing technical features of the accused infringing product do not constitute the identical features in a literal sense to the corresponding technical features of Claim 1 of the patent involved.

Finally, concerning whether the above technical features of the accused infringing product are equivalent to the corresponding technical features of Claim 1 of the patent involved, although the distinguishing technical features of the accused infringing product and the corresponding technical features recited in Claim 1 of the patent involved realize basically the same functions, the technical means adopted are substantially different and the technical effects achieved are not completely the same. Therefore, the two do not constitute equivalent features.

In this case, the Supreme People's Court clearly pointed out the scope of application of the "All Elements Rule." From the point of view of the judgment, it first demonstrated that the accused infringing product and the patent involved do not constitute the identical infringement. Under the premise of difference, the Court then explored the problem of whether they constitute the equivalent features. It can be clearly known therefrom that the "All Elements Rule" is applicable not only to the determination of the identical infringement but also to the determination of the equivalent infringement

[C] Specific Application of the "All Elements Rule"

[1] If the Accused Infringing Technical Solution Contains All the Technical Features of the Patent, It Constitutes an Infringement

Exactly the same situations include: situation a, literal infringement, only by literal analysis and comparison, it can be determined that the technical features of the accused technical solution and the claims are characterized in that the literal expressions of the technical features are identical; and situation b, generic terms are used in the claims, and the technical features used in the accused technical solution belong to the specific terms of the generic terms. An introduction is made below to situation b with reference to related cases.

Case 4: In an infringement dispute over a patent right for utility model between Wuxi Guowei Ceramic Electric Appliances Co. Ltd., JIANG Guoping and Changshu Linzhi Electric Heating Device Co. Ltd. as well as Suning.Com Co. LTD. ((2018) Zui Gao Fa Min Zai No. 111), the Court of Second Instance (Jiangsu High People's Court) determined that although Claim 2 of the patent, in this case, does not directly define the presence of grooves on the upper and lower surfaces of the heat-conducting aluminum pipe, due to the errata interpretation, the definitive effect of the technical feature "the upper and lower surfaces of the heat-conducting aluminum pipe are provided with grooves respectively" must be considered. Because there are no grooves on the upper and lower surfaces of the heat-conducting aluminum pipe of the accused infringing product, and because the grooves in the patent, in this case, are not dispensable, it has the function of "ensuring that the width of the upper and lower surfaces is consistent with the width of the heat sink strip." Accordingly, the accused infringing product lacks the technical features implied in Claim 2 of the patent in this case: grooves are also present on the upper and lower surfaces of the heat-conducting aluminum pipe, and the grooves have the function of ensuring that the width of the upper and lower surfaces is consistent with the width of the heat sink aluminum strip. Therefore, according to the "All Elements Rule," the accused infringing product does not fall into the protection scope of Claim 2 of the patent in this case.

The Supreme People's Court determined that the expression "stuck" in the feature E of Claim 2, "the heat sink aluminum strip is stuck to the left and right sides of the heat-conducting aluminum pipe in the heating core," needs to be understood from the perspective of those skilled in the art, and overall understanding is needed in combination with the information given in the description. The heat sink aluminum strip in feature E is "stuck" to the upper and lower surfaces of the heat-conducting aluminum pipe in order to make the heating core and the heat sink aluminum strip fully fit to ensure that the heat of the heating core can be efficiently conducted out through the heat sink aluminum strip. For this purpose, it can be considered that "stuck" should be understood as "fitting." As for how to realize the fitting between the heating core and the heat sink aluminum strip, there is no strict definition. It can be fixed by welding and slot wedge or can be fixed by other means such as adhesive.

On this basis, the Supreme People's Court determined that the feature "the heat sink aluminum strip is fixed on the upper and lower surfaces by braze welding or through the slot wedge on the heat-conducting aluminum pipe" of the accused infringing product constitutes the feature identical to the feature E "the heat sink aluminum strip is stuck to the upper and lower surfaces of the heat-conducting aluminum pipe in the heating core" of Claim 2 of the patent in this case.

[2] If the Accused Infringing Technical Solution Lacks Patent Technical Features, It Does Not Constitute an Infringement

Case 5: In an infringement dispute over a patent right for utility model between ZHANG Zhen and Yangzhou Golden Pride Shoes Co. Ltd. as well as Baotou Tongshengxiang Shoes Store ((2011) Min Shen Zi No. 630), the Supreme People's Court determined that the accused infringing product technical features were compared with the technical features of the patent involved, and they both relate to a heel shank for women shoes, which consisted of a cambered shank sheet and a heel post. However, the cambered shank sheet of the patent involved is provided with a plug on the lower right end, which is fixed to each other as a whole, inserted into the hole at the upper end of the heel post. And the cambered shank sheet and the heel post of the accused infringing product are an integral structure with grooves formed by bending a whole piece of material and do not have the technical feature that the cambered shank sheet of the patent involved is connected with the heel post through a plug. Therefore, the accused infringing product does not fall into the protection scope of the patent in this case.

It can be seen that the corresponding technical feature to the technical feature "a cambered shank sheet is connected with a heel post through a plug" of the patent involved is not found in the accused infringing product and does not conform to the "All Elements Rule" and thus the accused infringing product does not fall into the protection scope of the patent involved.

[3] If the Accused Infringing Technical Solution Is Added with a Technical Feature on the Basis of the Patent, It Will Not Be Considered and Still Constitutes an Infringement

In the foregoing Case 1 of the retrial of an infringement dispute over a patent right between ZHANG Qiang and Yantai Qixia Dayi Industry and Trade Co. Ltd. as well as WEI Eryou ((2012) Zui Gao Fa Min Shen No. 137[3]), one of the focuses of the dispute, in this case, is whether the addition of the lifting function to the accused infringing product is a reason for not constituting an infringement.

In this regard, the Supreme People's Court, upon retrial, held that: in the judgment of an infringement, there is no need to consider whether the accused infringing technical solution has added technical features compared with the patent involved. The accused infringing technical solution constitutes an infringement if it contains the technical features identical or equivalent to all the technical features recited in the claims of the patent involved. The accused infringing technical solution does not constitute infringement if it lacks more than one technical feature of the patent involved or contains more than one technical feature which is neither identical nor equivalent to the patent involved. The Court of Second Instance regarded the addition of the lifting function of the accused infringing product as one of the reasons that it does not constitute an infringement, and this is an improper application of the law.

It is easy to understand that the application of the "All Elements Rule" means that, as long as the accused infringing technical solution has all the features of the claims of the patent involved, it is considered as an infringement. Therefore, there is no need to pay attention to whether the accused infringing technical solution has more technical features than the claims.

In practice, the public may not understand this and may have the question why it should be counted as an infringement since the accused infringing technical solution has more features than the claims, and the performance may be better than the patented product. This is because the patent protects intellectual achievements. The subsequent product must obtain the others' permission if it uses others' patents and intellectual achievements and is improved on the basis of patented products, even if its performance may be better than that of the patented products. Otherwise, it is an infringement.

[D] Once Highly Controversial Principles of Infringement Comparison

[1] Inferior Technical Solution

Case 6: In an infringement dispute over a patent right for utility model between ZHANG Jianhua and Shenyang Zhilian Highrise Heating Technology Co. Ltd. as well as Shenyang Gaolian Highrise Heating Network Technology Co. Ltd. (Gaolian Company)

3. This case is the Case 01 in Intellectual Property Annual Report of the Supreme People's Court in 2012.

((2009) Min Ti Zi No. 83), the Supreme People's Court has given clear guidelines, that is, whether the accused infringing technical solution lacks a certain patent technical feature and thus causes an inferior technical effect is not a factor that should be considered in the determination of patent infringement. In this case, the accused infringing technical solution does not fall into the scope of patent protection due to the lack of more than one technical feature of the patent. ZHANG Jianhua and Gaolian Company did not constitute patent infringement.

There are situations where the accused infringer omitted or replaced a certain technical feature of the patent technical solution, resulting in its inferior technical effect to the patent technical solution. There were two different opinions in the past judicial practice on whether this inferior technical solution falls into the protection scope of the patent. One opinion holds that if the inferior technical solution is obviously caused by deliberate omission or replacement of a certain technical feature, the doctrine of equivalents should be used to determine that it constitutes an infringement. Another opinion is that the determination of patent infringement should adhere to the principle of all technical features. If an inferior technical solution lacks a certain technical feature of the patent technical solution or the corresponding technical feature is not identical or equivalent, it shall not be deemed to constitute an infringement.

Regarding the first opinion, if the doctrine of equivalents is used to determine an infringement, there are obstacles. The application of the doctrine of equivalents needs to meet three basic conditions. Since the accused infringing technical solution lacks the technical features of the patent or the functional effect has become inferior, it no longer accords with "achieving basically the same effect" and does not meet the application conditions of the doctrine of equivalents.

[2] Principle of Superfluity Establishing

The basic meaning of the principle of superfluity establishing is: ignoring non-essential technical features, that is, a certain technical feature recited in the claims is superfluous to the technical problem to be solved by the invention, and the technical feature can be ignored when determining the infringement. Even if the accused infringing product does not have this feature, it can be determined to fall into the protection scope of the patent right.

The most famous case in which the court applied the "principle of superfluity establishing" was the case of "Zhoulin Frequency Spectrum Instrument" in 1995. In the case of "Zhoulin Frequency Spectrum Instrument," the plaintiff argued that the feature b "a stereo sound play system and a music current acupoint stimulator are placed in the whole machine body" is not the essential technical feature for realizing the therapeutic function of the patent product, and the defendant constitutes the infringement under the doctrine of equivalents

The Court of Second Instance determined that although technical feature b is written into the independent claims, combined with the description in the patent description, and in terms of the essence of the patent's overall technical solution, technical feature b does not produce substantive and essential functions and effects.

Obviously caused by the applicant's misunderstanding and lack of experience in drafting application documents, technical feature b should be regarded as an additional technical feature. The judgment rejected the appeal and upheld the infringement judgment made in the first instance.

However, the Supreme People's Court has explicitly denied the application of the principle of superfluity establishing.

Case 7: In an appellate infringement dispute over a patent right between Dalian Xinyi Building Material Co. Ltd. and Dalian Renda New Wall Building Material Plant ((2005) Min San Ti Zi No. 1), the Supreme People's Court clearly determined that the independent claims should reflect the technical solution of the invention or utility model as a whole and recite the essential technical features to solve the technical problem. It should be considered that all the technical features written into the independent claims by the patentee are essential technical features and should not be ignored, and all should be included in the comparison of technical features. This court does not approve of rash application of the so-called principle of superfluity establishing for reference.

Historical significance of existence: in the early days of the establishment of our country's patent system, the level of the patent agency was not high. When drafting the Claims, it often happens that some non-essential technical features are written into independent claims. If the infringement is determined according to the "All Elements Rule," only non-infringement can be obtained. In order to protect the interests of the inventor of the invention, in judicial practice, the courts represented by the Beijing High People's Court have developed the principle of superfluity establishing, designating non-essential technical features as surplus features, which will not be considered when determining the protection scope of the claims. This thus gives the patentee the opportunity to remedy the writing of the non-essential technical features when drafting the claims due to lack of experience.

Of course, with the establishment of the "All Elements Rule" by the Supreme People's Court in the *Interpretation on Several Issues Concerning the Application of Law in the Trial of Patent Infringement Dispute Cases* of in 2009, the principle of superfluity establishing has officially withdrawn from the historical arena.

§15.04 CONCLUSION

In 2009, the *Interpretation on Several Issues Concerning the Application of Law in the Trial of Patent Infringement Dispute Cases* clearly adopted the "All Elements Rule" in the determination of an infringement over a patent right for the first time: all the technical features recited in the claim asserted by a right holder shall be examined. Previously, the principle of superfluity establishing was adopted for the determination of an infringement over a patent right in China; that is, the relevant patent judicial interpretation stipulates that the essential technical features in the claims are used to determine the scope of patent protection. This practice has become the history of China's patent system. However, the current principle of determining patent infringement clarifies the application of the "All Elements Rule," that is, the protection scope of the claim asserted by the right holder is determined by all the technical features recited thereby, and it is no longer necessary to determine whether the technical feature is an essential technical feature. The establishment of the "All Elements Rule" marks that the effort of demonstration of the scope of patent protection has been clarified and that the public can determine the boundary of the scope of patent protection and what kind of technical solutions are infringing.

CHAPTER 16
Doctrine of Equivalents

He Yibo & Ge Xiaomei

The Doctrine of Equivalents, which originated in the United States in 1853, has been applied around the world. Since 2002 when the Doctrine of Equivalents was first applied by Chinese courts to determine an infringement upon a patent, this doctrine has gradually become an important legal basis for a determination of a patent infringement. This report discusses the basic problems and methods of the application of the Doctrine of Equivalents with nine typical judicial precedents and various situations of analyzing and judging "three 'basically the same'" + "no creative work is required."

§16.01 BASIC PROVISIONS OF LAWS

***Interpretation of the Supreme People's Court on Several Issues concerning the Application of Law in the Trial of Patent Infringement Dispute Cases* (hereinafter referred to as "*Judicial Interpretation I*")**

Article 7 When determining whether the alleged infringement technical solution falls within the protection scope of a patent, the people's court shall examine all the technical features recited in the claims claimed by the patentee. Where the alleged infringement technical solution contains technical features identical or equivalent to all the technical features recited in the claims, the people's court shall determine that it falls within the protection scope of the patent; or where, compared with all the technical features recited in the claims, the technical features of the alleged infringement technical solution are lack of one or more technical features as recited in the claims or contain one or more technical features which are neither identical nor equivalent to any technical feature as recited in the claims, the people's court shall determine that it does not fall within the protection scope of the patent.

Several Provisions of the Supreme People's Court on Issues concerning the Application of Law in the Trial of Cases on Patent Disputes (amended in 2015) **(hereinafter referred to as "*the Provisions*")**

Article 17 The provision that "the extent of protection of the patent right for invention or utility model shall be determined by the terms of the claims. The description and the appended drawings may be used to interpret the content of the claims" as mentioned in Article 59.1 of the Patent Law means that the protection scope of the patent shall be determined by the extent determined by all technical features recited in the claims, and shall also include the scope determined by the features that are equivalent to those technical features.

Equivalent features refer to the features that use basically the same means, realize basically the same function and achieve basically the same effect as the technical features recited in the claims, and that persons of ordinary skill in the art can envisage without any creative work when the alleged infringement action occurs.

Interpretation (II) of the Supreme People's Court on Several Issues concerning the Application of Law in the Trial of Patent Infringement Dispute Cases **(hereinafter referred to as "*Judicial Interpretation II*")**

Article 8 Functional features mean the technical features which define the structure, component, step, condition or the relationship thereof, among others, through the function or effect thereof in the invention-creation, except when persons of ordinary skill in the art can directly and unambiguously determine the specific embodiments for achieving the above function or effect only by reading the claims.

Where the corresponding technical feature of the alleged infringement technical solution adopts basically the same means, realizes the same function and achieves the same effect as the indispensable technical feature for achieving the function or effect as mentioned in the preceding paragraph as recited in the Description and the Drawings, which can be readily envisaged by persons of ordinary skill in the art without any creative work when the alleged infringement action occurs, the people's court shall determine the corresponding technical feature is identical with or equivalent to the functional feature.

§16.02 INTERPRETATION OF THE PROVISIONS

In judicial practice, an actual action of identical infringement is less common, while an action of equivalent infringement is more common. Many alleged infringers study a patented technical solution of a patentee and simply replace or change the patented technical solution with a conventional technical means in the technical field. That is, they manufacture and sell an infringement product or use an infringement method for the purpose of production and operation so as to achieve the purpose, advantage or positive effect of invention that can only be obtained by the patented technical solution. Therefore, the Doctrine of Equivalents emerged as required in the international and domestic judicial countermeasures.

According to the relevant provisions of the *Judicial Interpretation I*, the so-called equivalent refers to a technical feature equivalent to a technical feature rather than an equivalent to the whole claims of the patent. The *Provisions* further explains the meaning of an equivalent feature, that is, an equivalent feature must meet two conditions at the same time: (1) the equivalent feature adopts basically the same means, realizes basically the same function and achieves basically the same effect as the technical feature in the claims; and (2) the equivalent feature can be readily envisaged by persons of ordinary skill in the art without any creative work when the alleged infringement action occurs, that is, it is obvious to persons of ordinary skill in the art.

When amending the *Provisions* in 2015, the Supreme People's Court added a time limit, that is, "when the alleged infringement action occurs," to the definition of equivalent features on the basis of the previous version of the *Provisions* in order to strengthen the patent protection. Upon such an amendment, the equivalents caused by the development of new technologies from the filing date of the patent to the date of alleging an infringement are incorporated into the protection scope of the patent. Therefore, whether a technical feature constitutes equivalence or not should be judged by taking the occurrence of the alleged infringement as a basis time point. Such an amendment also makes the *Provisions* consistent with the *Judicial Interpretation I* in the determination of the protection scope of the patent and the time point of infringement judgment.

§16.03 ISSUES/DISPUTES ARISEN IN THE APPLICATION

[A] Replacement of Equivalents Pertains to an Issue of a Technical Fact, and Equivalent Infringement Pertains to a Legal Issue

Case 1: In an infringement dispute over a patent between Ningbo Dongfang Movement General Factory (hereinafter referred to as "Movement General Factory") and Jiangyin Jinling Hardware Products Co. Ltd. (hereinafter referred to as "Jinling Company") (A Civil Judgment of the Supreme People's Court (2001) Min San Ti Zi No.1),[1] the focus of the dispute between the two parties related to the issue concerning the functions or effects of the anti-vibration limiting plate in the alleged infringement product and method and the guide plate in the patent.

Since whether the alleged infringement product and method are equivalent to the patented technology relates to professional technical issues, it is necessary to rely on the judgment of professionals skilled in the art. Therefore, the Supreme People's Court entrusted relevant professionals to appraise the professional technical issues involved in this case.

Regarding the above appraisal opinion, Jinling Company at least held the following opinions: 1. the conclusion in the appraisal that "the main functions of the

1. This case is the first one in China where the Doctrine of Equivalents was applied in determination of a patent infringement.

two features are basically the same" regarding the guide plate in the patent and the anti-vibration limiting plate in the alleged infringement product is not objective and comprehensive. The guide plate in the patented technology performs not only the guiding, anti-vibration and positioning function of the grinding wheel but also the functions of supporting and fixing a workpiece. However, the anti-vibration limiting plate of the alleged infringement product does not have the functions of supporting and fixing a workpiece; and 2. "whether it pertains to equivalent substitution" should be judged within the jurisdiction of the people's court and should not be solved through the technical appraisal.

In this regard, the Supreme People's Court held that: first of all, equivalent substitution or equivalent replacement should pertain to an issue of a technical fact, that is, the necessary technical feature in the claims of the patent is basically the same as the corresponding feature of the alleged infringement product in terms of technical means, functions and effects; the mutual replacement of the two features can be realized without any creative work for persons of ordinary skill in the art. The people's court sometimes needs the assistance of the judgment of professionals skilled in the art when determining whether the two features pertain to equivalent replacement. Equivalent replacement does not always constitute an infringement upon a patent. When judging whether equivalent replacement constitutes a patent infringement, other elements should also be considered. Therefore, it should be a legal issue within the jurisdiction of the people's court to determine whether the equivalent replacement itself constitutes a patent infringement.

Second, the working principles and methods are the same, and the structural shapes of the main working surfaces of the two important parts, i.e., the guide plate and the anti-vibration limiting plate, are similar; and the differences between the technical features of the two parts can be realized without any creative work for persons of ordinary skill having mechanical professional knowledge. Therefore, the two parts can be determined as basically the same in the technical means. The main functions of the two important parts, i.e., the guide plate in the patent and the anti-vibration limiting plate in the alleged infringement product, are basically the same, and thus it can be determined that the functions to be realized by the two parts are basically the same. Particularly when the anti-vibration limiting plate and the work-piece carriage of the alleged infringement product are taken as a whole, the function thereof is not substantively different from that of the guide plate in the patent. It is not beneficial to reducing the processing vibration of the workpiece to fix a workpiece on the workpiece carriage in the alleged infringement product rather than on the anti-vibration limiting plate, compared with fixing the workpiece on the guide plate in the patent. As stated in the appraisal, the guide plate in the patent has the function of supporting the workpiece (blind plate), which is beneficial to reducing the processing vibration of the workpiece and improving the processing quality. However, it cannot be held that the anti-vibration limiting plate in the alleged infringement product does not have the damping effect or the damping effect thereof is fundamentally different. This can be confirmed from the Description of the alleged infringement product for application for the patent for utility model. The Description of the patent for utility model discloses that: "the purpose of the present utility model is to provide a simple soundboard slitting device, which can effectively prevent the quality of the soundboard from being affected by the vibration of the grinding wheel." "In the present utility model, a comb-shaped anti-vibration limiting device fixed with the machine body is provided under the soundboard, and the grinding wheel is embedded in the comb slit of the comb-shaped anti-vibration limiting device. This can prevent vibration and limit position, thereby improving the quality of soundboard processing and production, and reducing the breakage rate of the grinding wheel." Therefore, the technical effects of the two parts are considered to be basically the same.

In this case, the Supreme Court clarified the following contents. Basically, the same means generally refers to the technical features for conventional replacement in the relevant art of the patent and the technical features with basically the same working principle before the date when the alleged infringement action occurs. Basically, the same function refers to that the replacement means in the alleged infringement technical solution performs basically the same function as the corresponding technical feature of the claims in the technical solution of the patent. Basically, the same effect generally refers to that the effect achieved by the replacement means in the alleged infringement technical solution is not substantially different from the technical effect of the corresponding technical feature of the claims. Being envisaged without any creative work means that it is obvious for persons of ordinary skill in the relevant art that the replacement means in the alleged infringement technical solution and the corresponding technical feature of the claims are replaced with each other.

[B] The Court Can Determine Whether an Equivalent Infringement Is Constituted by Jurisdiction

Case 2: In an infringement dispute over a patent for invention between Wenzhou Qianfeng Technology Co. Ltd and Wenzhou Ningtai Machinery Co. Ltd (A Civil Decision of the Supreme People's Court (2017) Zui Gao Fa Min Shen No. 2073), in the case that the patentee claims for identical infringement, it is one of the disputes whether there is an error in the application of law in the determination of equivalent infringement by the second instance judgment.

In this regard, the Supreme Court held in retrial that according to the provisions of Article 17 of the *Provisions II* and Article 7 of the *Judicial Interpretation I*, whether it constitutes an identical infringement or an equivalent infringement is only a specific reason for the constitution of a patent infringement, rather than the legal claim of the patentee. The *Patent Law of the People's Republic of China* (hereinafter referred to as the *Patent Law*) and relevant judicial interpretations thereof do not restrict the people's court from taking the initiative to determine the constitution of an equivalent infringement. On the basis of finding out relevant technical facts, the people's court can determine that an infringement is constituted on the ground of equivalent infringement according to the specific circumstances of the case, which is not limited by the patentee's understanding and claim.

In this case, the Supreme Court clearly pointed out that: in the case that the patentee claims an identical infringement, the people's court can initiatively determine whether an equivalent infringement is constituted. However, equivalent infringement determination by jurisdiction does not mean that the patentee can take no action at all in the litigation.

In practice, if the patentee does not claim an equivalent infringement in litigation, the people's court should explain that it is required to hear whether an equivalent infringement is established and clearly inform the legal consequences of not providing evidence or sufficient evidence. Assuming that the patentee neither provides evidence nor makes sufficient explanation, adverse legal consequences should still be borne by the patentee.

[C] Basic Steps of Determination of Equivalent Features: Comparison + Analysis + Judgment

Case 3: In an infringement dispute over a patent for utility model between XUE Shengguo and ZHAO Xiangmin et al. ((2009) Min Shen Zi No. 1562),[2] Claim 1 recites the following technical features: 5. Two inter-communicated U-shaped kneading buckets are arranged side by side on the frame above the discharge outlet, and the bottom of one of the kneading buckets is connected with the discharge outlet; 6. A kneading hammer is arranged on the frame above each U-shaped kneading bucket, respectively, and the support frames of the two kneading hammers are connected with the power shaft of the driving motor through a crank connecting rod mechanism. The focus of the dispute lies in whether the corresponding technical features of the alleged infringement product constitute the equivalent features to the above features of Claim 1.

In this regard, the Supreme Court held in retrial as follows.

For the fifth corresponding technical feature, the two U-shaped kneading buckets of the patent are located above the discharge outlet, the bottom of one of the kneading buckets is connected with the discharge outlet, and the dough is compressed into the kneading bucket from bottom to top after reaching the discharge outlet under the action of the conveying auger. The two U-shaped kneading buckets of the alleged infringement product are located below one side of the discharge outlet, and the dough enters the kneading bucket from top to bottom under the double actions of compression by the conveying auger and its gravity after reaching the discharge outlet.

The alleged infringement product only moves the hopper up relative to the kneading bucket on the basis of the patent, thus taking advantage of the gravity of the dough itself. However, since the dough itself has a property of poor flowability, it is difficult to realize the purpose of conveying the dough in the hopper to the kneading bucket only by the gravity of the dough itself without the compression of the conveying auger. Conversely, if the purpose that the dough in the hopper flows into the kneading bucket naturally can be realized only by the gravity of the dough itself, it is unnecessary to adopt the technical means of the conveying auger. (Differences are obtained by

2. This case is the Case 04 in the Intellectual Property Annual Report of the Supreme People's Court in 2009.

comparing the features of the patent and the corresponding features of the alleged infringement product.)

Therefore, the alleged infringement product substantively still uses the compression of the conveyor auger to convey the dough to the kneading bucket through the discharge outlet. Like the patent, the alleged infringement patent also requires using the part, i.e., the conveyor auger, to realize the function of compressing and conveying the dough from the hopper to the kneading bucket. Accordingly, compared with this technical feature of the patent, the alleged infringement product adopts basically the same means, realizes basically the same function and achieves basically the same effect. (Whether "the means, functions and effects are basically the same" is analyzed.)

It is common sense in life that an object can slide downwards because of its own gravity. Therefore, it does not require any creative work for persons of ordinary skill in the relevant art to envisage moving the hopper up with respect to the kneading bucket. (Whether creative work is required is judged).

According to the provisions of the above judicial interpretations, the technical feature of the alleged infringement product constitutes an equivalent feature of the corresponding technical feature of the patent.

In this case, the Supreme People's Court made a relatively in-depth analysis on how to specifically judge "three 'basically the same'" and "obviousness" when applying the Doctrine of Equivalents. The determination of equivalent features can usually follow the steps below: (1) comparing the features of the patent with the corresponding features of the alleged infringement product to obtain differences; (2) analyzing "whether the means, functions and effects are basically the same"; and (3) judging whether creative work is required.

Similarly, the above method is also used in the determination of equivalence of the technical feature 6.

As for the sixth corresponding technical feature, there are two differences between the patent of XUE Shengguo and the alleged infringement product. The two kneading hammers in the patent share one support frame and are driven by the crank connecting rod mechanism and the power driving device to move up and down reciprocally in the same direction. However, each of the two kneading hammers of the alleged infringement product has a support frame, and the support frames of the two kneading hammers are connected by a lever. The support frame of one of the kneading hammers makes the two kneading hammers move up and down reciprocally in opposite directions through the crank connecting rod mechanism and the power driving device. (Differences are obtained by comparing the features of the patent and the corresponding features of the alleged infringement product.)

Although both the patent and the alleged infringement product have the basic functions of supporting the kneading hammer through the support frame and driving the support frame of the kneading hammer up and down by the power drive device through the crank connecting rod mechanism, they obviously adopted different technical means from the view of the working principles and movement manners of their respective kneading hammers, and it should not be deemed that they adopted basically the same means. Meanwhile, the power driving device of the alleged infringement product drives the support frame of one kneading hammer, while the driving device of the patent drives the support frame of both kneading hammers. Thus, the design of the alleged infringement product saves more kinetic energy and can use a driving motor with relatively low power. Moreover, the alleged infringement product uses the leverage principle to make the two kneading hammers move up and down reciprocally in opposite directions, which avoids the useless work done by the two kneading hammers sharing one support frame when moving upward in the same direction. Accordingly, the patent and the alleged infringement product are obviously different in the technical effects. (Whether "the means, functions and effects are basically the same" is analyzed.)

Moreover, this transformation means of the alleged infringement product is not a feature that persons of ordinary skill in the art can envisage without any creative work, which is also the distinguishing technical feature between the patent for utility model, i.e., "Dough Kneading Machine for Vermicelli Processing (No. ZL200620175922.7)" applied later by the respondent ZHAO Zhangren and allowed, and the prior art (i.e., the patent involved of XUE Shengguo). This also confirms, to a certain extent, that this transformation means is not obvious to persons of ordinary skill in the art. (Whether creative work is required is judged.)

Therefore, the corresponding technical features of the patent and the alleged infringement product are neither identical nor equivalent.

[D] Both Conditions Should Be Met: "Three 'Basically the Same'" and "No Creative Work Is Required"

Case 4: In an infringement dispute over a patent for utility model between Shaanxi Jingye FRP Co. Ltd and Yongchang Jishui Composite Material Co. Ltd ((2010) Min Shen Zi No. 181),[3] the focus of the case is whether the alleged infringement product has a technical feature identical or equivalent to the feature "the diameters of the pipe head and the pipe tail are consistent" in Claim 1.

In this regard, the Supreme Court held in retrial that, while judging whether the technical feature of the alleged infringement product and the technical feature of the patent are equivalent, it should be considered not only whether the technical feature of the alleged infringement product pertains to one that persons of ordinary skill in the art can envisage without any creative work, but also whether the technical feature of the alleged infringement product and the technical feature of the patent pertain to basically the same technical means, realize basically the same function and achieve basically the same effect. Only when the above two conditions are met at the same time can the two technical features be determined to be equivalent.

Although the inner diameters of the pipes of the spigot and the socket of the alleged infringement product are the same, the outer diameters thereof are different. It is specifically represented as follows: the outer diameter of the socket pipe is provided with a horizontal concave platform for installing the steel collar, and the outer diameter

3. This case is the Case 04 in the Intellectual Property Annual Report of the Supreme People's Court in 2010.

of the socket pipe is closely matched with the steel collar, while the outer diameter of the spigot pipe is irregularly step-shaped. Although the *Pipe Jacking Construction Technology* has disclosed the working principle of resistance reduction by grouting and the technical features of a grouting hole and a step-shaped outer diameter of a pipe, in order to achieve the purpose of resistance reduction by grouting in pipe jacking construction, persons of ordinary skill in the art can obviously envisage the technical features such as the grouting hole and the step-shaped outer diameter of the spigot pipe in the alleged infringement product under the technical enlightenment provided in the *Pipe Jacking Construction Technology*, which does not require any creative work.

However, the outer diameter of the spigot pipe in the alleged infringement product is irregularly step-shaped. As a result, on the one hand, the outer diameter of the spigot pipe and the steel collar cannot be closely matched, failing to realize the function and effect of enhancing the sealing of pipe connection. And on the other hand, an annular space for the resistance reducing mortar to pass through can be formed between the outer diameter of the pipe and the steel collar so that the resistance reducing mortar injected from the grouting hole can be uniformly distributed around the pipe through the annular space to form a lubricating sleeve, which realizes the beneficial function and effect of reducing the friction resistance between the outer wall of the pipe and the soil and improving pipe jacking efficiency. Therefore, the function and effect realized by the technical feature "the outer diameter of the spigot pipe is irregularly step-shaped" in the alleged infringement product are substantively different from that realized by the feature "the diameters of the pipe head and the pipe tail are consistent" in Claim 1. Thus, the two features do not pertain to equivalent technical features, and the alleged infringement product does not fall within the protection scope of the patent involved.

In this case, the Supreme Court clarified that two conditions should be considered simultaneously for determination of equivalent features: first, whether the technical feature of the alleged infringement product pertains to one that persons of ordinary skill in the art can envisage without any creative work; and second, whether the technical feature of the alleged infringement product and that of the patent pertain to basically the same technical means, realize the basically the same function, and achieve basically the same technical effect.

[E] Equivalent Infringement Should Be Judged Based on Comparison of the Technical Features One by One Rather than the Technical Solutions as a Whole

Case 5: In an infringement dispute over a patent for invention between Suzhou Antiwear Valves Co. Ltd. and Shanghai Kaiweixi Group Co. Ltd. (A Civil Decision of the Supreme People's Court (2017) Zui Gao Fa Min Shen No. 4626), the focus of the dispute between the two parties relates to whether it requires considering the effect of the below feature in the technical solution of the whole patent involved when the structural, technical features of the two components, i.e., "a horizontal shaft and a fixed valve shaft connected by flat keys and fastening screws" of the alleged infringement product and "a horizontal shaft welded on a fixed valve shaft" of the patent involved, are compared.

In this regard, the Supreme Court held in retrial that according to Article 17 of the *Provisions*, the judgment of equivalent infringement should be conducted by comparing the technical features one by one, rather than comparing the alleged infringement product with the technical solution of the patent as a whole. Claim 1 of the patent involved defines "a horizontal shaft welded on the fixed valve shaft" and "a driving member welded with the horizontal shaft." The original court determined that the alleged infringement product was different from the patent involved in the manners of connection between the horizontal shaft and the fixed valve shaft, as well as the driving member and the horizontal shaft, and this comparison manner is not improper. There lacks evidence for the claim of the retrial applicant that the original judgment is irrelevant to the purpose of the invention and the technical effect it intends to achieve, evaluates the similarities and differences between the technical features in an isolated and one-sided way, and violates the basic principle of equivalent infringement.

In this case, the Supreme Court clarified that the judgment of equivalent infringement should be conducted by comparing the technical features one by one, rather than comparing the alleged infringement product and the technical solution of the patent as a whole. The application of the Doctrine of Equivalents is also an adoption of the rule of comparing all the technical features; that is, it emphasizes the equivalence with the technical features in the claims, rather than considering the equivalence of the technical solution as a whole. Moreover, regarding the method of comparing technical features, it can be seen from the current trial practice by the courts in China, the method of comparing the technical features one by one is more commonly adopted.

[F] Adoption of a Technical Solution Opposite to the Patented Technical Means Does Not Constitute Equivalent Infringement

The judgment of the technical means is primary in the judgment of "three 'basically the same'."

Case 6: In an infringement dispute over a patent for utility model between Beijing Jerrat Springs Damper Technology Research Center and the respondent Beijing Jinzi Tianhe Buffer Technology Co. Ltd, WANG Hanxia ((2013) Min Shen Zi No.1146),[4] the focus of the dispute in the case is whether the installation manner of the unidirectional current limiting device in the alleged infringement product is equivalent to that of Claim 1 in the patent involved.

In this regard, the Supreme Court held in retrial that it can be seen from the disclosure of the Description of the patent involved that the invention purpose of the patent involved is to provide a fast-in and slow-out elastic damping body buffer. To achieve this purpose of the invention, the patent involved adopts an installation

4. This case is the Case 04 in the Intellectual Property Annual Report of the Supreme People's Court in 2013.

method for the unidirectional current limiting device to open in the compressing stroke and close in the returning stroke so as to achieve the effect of fast-in and slow-out of the bumping receiving head. In this regard, Claim 1 of the patent also involved clearly defines the installation manner of the unidirectional current limiting device. However, the alleged infringement product, in this case, adopts an installation manner for the unidirectional current limiting device to close in the compressing stroke and open in the returning stroke, and the effect realized is slow-in and fast-out of the bumping receiving head. Therefore, the installation manner of the unidirectional current limiting device in the alleged infringement product, in this case, is neither identical nor equivalent to that defined in Claim 1 of the patent involved. And thus, the alleged infringement product does not fall within the protection scope of the patent involved.

In this case, the Supreme court held that the technical means of the alleged infringement technical solution is opposite to that clearly defined in the claim and then analyzed that the technical effects that can be achieved by the two technical means are also opposite, and the purpose of invention cannot be achieved, and thus it came to the conclusion that equivalent infringement is not constituted. There are important differences in the determination of equivalence between functional features and ordinary technical features.

[G] Amendment of an Invention to an Inferior One, Which Results in a Technical Effect Thereof Different from That of the Patented Technology, Does Not Constitute an Equivalent Infringement

Case 7: In an infringement dispute over a patent for utility model between Guangxi Nanning Fuhuida Electromechanical Co. Ltd (hereinafter referred to as "Fuhuida Company") and Guangxi Laibin Xiaopingyang Sungain Sugar Co. Ltd (A Civil Decision of the Supreme People's Court (2019) Zui Gao Fa Zhi Min Zhong No 24), one of the focuses of a dispute between the two parties is whether the technical features of the alleged infringement product "① a steam heating system for a sugar-producing process" and "④ a manual adjustment valve control system" are equivalent to the corresponding technical features recited in Claim 1 "(1) an automatic steam balance heating system for a sugar producing process" and "(4) PLC controlling the operation of a steam flow adjustment valve."

In this regard, the Supreme Court held that: while judging whether the technical features of the alleged infringement product and the technical features of the patent are equivalent, it should be considered not only whether the technical feature of the alleged infringement product pertains to one that persons of ordinary skill in the art can envisage without any creative work, but also whether the technical feature of the alleged infringement product and the technical feature of the patent pertain to basically the same technical means, realize basically the same function and achieve basically the same effect. Only when the above two conditions are met at the same time can the two technical features be determined as equivalent technical features. If the alleged infringement product adopts more primitive means than the patented technology, resulting in that the technical effect of the alleged infringement product is different from that of the patented technology, even if the means adopted by the alleged infringement product pertains to technical features that persons of ordinary skill in the art can envisage without any creative work, the two technical features cannot be determined to be equivalent because of the different effects achieved thereby.

In this case, as a necessary technical feature in Claim 1, the presence of PLC enables the heating system in the sugar producing process of the patent involved to automatically adjust and control the opening of the steam flow control valve according to the temperature and/or pressure set by the program. In contrast, the alleged infringement product adopts the manual control manner. The operator determines the opening of the steam flow control valve at the high-pressure end by observing the steam temperature at the outlet at the low-pressure end. When the temperature is too high, the high-temperature steam flow is reduced with a manual operation device, and when the temperature is too low, the high-temperature steam flow is increased with the manual operation device. This process depends on the operator's observation and manual adjustment, and control of the operation. The automatic control is more accurate in adjustment and control than the manual operation. Since the alleged infringement product adopts a manner of observing temperature by human eyes combined with controlling valve opening by the manual operation device, the technical effect thereof is different from that of the patented technology in terms of adjustment and control accuracy. Fuhuida Company also recognized in the appeal that the function and effect of the PLC adjustment valve are far better than that of the manual adjustment valve. Features ① and ④ and features (1) and (4) do not constitute equivalent technical features, and thus the alleged infringement product does not fall within the protection scope of Claim 1.

In the judgment of equivalent infringement, if the replacement means in the alleged infringement technical solution generates an unexpected technical effect relative to the corresponding technical features of the claims, it should not be determined as an equivalent feature. On the contrary, if the replacement means causes the alleged infringement technical solution to become obviously inferior to the patented technical solution, it should not be determined as an equivalent feature.

[H] Determination of Functions and Effects Shall Be Based on the Understanding of Those Skilled in the Art

Case 8: In an infringement dispute over a patent for invention between Thunder-sky Winston Battery Technology Co. Ltd (hereinafter referred to as "Thunder-sky Company") and China Aviation Lithium Battery (Luoyang) Co. Ltd (hereinafter referred to as "China Aviation Company") (A Civil Ruling of the Supreme People's Court (2018) Zui Gao Fa Min Shen No. 972), the key to judge whether the alleged infringement product falls within the protection scope of the patent involved lies in whether the feature "the uncoated substrate surface ends of the positive and negative plates of the core body are arranged in the same direction, with the electrode poles pointing to the same direction and derived from the same end of the shell" of the alleged infringement product is equivalent to the feature "the uncoated substrate surface ends of the positive and negative plates of the core body are arranged in opposite directions with the electrode poles pointing to opposite directions and derived from two ends of the shell, respectively" of Claim 1 of the patent involved.

Regarding the above technical features, the retrial applicant, Thunder-sky Company, stated that: (1) No matter whether the electrode poles of the lithium battery point to the same direction or opposite directions, their basic functions of conducting electricity are the same, and will not change as the change in the guiding directions of the electrode poles. (2) The effect of the lithium battery will not be changed by the change in the guiding directions of the electrode poles of the lithium battery. (3) The change in the guiding directions of the electrode poles of the lithium battery can be envisaged without any creative work. Both the patent involved and the alleged infringement product are lithium batteries (including electrolytes) with a large capacity and have the same working principle, no matter whether the guiding directions of the electrode poles are the same or opposite. It is only a simple replacement relationship with no substantive difference to arrange the same or opposite guiding directions of the electrode poles. Therefore, it is believed that the two features constitute equivalents.

In this regard, the Supreme Court held in retrial that *the following technical features shall not be determined as equivalent features: those failing to realize the purpose of the patent for invention or being the technical defects to be overcome by the patent for invention, which can be recognized by those skilled in the art after reading the Claims, the Description and the Drawings in combination with the purpose of invention.*

The claims of the patent involved clearly define that "the uncoated substrate surface ends of the positive and negative plates of the core body are arranged in opposite directions with the electrode poles pointing to opposite directions and derived from two ends of the shell, respectively." The summary of the invention on page 2 of the Description of the patent involved clearly discloses that the main difference of the patent involved over the background art is to change the guiding directions of the electrode poles to meet the use requirements in different fields and under different load conditions. Moreover, according to the relevant contents of the Invalidation Decision No. 29942, the Patent Reexamination Board determined that the above distinguishing technical feature had a beneficial technical effect, and on this basis, it determined that Claim 1 of the patent involved possessed an inventive step. Accordingly, one of the reasons why Claim 1 of the patent involved possesses an inventive step is that Claim 1 of the patent involved possesses the technical feature "the uncoated substrate surface ends are arranged in opposite directions, and after being bound and connected by the electrode poles with binding heads, the electrode poles thereof point to opposite directions," which has a beneficial technical effect.

Accordingly, the technical feature "the uncoated substrate surface ends of the positive and negative plates of the core body are arranged in the same direction, with the electrode poles pointing to the same direction and derived from the same end of the shell" of the alleged infringement product is one of the technical defects to be overcome by the patent involved, and is significantly different from the technical feature "the uncoated substrate surface ends of the positive and negative plates of the core body are arranged in opposite directions with the electrode poles pointing to opposite directions and derived from two ends of the shell, respectively" of Claim 1 of the patent involved in terms of means, functions and effects. Therefore, the two features are not equivalent.

When the equivalent features are judged, *the function and effect realized by the relevant technical feature of the patent shall be based on the understanding of the corresponding technical feature by those skilled in the art after reading the Claims, the Description and the Drawings of the patent. All the technical features that cannot realize the functions and effects emphasized in the Description of the patent shall not be determined as equivalent features*. The Description of the patent involved clearly emphasizes the function and effect generated by the electrode poles pointing to opposite directions. In judging whether the corresponding feature of the alleged infringement technical solution pertains to an equivalent feature, the functions and effects emphasized in the Description of the patent involved should be taken as the judgment basis. Since the corresponding technical feature of the alleged infringement product cannot realize the functions and effects emphasized in the Description of the patent involved, it does not pertain to an equivalent feature of the patent in the case.

In this case, from the perspective of the invention purpose, the Supreme Court held that the following technical features shall not be determined as equivalent features: those failing to realize the purpose of the patent for invention or being the technical defects to be overcome by the patent for invention, which can be recognized by those skilled in the art after reading the Claims, the Description and the Drawings in combination with the purpose of invention.

[I] Important Differences Exist in the Determination of Equivalence to a Functional Feature and to an Ordinary Technical Feature

Case 9: In an infringement dispute over a patent for utility model between Linhai Linong Machinery Factory and LU Jie (A Civil Ruling of the Supreme People's Court (2017) Zui Gao Fa Min Shen No. 1804),[5] both parties held different opinions on whether the "transmission sprocket (6)" in Claim 1 of the patent involved pertains to a "functional feature" and whether the provision of Article 8.2 of the *Judicial Interpretation II* is correctly applied to the second instance judgment on this feature.

In this regard, the Supreme Court held in retrial that: the transmission system of the patent involved includes a motor, a transmission sprocket, a rotating sprocket and a transmission shaft, and the transmission sprocket in Claim 1 is a commonly used mechanical component for transmitting the power generated by the motor to the transmission shaft to rotate the transmission shaft and the rotating sprocket. The provision of Article 17 of the *Provisions* is applicable to judging whether equivalent features are constituted.

The Supreme Court further clarified that the determination of "equivalent features" stipulated in Article 17 of the *Provisions* is different from the determination that "the corresponding technical feature is ... equivalent to the functional feature"

5. This case is the Case No. 03 in the Intellectual Property Annual Report of the Supreme People's Court in 2018.

stipulated in Article 8.2 of the *Judicial Interpretation II*. Although both provisions require to meet the standards "use basically the same means" and "can be envisaged without any creative work," they still have important differences, including the following two aspects:

> First, the applicable objects and the comparison basis are different. The applicable objects of the "equivalent features" stipulated in Article 17 of the *Provisions* are broader, relating to other technical features than the "functional features", and the comparison basis is the technical features per se recited in the Claims. However, the applicable objects of Article 8.2 of the *Judicial Interpretation II* are the "functional features" as stipulated in Article 4 of the *Judicial Interpretation I* and Article 8.1 of the *Judicial Interpretation II*, and the comparison basis is the "indispensable technical feature" disclosed in the Description and the Drawings for realizing the function or effect of the functional feature.
>
> Second, the determination standards are different. Regarding the "equivalent features" stipulated in Article 17 of the *Provisions*, "realizing basically the same function" and "achieving basically the same effect" should be used as the determination standards. However, "being... equivalent to the functional feature" stipulated in Article 8.2 of the *Judicial Interpretation II* requires to meet the standards "realize the same function" and "achieve the same effect," which are stricter.

In this case, the court of the second instance did not determine the "transmission sprocket" of the patent involved as a "functional feature" but determined that the "worm transmission" of the alleged infringement product and the "transmission sprocket" in the patent involved constituted "equivalence of technical features" based on Article 8 of the *Judicial Interpretation II*. This substantively confused the "equivalent features" stipulated in Article 17 of the *Provisions* with "being ... equivalent to the function feature" stipulated in Article 8 of the *Judicial Interpretation II*. The application of law was improper and was corrected by the Supreme Court.

In this case, the Supreme Court clarified the following important differences between "equivalent features" and "equivalent to the function feature": 1. Applicable objects. When the technical features comply with the "functional features" provided in Article 4 of the *Judicial Interpretation I* and Article 8.1 of the *Judicial Interpretation II*, the provision of Article 8.2 of the *Judicial Interpretation II* shall apply, and the provision of Article 17 of the *Provisions* shall apply to other technical features. 2. Comparison basis. The comparison basis of "equivalent features" is the technical feature itself recited in the claims, while the comparison basis of "equivalent to the functional feature" is the "indispensable technical feature" disclosed in the Description and the Drawings, for realizing the function or effect of the functional feature. 3. Determination standard. "Equivalent features" should be determined by the "three 'basically the same'" standard, while "equivalent to the functional feature" requires to meet the standards "realize the same function" and "achieve the same effect" which are stricter.

§16.04 CONCLUSION

According to Article 7.2 of the *Judicial Interpretation I*, the protection scope of the patent is constituted by the technical features identical with and equivalent to all the technical features recited in the claims. In judging whether constituting equivalent features, the technical features per se recited in the claims are compared with the technical features of the alleged infringement technical solution generally based on Article 17 of the *Provisions*, to determine whether equivalence is constituted according to the judgment standards of "three 'basically the same'" and "readily envisaged." However, if the technical features recited in the claims are "functional features," it is required to compare the "indispensable technical features" disclosed in the Description and the Drawings for realizing the function or effect of the functional feature with the technical features of the alleged infringement technical solution based on the provision of Article 8.2 of the *Judicial Interpretation II*, to determine whether equivalence is constituted according to the judgment standards of one "basically the same," two "the same" and "readily envisaged."

When the Doctrine of Equivalents is applied, a one-by-one comparison of the technical features, rather than a comparison of the alleged infringement product with the patented technical solution as a whole, is taken as the determination method. In judicial practice, we can further find the substantive differences between the alleged infringement object and the patented technology by combining and decomposing the technical features so as to achieve more effective protection to the patentee.

CHAPTER 17

Dedication Rule

Zhang Junjie & Ge Xiaomei

§17.01 BASIC PROVISIONS OF LAWS

Interpretation of the Supreme People's Court on Several Issues concerning the Application of Law in the Trial of Patent Infringement Dispute Cases **(hereinafter referred to as "*Judicial Interpretation I*")**

Article 5 Where a right holder includes a technical solution, which is described only in the Description or Drawings, not in the claims, in the scope of protection of a patent in a patent infringement dispute case, the people's court shall not support it.

§17.02 INTERPRETATION OF THE PROVISIONS

The dedication rule is introduced mainly for the reason that the exclusivity of a patent is shown to the public through the Claims instead of the Description, which makes it necessary to protect the reliance interest of the public regarding the public notice of the claims of the patent. The dedication rule is substantially a restriction on the application of the doctrine of equivalents to prevent the patentee from gaining profits in both patenting and infringement procedures, which is beneficial to safeguarding the publicity of the Claims and balancing the interest relationship between the patentee and the social public.

According to the above legal provision, the application of the dedication rule shall conform to the following conditions:

(1) it is first required to ensure that the technical solution is described in the Description and Drawings;
(2) the technical solution is specialized as another option;

(3) the technical solution is not recited in the claims;
(4) the dedication covers the parallel solutions disclosed but not recited in the claims and the specific terms thereof;
(5) there is a view that the application of the dedication rule is conditional upon the potential formation of equivalence, and the dedication rule is necessarily inapplicable if it is affirmed that equivalence is not formed;
(6) the dedicated solution is not protected by another application.

§17.03 POTENTIAL ISSUES/DISPUTES ARISING IN THE LAW APPLICATION

[A] Can the Court Take the Initiative to Apply the Dedication Rule?

The scholars hold different views as to the issue of whether the court can take the initiative to apply the dedication rule. Some scholars think that the accused infringer should make the proposal and produce evidence, and then the court determines whether to apply the dedication rule or not.[1] There is also a view that[2] the dedication rule has the same significance as the prosecution history estoppel, and the Supreme People's Court has determined that the court can take the initiative to apply the prosecution history estoppel.[3] Compared with the application of the prosecution history estoppel, the application of the dedication rule does not require any additional evidence produced by the parties, and just a check on the Description can bring about a conclusion. In such a case, no restrictions should be imposed on the initiative of the court to apply the dedication rule.[4] We also accept the latter point of view and opine that the people's court, on the basis of finding relevant facts, can take the initiative to apply the dedication rule according to the particulars of the case.

[B] Can the Dedication Rule Apply to Patent Confirmation Procedure?

It seems to become a consensus in the theoretical circle that the dedication rule is derived from the patent infringement procedure and acts as a restriction on the application of the doctrine of equivalents. However, the dedication rule functions to further identify the protection scope of the claims and prevent the patentee from "gaining profits on both sides." In the patent confirmation process, the technical solutions likewise exist, which are not recited in the claims but are explicitly described

1. SUN Ping, On the Application of the Dedication Rule in China [J]. Study on Patent Law, 2010, P403.
2. YAN Wenjun, Dedication Rule in the Determination of Patent Infringement—Case of Patent Infringement Between CHEN Shundi and Zhejiang LeXueEr. Household Articles Co. Ltd., China Invention & Patent, 2019 (1) 16, P103-106.
3. Civil Ruling Paper (2009) Min Shen Zi No. 239 issued by the Supreme People's Court.
4. YAN Wenjun, Dedication Rule in the Determination of Patent Infringement—Case of Patent Infringement Between CHEN Shundi and Zhejiang LeXueEr Household Articles Co. Ltd., China Invention & Patent, 2019 (1) 16, P103-106.

in the Description or Drawings. On that occasion, the protection scope of the patent also needs to be further determined in the first place, and then the distinguishing technical features in the claims can be determined more effectively. Consequently, it is held that[5] there is a basis and necessity for introducing the determination method for the dedication rule to the patent confirmation process.

Case 1: In the case of administrative dispute between CHEN Huaqing and the Patent Reexamination Board of China National Intellectual Property Administration and Dongguan City Minch Optoelectronic Technology Company Limited ((2017) Jing Xing Zhong No. 1082), the patentee CHEN Huaqing has alleged that the technical feature "the battery case has a base whose shape is designed to fully match a shape of the bottom of the bottle and which can be concealed at the bottom of the bottle" in Claim 2 of the patent only pertains to a technical solution that the battery case is completely concealed at the bottom of the bottle. However, Evidence 1 shows a battery case of base type with the battery exposed to the outside at the bottom of the bottle and thus does not disclose the above distinguishing technical feature.

In this regard, the Beijing High People's Court has held that, according to the "contextualism" rule for the interpretation of claims, the Description and Drawings shall be taken into account for the interpretation of claims. That is, for any term in the claims which has a general meaning in the technical field and also has a specially defined meaning in the Description, if the defined meaning is clear and can be determined by those skilled in the relevant art, the meaning defined in the Description shall be taken to determine the meaning of the term; if the Description contains no specially defined meaning or does not define the meaning clearly, and those skilled in the relevant art cannot determine the specific meaning defined therein, then the general meaning in the technical field shall be adopted. The Description of the patent explicitly discloses two arrangement modes for battery case: one is "can be mounted at the bottom of the bottle very concealedly," and the other one is the bottle "is placed on the base." Such two arrangement modes are parallel technical solutions. The protection scope of a patent is subject to the claims. When drafting Claim 2, the patentee only recites that the base of the battery case "can be mounted at the bottom of the bottle very concealedly" and does not seek to protect the technical solution of "placed on the base." Any technical solution apparently excluded from the protection scope of the claims shall be deemed "dedicated" and not be included in the claims. Accordingly, Claim 2 of the patent only pertains to the technical solution that the battery case is completely concealed at the bottom of the bottle and does not include the technical solution that the battery case is exposed to the outside at the bottom of the bottle. When commenting on the inventive step of Claim 2, the Patent Reexamination Board has omitted the distinguishing technical feature "the battery case has a base whose shape is designed to fully match a shape of the bottom of the bottle and which can be mounted at the bottom of the bottle very concealedly." The relevant grounds of appeal held by CHEN Huaqing are tenable and shall be supported.

5. LI Xiangqun, Application of the Dedication Rule in the Patent Confirmation Process, http://www.iprdaily.cn/news_19946.html

In this case, the Beijing High People's Court has analogically applied the "dedication rule" to determine the protection scope of the claims, thereby precisely identifying the distinguishing technical feature of the patent involved from the reference document. As can be seen, the dedication rule is not only applicable to the patent infringement procedure but also conducive to precise determination of the protection scope of claims in the patent confirmation procedure.

[C] Application Conditions of the Dedication Rule

According to the above provision, we opine that the application of the dedication rule needs to conform to the conditions in the following three aspects:

(1) the technical solution is described in the Description and Drawings, and persons of ordinary skill in the art upon reviewing the Description can determine that it has been disclosed;
(2) the disclosed technical solution is specifically disclosed in the Description as another clear option of any technical feature in the claims;
(3) the disclosed technical solution is not recited in the claims.

[1] It Is First Required to Ensure That the Technical Solution Is Described in the Description and Drawings

Case 2: In the case of dispute over patent infringement between Gree Electric Appliances, Inc. of Zhuhai and GD Midea Air-Conditioning Equipment Co. Ltd. ((2013) Yue Gao Fa Min San Zhong Zi No. 615), the dispute focus has been on whether the distinguishing technical feature "1. A non-detachable air conditioner indoor unit pipeline installation baffle, consisting of two portions: a fixed plate and a sliding plate" of the accused infringing technical solution is equivalent to the corresponding technical feature "a removable air conditioner indoor unit pipeline installation baffle, comprising a fixed plate and a sliding plate" of Claim 1 of the patent involved.

In this regard, the Higher People's Court of Guangdong Province has held that:

> The feature "removable" in the patent involved includes the functions of "detachability" and "installability." As understood by persons of ordinary skill in the art, the detachment and installation shall be carried out without any damage to the basic structure and use function of the product. After the accused infringing installation baffle is mounted on the air conditioner unit, the clamping jaw is damaged in the detachment course and cannot function normally. Thus, the accused infringing installation baffle does not have the functional technical feature of "detachability" as recited in the patent involved.

The Description of the patent involved does not support the functional technical feature of "detachability." However, when drafting the claims of the patent, the patentee has explicitly added the function of "detachability," thereby objectively reducing the protection scope of the patent. According to the above dedication rule, in the infringement case, the patentee is no longer free to include the dedicated technical solution into the protection scope of the patent.

It should be noted that, in the retrial case of this case ((2014) Min Shen Zi No. 1812), the Supreme People's Court has not responded to the application by the Higher People's Court of Guangdong Province of the dedication rule but has only reached a conclusion of noninfringement based on the interpretation of the feature "removable."

We opine that a technical solution has the potential for being dedicated on a precedent condition that the description of the solution in the Description and Drawings is ensured. Otherwise, the dedication will not happen. The application of dedication rule will be unsuitable in the above Case 2 if the solution "non-detachable" is not specifically described as another option in the Description of the patent involved; that is, the technical solution of the accused infringing product is never disclosed therein.

[2] The Technical Solution Is Specialized as Another Option

Case 3: in the case of infringement dispute over a patent for invention between CHEN Shundi and Zhejiang LeXueEr Household Articles Co. Ltd., etc. ((2013) Min Ti Zi No. 225[6]), LeXueEr has argued in the petition for retrial that Steps 10 and 11 in Claim 1 of the patent involved are in reverse sequence in the accused infringing process. The Description of the patent involved discloses reversing Steps 10 and 11. According to the dedication rule, the other sequence of steps disclosed in the Description should not be included in the protection scope of the patent involved. Therefore, the accused infringing process with the change in the sequence of steps does not fall within the protection scope of the patent involved.

In this regard, the Supreme People's Court has held that:

> The accurate determination of the protection scope of a patent is necessary not only for providing effective legal protection for the patentee, but also for respecting the role of publicity and delimitation of claims and safeguarding the reliance interest of the social public. The establishment of dedication rule in the interpretation of claims is exactly a product of balancing the interests between protection function and publicity function of the patent. The meaning of the rule lies in that any technical solution disclosed in the Description of the patent but not reflected in the claims cannot be included into the protection scope of the claims. For any technical solution disclosed in the Description but not recited in the claims, non-application of dedication rule provides adequate protection for the patentee, but on the one hand, the patent applicant obtains advantages in avoiding the examination of a broader range of claims, and on the other hand, the delimitation role of claims is reduced, and thus the determination of protection scope of the patent becomes a too flexible and uncertain thing, which makes it more difficult for the public to predict the protection scope of the patent and goes against the publicity role of the patent and the safeguarding of public interests.

6. Annual Report on Intellectual Property of the Supreme People's Court (2013), *Gazette of the Supreme People's Court of the People's Republic of China*, 2015, Issue 10.

As stipulated in Article 5 of the *Interpretation, if those skilled in the art upon reviewing the Description can determine that a technical solution disclosed but not claimed is* ***specialized*** *by the patentee as another option of any technical feature in the claims, then the technical solution will be deemed to be dedicated to the society*. The above provision exactly applies to this case. The Description of the patent involved explicitly discloses on page 3 that Steps 10 and 11 can be reversed. However, the reversed steps are not reflected in the claims and thus cannot be included in the protection scope of the patent involved.

In this case, the Supreme People's Court has held that: on the one hand, the reversion of steps produces a substantial difference in technical effect, and the reversed steps do not constitute an equivalent technical feature to Steps 10 and 11 in Claim 1 of the patent involved; on the other hand, with the application of the dedication rule, it has been affirmed that the reversed steps do not fall within the protection scope of the patent. In essence, the Supreme People's Court has held that *the reversion of steps in this case does not conform to the application criteria of doctrine of equivalents. Even if it conforms to the application criteria of doctrine of equivalents, the infringement cannot be affirmed under the dedication rule.*

This case is a typical case to which the dedication rule applies. In the determination of patent infringement, if the technical feature in the accused infringing solution has a different literal meaning from the corresponding technical feature in the claims of the patent, the patentee may allege that the former is still an equivalent feature, resulting in that the infringer is accused of the infringement under the doctrine of equivalents. However, can the infringement under the doctrine of equivalents still be affirmed if the technical solution used by the accused infringer is disclosed in the Description of the patent but not recited in the Claims? The dedication rule is applicable to this case, with the exclusion of said situation.

Case 4: In the case of dispute over patent infringement between Jiangsu Youning Sureblock Building Materials Co. Ltd. v. Changzhou Navigation Project Co. Ltd. and Jingjiang Hongxing Cement Member Factory ((2013) Su Zhi Min Zhong Zi No. 0209), the dispute focus has been on whether the locking structure of retaining block used in the accused infringing product is equivalent to the locking structure defined in the claims.

In this regard, the Higher People's Court of Jiangsu Province has held that no equivalent feature is formed for the following reasons:

> The protection scope of a patent for invention shall be determined on the basis of the contents stated in the claims thereof. If the patentee discloses a certain technical solution in the Description or Drawings of the patent but does not recite it in the claims, the patentee cannot bring it back into the protection scope of the claims by means of the doctrine of equivalents in the patent infringement proceedings. *The reason for establishing such legal provision lies in that*: the doctrine of equivalents is taken into account in the determination of patent infringement because it is virtually impossible for the patentee when drafting the claims to predict all the potential infringement ways taken by the infringer in the future, in which case, the protection scope literally expressed by the claims is appropriately expanded, and the infringement is affirmed in the case that non-substantial changes have been made to the technical solution of the patent, so as

> to protect the patentee's legitimate interests. *If the patentee discloses a certain technical solution in the Description or Drawings of the patent but does not recite it in the claims, it indicates that when drafting the claims of the patent, the patentee has predicted the technical solution but not intended to include it into the protection scope of the patent.* In that case, the people's court can no longer bring the technical solution back into the protection scope of the patent by the application of the doctrine of equivalents, which is conducive to safeguarding the publicity of the patent and balancing the interest relationship between the patentee and the social public.

The "locking structure" described in Claim 1 of the patent for invention involved is a front flange (31) that is disposed at the front end of the retaining block and protrudes from the upper surface of the retaining block, or a protrusion (41) disposed on the upper surface of the retaining block and a matching groove disposed on the lower surface of the retaining block. However, the Description discloses both an example of a front flange that is disposed at the front end of the retaining block and protrudes from the upper surface of the retaining block (corresponding to Figure 2 for the Description) and an example of a protrusion disposed on the upper surface of the retaining block and a matching groove disposed on the lower surface of the retaining block (corresponding to Figure 4 for the Description), and further discloses an example of a rear flange (21) that is disposed at the rear end of the retaining block and protrudes from the lower surface of the retaining block (corresponding to Figure 3 for the Description). *The technical solution of "a rear flange that is disposed at the rear end of the retaining block and protrudes from the lower surface of the retaining block" not recited in the claims does not fall within the protection scope of the patent as defined by the equivalent feature, and the retaining block used by Changzhou Navigation takes the technical solution of a rear flange that is disposed at the rear end of the retaining block and protrudes from the lower surface of the retaining block.* Accordingly, the technical feature in the construction practice of Changzhou Navigation is not equivalent to the technical feature in Claim 1 of the patent for invention involved.

Figure 2 for the Description

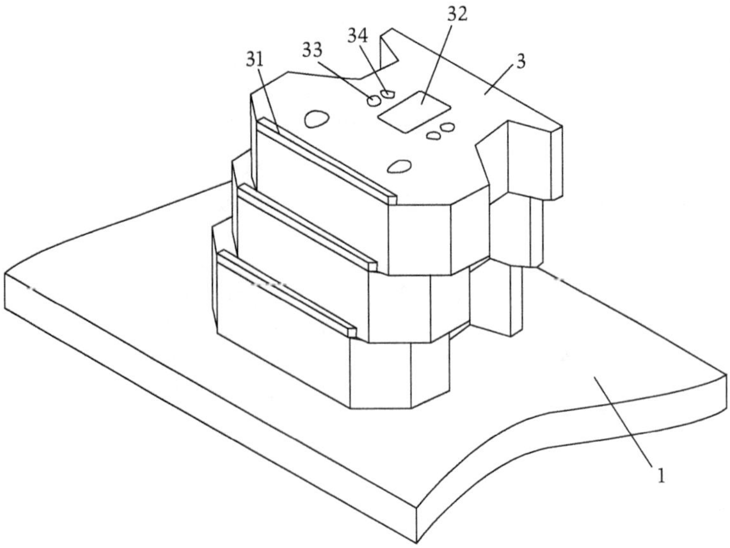

Figure 3 for the Description

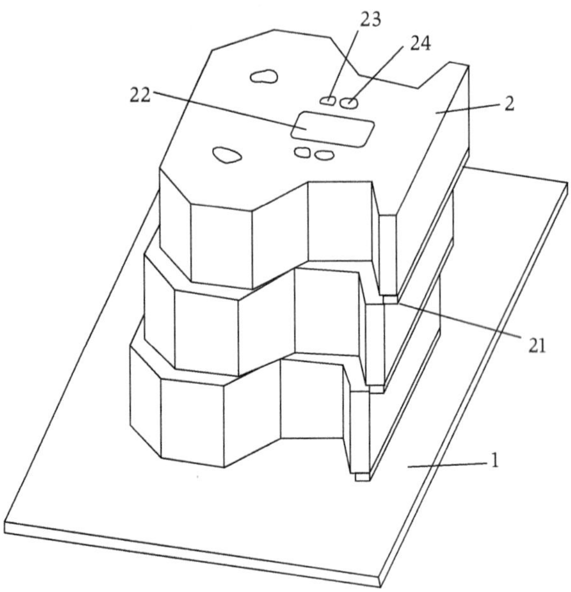

Figure 4 for the Description

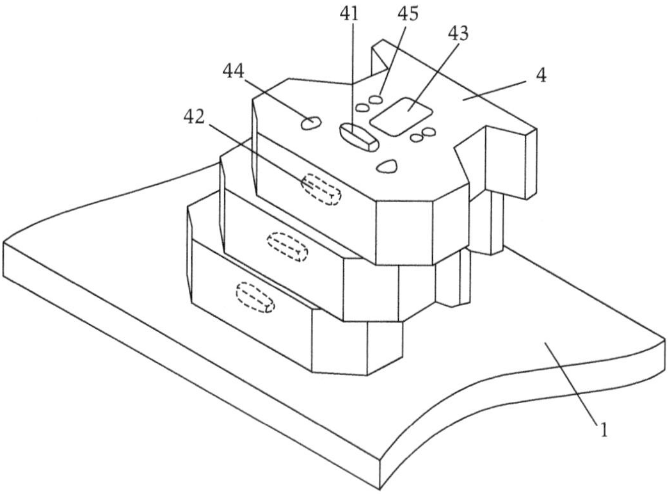

In this case, the Higher People's Court of Jiangsu Province has held that the protection scope of a patent for invention should be determined on the basis of the contents stated in the claims thereof. The patentee has disclosed three locking structures of the retaining block in the Description. The first and third locking structures are recited, and the second locking structure is not recited in the claims, *which indicates that when drafting the claims of the patent, the patentee has predicted the technical solution but not intended to include it into the protection scope of the patent.* In the patent infringement proceedings, the second locking structure could not be included in the protection scope of the claims of the patent by means of the doctrine of equivalents.

[3] The Technical Solution Is Not Recited in the Claims

Case 5: In the case of infringement dispute over a patent for utility model between Nantong BEITE Pharmaceutical Machinery Co. Ltd. and Nantong Fengwei Machinery Co. Ltd. ((2018) Zui Gao Fa Min Shen No. 1727), Fengwei Company has argued in the petition for retrial that: (1) the reversing mechanisms of the accused infringing equipment are not directly connected on the output ends of the motor but are connected to the motor through the connecting shaft and shaft coupling, and BEITE Company has explicitly stated that "connection by shaft coupling" and "direct connection" are different technical features in its related patent; and (2) Since the technical solutions of the connecting shaft and shaft coupling are disclosed in the Drawings for the Description of the patent involved but are not recited in the Claims, according to the dedication rule, the technical solution of "connection by shaft coupling" should not be included in the protection scope of the patent.

In this regard, the Supreme People's Court has held that:

> "A technical solution, which is described only in the Description or Drawings, not in the claims" in the provision of Article 5 of the *Interpretation* refers to a circumstance where the technical solution is only disclosed in the Description or Drawings, but not covered under the protection scope as defined by the claims. In this case, Claim 1 of the patent involved explicitly recites the feature "two output ends of the motor (3) are respectively connected with a reversing mechanism" but does not define that it must be a direct connection. The connection mode disclosed in Figure 1 for the Description of the patent involved is substantially covered under the protection scope defined by Claim 1, which does not pertain to the circumstance described by the above provision. The grounds of petition for retrial, as proposed by Fengwei Company, that the connection by connecting shaft and shaft coupling is not included in the protection scope of the patent involved, are untenable.

In this case, the Supreme People's Court has pointed out that "a technical solution, which is described only in the Description or Drawings, not in the claims" refers *to a circumstance where the technical solution is only disclosed in the Description or Drawings, but not covered under the protection scope as defined by the claims*. The dedication rule does not cover a circumstance where a technical solution described in the Description or Drawings has been covered under the protection scope of the claims.

[D] The Dedication Covers the Parallel Solutions Disclosed but Not Recited in the Claims and the Specific Terms Thereof

Case 6: In the case of second instance regarding infringement dispute over a patent for invention between Shaanxi Yinhe Fire-Fighting Technology and Equipment Co. Ltd. and Shandong Tianhe Fire Vehicle Equipment Co. Ltd. ((2015) Lu Min San Zhong Zi No. 151[7]).

The appealer has alleged that the court of original trial had misapplication of laws, and the "dedication rule" should not be applied in this case. First, the Description of the patent involved does not disclose the technical solution of the "wired controller." Second, either "wired controller" or "wireless controller" is prior art, and the control system is not the inventive or innovative point of the patent involved. The feature that a control system includes a wireless controller makes no contribution to patenting the application for the patent involved. Consequently, the application of the "dedication rule" does not conform to the legislative intent.

In this regard, the Higher People's Court of Shandong Province has held that:

> According to Claim 1, the control system of the patent involved consists of a "wireless controller" and a "receiving device". As can been seen from the disclosure "the present invention adopts a wireless control system, which includes a wireless controller and a receiving device" in the Description of the patent involved, the technical features are definite for the control system in Claim 1 of the

7. 50 Typical Intellectual Property Cases in Chinese Courts in 2015, Top Ten Intellectual Property Cases of First Instance in Jinan in 2015.

> patent involved, that is, the control system of the patent involved is a "wireless control system" consisting of a "wireless controller" and a "receiving device". Moreover, the Description of the patent involved discloses that "A control system is provided in this patent. The control system can be a wireless control system or a wired control system. The present invention adopts a wireless control system, which includes a wireless controller and a receiving device", while the technical solution of wired control system is not recited in the claims. According to the provision of Article 5 of *Interpretation of the Supreme People's Court on Several Issues concerning the Application of Law in the Trial of Patent Infringement Dispute Cases*, the technical solution of wired control system shall not be included into the protection scope of the patent.

In this case, the Higher People's Court of Shandong Province, after construing the technical features of the claims based on the Description, has defined the protection scope of the claims as a "wireless control system" consisting of a "wireless controller" and a "receiving device," and applied the dedication rule to exclude the technical solution of "wired control system." Given the use of a wired control system, the accused infringing product has been affirmed not to fall within the protection scope of the patent.

Case 7: In the case of infringement dispute over a patent for invention between WANG Zaihe and Shanghai Christine Foodstuff Co. Ltd. ((2017) Zui Gao Fa Min Shen No. 5147), the dispute focus has been on whether "soybean flour" defined in the technical feature 2 of Claim 1 of the patent involved is identical with or equivalent to the corresponding technical feature "soybean fiber D of bean curd residue flour" of the two accused infringing processes.

In this regard, the Supreme People's Court has held that:

> In this case, the technical feature 2 of Claim 1 of the patent involved is described as "3-39% of one or more of soybean flour, peanut flour, and mixed bean flour," while the Description correspondingly discloses "soybean flour, peanut flour, mixed bean flour, ..., and extract flour thereof" in paragraph 5. Accordingly, *the Description has disclosed the soybean flour and the "extract flour" of soybean as two parallel technical solutions. The patentee fails to include the "extract flour" of soybean into the protection scope of the claims of the patent involved, and thus it should be deemed that the patentee has excluded the technical solution of the "extract flour" of soybean from the protection scope of the patent involved.* Consequently, in the patent infringement case, the patentee can no longer include the technical solutions dedicated to the society into the protection scope of the patent.

As to the issue of whether the technical feature "soybean fiber D of bean curd residue flour" in the technical feature II of the two accused infringing processes is equivalent to the technical feature "soybean flour" of the patent involved, *given that the "soybean fiber D of bean curd residue flour" is one kind of "extract flour" of soybean, and that the patentee has excluded the technical solution of the "extract flour" of soybean from the protection scope of the patent involved*, it is appropriate that it has not been affirmed that the two constitute equivalent features in the order of second instance.

In this case, the Supreme People's Court has first *identified the parallel relation between "soybean flour" and "extract flour" of soybean according to the Description*. The patentee fails to include the "extract flour" of soybean into the protection scope of the claims of the patent involved, and thus it should be deemed that the patentee has excluded the technical solution of the "extract flour" of soybean from the protection scope of the patent involved. *The "soybean fiber D of bean curd residue flour" is one kind of "extract flour" of soybean, and thus a dedication is constituted.*

Reminder: regarding the scope of dedication, there are three different views in the theoretical circle, which correspond to the small, middle and large scopes accordingly. We opine that each dedication scope is inevitably biased, and the determination criteria should come back to the knowledge of those skilled in the art; that is, a solution is deemed as a dedication if those skilled in the art upon reviewing the Description can determine that the solution has been disclosed and not recited in the claims.

[E] Restrictions on the Application of the Dedication Rule

[1] The Application of the Dedication Rule Is Conditional upon the Potential Formation of Equivalence, and the Dedication Rule Is Necessarily Inapplicable If Nonequivalence Is Affirmed

Case 8: In the case of infringement dispute over a patent for utility model between Jianke Machinery (Tianjin) Co. Ltd. and Tianjin Yinfeng Machinery Equipment Co. Ltd. ((2015) Jin Gao Min San Zhong Zi No. 0022[8]), the dispute focus has been on whether the technical feature "there is one material moving and conveying device located above one side of two bending heads" in the accused solution is equivalent to the corresponding technical feature "there are two or more separated type material moving and conveying devices each located above one side of one of bending heads" in the claims.

The Court of First Instance has held that the above features are neither identical with nor equivalent to each other and then applied the dedication rule to affirm that the accused solution does not fall within the protection scope of the claims. In this regard, the Tianjin High People's Court has held in the second instance that:

> Under the dedication rule, a technical solution disclosed by the patentee in the Description of the patent but not recited in the Claims should be deemed to be dedicated to the public, and the patentee cannot intend to bring it back into the protection scope of the claims by means of the doctrine of equivalents in the patent infringement proceedings. As a consensus in the theoretical circle, the dedication rule is a restriction on the application of the doctrine of equivalents, and it serves for a precaution against circumstances where an applicant for patent submits claims with a narrow protection scope in the application phase to pass the examination of the patent office more easily, while after the patent right is granted, the applicant alleges an infringement under the doctrine of equivalents based on the equivalent features disclosed in the Description. Based on the above analysis, *the dedication rule is applied on condition that one or more technical features in the technical solution of the accused infringing product may be equivalent to the corresponding technical features in the claims drafted by the patentee. In the event*

8. Selected Series of Tianjin Legal Cases (2015-2017): Judges Volume, Top-rated Cases.

of non-application of the dedication rule, the infringement under the doctrine of equivalents should be affirmed. On the contrary, it is unnecessary to apply the dedication rule if it has been affirmed that the technical features of the accused infringing product are essentially not equivalent to the technical features of the claims of the patent.

By the analysis of this case, the Court of First Instance has cited the dedication rule for reasoning in its judicatory ground, but before that, the Court of First Instance had affirmed that the technical feature 5 of the accused infringing product was neither identical with nor equivalent to the corresponding technical feature 5 of the patent, resulting in no precondition for the application of the dedication rule in this case. Consequently, it is not required to comment on if the dedication rule applies in this case.

In this case, the Tianjin High People's Court has held that the dedication rule is applied on condition that one or more technical features in the technical solution of the accused infringing product may be equivalent to the corresponding technical features in the claims drafted by the patentee. In the event of nonapplication of the dedication rule, the infringement under the doctrine of equivalents should be affirmed. The dedication rule is necessarily inapplicable if it has been affirmed that the technical features of the accused infringing product are not equivalent to the technical features of the claims of the patent.

Reminder: this view has certain typicality, while there is another view that[9] the priority can be given to the dedication rule for simplicity of operation during the determination of infringement under the doctrine of equivalents. If the dedication rule takes effect, the conclusion of noninfringement can be drawn, and thus the comparison of the patented technical solution with the accused infringing technical solution is skipped. If the dedication rule does not apply, then the comparison of the patented technical solution with the accused infringing technical solution can be performed.

[2] The "Dedicated Technical Solution" Is Not Protected by Another Application

Case 9: In the case of infringement dispute over a patent for utility model between CHEN Shaodong and Zhejiang Taobao Network Co. Ltd. ((2016) Zhe 01 Min Chu No. 1379[10]), as to the issue of whether the feature of the accused infringing product that the bottom plate is arranged above the U-shaped frame is equivalent to the feature of the patent involved that the bottom plate is arranged on the two connecting rods below, the plaintiff CHEN Shaodong has alleged that, as disclosed in Examples 4 and 5 of the Description of the patent, the bottom plate can be arranged on the upper connecting

9. Intellectual Property Trial Division of the Beijing High People's Court, Interpretation and Application of *Guidelines for Patent Infringement Determination (2017)* of Beijing High People's Court, [M]. Beijing: Intellectual Property Publishing House, 2020.6:240-242.

10. Intellectual Property Trial Division of the Beijing High People's Court, Interpretation and Application of *Guidelines for Patent Infringement Determination (2017)* of Beijing High People's Court, [M]. Beijing: Intellectual Property Publishing House, 2020.6:240-242.

rod to serve as a bench for rest. Thus, the accused infringing product has infringed on the patent.

In this regard, the Hangzhou Intermediate People's Court has held that:

> The Description and the examples can be used to interpret the claims, while the protection scope of the patent shall be defined by the claims, which is explicitly stipulated in Article 59 of the *Patent Law of the People's Republic of China*. For any technical solution not recited in the claims, the patentee can claim the priority in another application for patent. Otherwise, the technical solution shall be deemed dedicated. Considering that the plaintiff of this case has not held the patent right of the alleged technical solution that the bottom plate is arranged on the upper connecting rod, the plaintiff's allegation of accusing the product of infringing on his patent lacks a factual basis and is thus untenable.

In this case, the Hangzhou Intermediate People's Court has held that: a technical solution is not necessarily dedicated if it is disclosed by the patentee in the Description but not recited in the claims. It should be further determined if the patentee claims the priority in another application for patent. If not claimed, the technical solution shall be deemed dedicated. We opine that if the patentee files a divisional application based on the patent involved as the parent application, the application of the dedication rule shall be restricted for the same reasons.

§17.04 CONCLUSION

In general, the introduction of the dedication rule is favorable for the public to accurately determine the protection scope of the claims by comparing the Description and the claims, thus enabling the claims to play the due roles of publicity and delimitation, and it can also guide the industry insiders to attach importance to the drafting quality and improve the drafting level. However, we also notice that, under the circumstance that the drafting level of our country is relatively backward at present, we should strictly regulate the application conditions of the dedication rule.

CHAPTER 18

The Application of Prosecution History Estoppel

Zhang Qiulin & Sun Changlong

§18.01 BASIC PROVISIONS OF LAWS

***Interpretation of the Supreme People's Court on Several Issues concerning the Application of Law in the Trial of Patent Infringement Dispute Cases* (hereinafter referred to as "*Judicial Interpretation I*")**

Article 6 Where a patentee includes a technical solution, which the patent applicant or patentee has abandoned through an amendment of claims or Description or through observations in the procedures of granting or announcement for invalidation of a patent, in the protection scope of a patent in a case of a dispute over infringement of a patent right, the people's court shall not support it.

***Interpretation (II) of the Supreme People's Court on Several Issues concerning the Application of Law in the Trial of Patent Infringement Dispute Cases* (hereinafter referred to as "*Judicial Interpretation II*")**

Article 13 Where the patentee can prove that the restrictive amendments made to the Claims, Description and Drawings or observations made by the patent applicant or patentee in the patent granting and confirmation procedures are definitely negated, it shall be determined by the people's court that the amendments or observations do not lead to the abandonment of the technical solution.

Guidelines for Patent Infringement Determination (2017) Beijing High People's Court

61. In the determination as to whether a technical feature in the accused infringing technical solution is equivalent to a technical feature in the claim, the accused infringer may defend on the grounds that this equivalent feature has been abandoned by the patentee and prosecution history estoppel shall be applied.

Prosecution history estoppel refers to the prohibition of the patentee from reincorporating the abandoned content into the protection scope of the patent in determining whether equivalent infringement is found in patent infringement litigation, where the abandoned content is the protection scope abandoned by the patent applicant or patentee by means of restrictively amending the claim or the Description or making observations in the patent granting or invalidation procedure.

62. The restriction or partial abandonment of the protection scope by the patent applicant or patentee shall be required for overcoming such substantial defects as lack of novelty or inventiveness, lack of essential technical features, lack of support of the claims by the Description and insufficient disclosure of the Description, which render an application unpatentable.

Where the right holder fails to explain the reason for amending the patent documents by the patent applicant or patentee, it may be presumed that the amendment is made for the purpose of overcoming the substantial defects which render the application unpatentable.

63. The restrictive amendment to the protection scope of the claim or observations made by the patent applicant or patentee shall be expressly specified, and shall have been recorded in written statements, patent examination dossiers and effective legal documents.

Where the right holder can prove that the restrictive amendments made to the Claims, Description and Drawings or observations made by the patent applicant or patentee in the patent granting and confirmation procedures are definitely negated, it shall be determined that the amendments or observations do not lead to the abandonment of the technical solution.

64. Prosecution history estoppel shall be applied on the premise that the accused infringer files a request and furnishes the corresponding evidence in respect of the estoppel of the patent applicant or patentee.

In the event that evidence in respect of estoppel of the patent applicant or patentee has been obtained, the court may, in light of the facts ascertained and by applying prosecution history estoppel, put necessary limit on the protection scope of the claim and determine reasonably the protection scope of the patent.

§18.02 INTERPRETATION OF THE ARTICLES OF LAWS

As one of the basic principles of civil law, the principle of good faith requires civil subjects to keep their promises and not damage the reasonable reliance or the legitimate expectation of a bona fide third party so as to balance the inequity that may be brought about by the free exercise of rights. In the practice of granting a patent, the patent applicant usually restricts the claim or the Description so as to quickly obtain the grant. However, in the patent infringement litigation, the patent applicant tries to reincorporate the abandoned technical solution into the protection scope of the patent right through equivalent infringement. In order to ensure the stability of the protection scope of the patent right and safeguard the reliance interest of the public, the patent system prevents the patentee from benefiting from both the infringement procedure and the granting and confirmation procedures through prosecution history estoppel. Therefore, where a patentee includes a technical solution which has been abandoned through an amendment to claims or Description or through observations in the procedures of granting or announcement for invalidation of a patent, in the protection scope of a patent in a case of a dispute over infringement of a patent right, the people's court shall not support it.[1]

The key of Article 6 of *Interpretation I* lies in the abandonment of the technical solution by the restrictive amendment or the observations, and the key of Article 13 of *Interpretation II* lies in the express negation of the restrictive amendment or the observations, both of which relate to the restrictive amendment or the observations. However, the conditions for the application of prosecution history estoppel as specified in Article 6 of *Judicial Interpretation I* are relatively general. As long as the technical solution is abandoned by the amendment or the observations in the procedures of granting or announcement for invalidation of a patent, prosecution history estoppel can be applied. That is to say, *Judicial Interpretation I* does not distinguish the types of the amendment or the observations and only sets the conditions for the application of prosecution history estoppel from the perspective of results. When the determination is made as to whether the "abandonment of technical solution" occurs, it is unnecessary to study in detail whether the purpose of the amendment or observations made by the applicant is to meet the substantive granting conditions or the formal granting conditions. The focus of the examination should be to judge whether a restrictive influence is made to the protection scope claimed by the patent by the amendment or observations of the applicant or patentee.[2]

According to Article 6 of *Judicial Interpretation I*, since the abandonment is made to the "technical solution," literally, the provision of this Article does not apply to disputes over infringement of a patent right for design. However, as described below, the Supreme People's Court indirectly indicated in judicial practice that prosecution history estoppel can be applied in such disputes. Similarly, based on the literal meaning of Article 6, the purpose of this provision is to prevent the applicant or patentee from continuing to obtain improper benefits in the infringement procedure after gaining benefits in the granting and confirmation procedures. Based on the original legislative intention of avoiding benefiting from both the infringement procedure and the granting and confirmation procedures, this provision should, in turn, be applicable to the

1. A dispute over infringement of a patent right for utility model between Zhongyu Electronics (Shanghai) Co. Ltd. and Shanghai Nine Eagles Electronic Technology Co. Ltd. [18(2011) Min Ti Zi No. 306].
2. SONG Jian; ZHANG Xiaoyang; A Few Issues on Estoppel in Patent Infringement Litigation [J]; Journal of Law Application (Judicial Case), 2018(08): 49-55.

granting and confirmation procedures. For details, please refer to the thesis of the Masters of China University of Political Science and Law of LI Debao.[3]

§18.03 ISSUES/DISPUTES ARISING IN THE LAW APPLICATION

[A] The Application of Prosecution History Estoppel

[1] The Application of Prosecution History Estoppel in Time

Since laws of China do not clearly prescribe the validity in time of judicial interpretation, there are different understandings of the retroactivity of judicial interpretation: first, according to the general principle "the law is not retroactive," judicial interpretation can only be applied to cases brought to the people's court after the promulgation and implementation of judicial interpretation, and the judicial interpretation cannot be applied to cases accepted before the implementation of judicial interpretation; second, based on the natural dependence of judicial interpretation to the law on which the judicial interpretation is based, the judicial interpretation specifies how the current laws are specifically applied in the hearing process, and thus the effectiveness of the judicial interpretation certainly can retrospect to the effective date of the interpreted law.

Judicial Interpretation I was adopted at the 1480th session of the Judicial Committee of the Supreme People's Court on December 21, 2009, promulgated on December 28, 2009, and took effect as of January 1, 2010.

Whether *Judicial Interpretation I* is only applicable to cases brought to court on or after January 1, 2010, according to the general principle "the law is not retroactive," or the effectiveness can be traced back to the implementation date of the interpreted *Patent Law*, that is, April 1, 1985, according to the *Patent Law* on which *Judicial Interpretation I* is based? In this regard, the Supreme People's Court gave a clear answer in the Civil Judgment (2013) Min Ti Zi No.127.

In a dispute over infringement of a patent right for invention between Changsha Shenxiang Universal Machine Co. Ltd. and Hunan Guangyi Technology Co. Ltd., and XIA Jiyong (1 (2013) Min Ti Zi No. 127), the Supreme People's Court held in the review that "the validity in time of judicial interpretation should not retrospect to the effective time of the interpreted law by simply applying the principle of 'retroactivity', or the validity in time of judicial interpretation is determined as the implementation date of judicial interpretation by the principle of 'non-retroactivity'." If the judicial interpretation specifically determines the standard of the retroactivity due to various considerations such as the content interpreted by the judicial interpretation and the application in judicial practice, such provision should apply. The *Judicial Interpretation I* involved in this case was promulgated on December 28, 2009 and would come into force on January 1, 2010. The judicial interpretation was formulated in accordance

3. LI Debao; Research on the Application of the Doctrine of Estoppel in Procedures of Patent Appllication Examination and Patent Invalidation [D]; China University of Science and Law; 2012.

with the relevant provisions of the Patent Law and in combination with the trial practice. Therefore, if there is no special provision, the applicable validity in time of the judicial interpretation shall be traced back to the effective time of the Patent Law. However, Article 19 of the Judicial Interpretation specifies that: where an alleged patent infringement occurred before October 1, 2009, the people's court shall apply the Patent Law before the amendment; or where it occurs after October 1, 2009, the people's court shall apply the Patent Law as amended. October 1, 2009 is the implementation date of the *Decision of the Standing Committee of the National People's Congress to Amend the Patent Law of the People's Republic of China* adopted at the 6th Session of the Standing Committee of the 11th National People's Congress. It can be seen that the judicial interpretation has made a special provision on its retroactivity, and the retroactivity depends on the time when the "patent infringement" occurs. Accordingly, the judicial interpretation has clearly specified the validity in time of its application and should be applied to patent infringement after the implementation of the judicial interpretation. The sued infringement in this case is earlier than October 1, 2009. Therefore, the Patent Law and relevant judicial interpretations before the amendment in 2008 shall apply, and *Judicial Interpretation I* shall not apply.

[2] A Court Can Voluntarily Apply Prosecution History Estoppel

Generally, prosecution history estoppel is a necessary restriction on the doctrine of equivalents. In patent infringement litigation, on the basis of the assertion that the sued infringing object constitutes the same infringement to the claim of the patent involved, the patentee generally further asserts the equivalent infringement on the side of caution, while the defendant may ignore using prosecution history estoppel against the assertion of the equivalent infringement made by the patentee. The treatment of this situation actually involves whether the court can voluntarily apply prosecution history estoppel. In this regard, in item 2 of Annual Work Report on Intellectual Property Rights Cases of the Supreme People's Court (2009) (Summary), the Supreme People's Court held that when the determination is made to whether the equivalent infringement is constituted, even if the alleged infringer did not assert to apply prosecution history estoppel, the people's court can reasonably determine the protection scope of the patent right by applying prosecution history estoppel to impose necessary restrictions on the scope of equivalence according to the ascertained facts.

Specifically, in a dispute over infringement of a patent right for utility model between SHEN Qiheng and Shanghai Shengmao Transportation Facilities Engineering Co. Ltd. (2 (2009) Min Shen Zi No. 239), the Supreme People's Court held in the retrial that "the current laws and judicial interpretations do not prescribe whether the people's court can voluntarily apply the doctrine of equivalents. In order to maintain the balance of interests between the patentee, the alleged infringer and the public, the people's courts should not be restricted from voluntarily applying prosecution history estoppel. Therefore, when the determination is made to whether the equivalent infringement is constituted, even if the alleged infringer does not assert to apply prosecution history estoppel, the people's court can reasonably determine the protection scope of the patent right by applying prosecution history estoppel to impose necessary restrictions on the scope of equivalence according to the ascertained facts.

Therefore, the application of prosecution history estoppel by the court of second instance is not improper."

The Supreme People's Court has basically the same view on the case of a dispute over infringement of a patent for utility model between SHEN Qiheng, and Shanghai Lvyu Real Estate Development Co. Ltd., and Shanghai Yisheng Lock Industry Co. Ltd. (3 (2009) Min Shen Zi No. 238).

[3] *The Application of Prosecution History Estoppel in a Case of a Dispute over Infringement of a Patent Right for Design*

As mentioned above, according to the expression per se of Article 6 of *Judicial Interpretation I*, prosecution history estoppel can only be applied in cases of disputes over infringement of patents for invention and utility model. However, for a patent for design, the patentee also has the intrinsic motivation to benefit from both the infringement procedure and the granting and confirmation procedures; that is, to restrict the protection scope in the confirmation procedure to maintain the validity of the patent right, and to expand the protection scope to cover the sued infringing product in the infringement procedure. Therefore, according to such consideration, prosecution history estoppel should be referred to in a case of a dispute over infringement of a patent right for design.

In a dispute over infringement of a patent right for design between Zhongshan Nabao Electrical Technology Co. Ltd. and Zhongcha Mingpin (Beijing) Technology Co. Ltd. (4 (2018) Zui Gao Fa Min Shen No. 4892), the respondent Zhongcha Mingpin Company replied that: Nabao Company stated in the administrative procedure against patent invalidation that the handle, protruding knob, concave display screen and the shape of heat-dissipation hole on the back of the product expressed in the patent for design were important manifestations to distinguish the patent for design from the prior art, with the aim of narrowing the protection scope of the patent to obtain the stability of the patent right. In the patent infringement litigation stage, Nabao Company tried to abandon the elements such as the handle, knob, display screen and the shape of heat-dissipation hole on the back of the product and only took the shape of the housing of the product as the protection content to expand the protection scope, which violated prosecution history estoppel.

Unfortunately, in this case, the Supreme People's Court did not respond to the assertion of the party.

In a dispute over infringement of a patent right for design between Jinan Sanxing Lighting Co. Ltd. and Sichuan Zhongxing Huaye Municipal Lighting Engineering Co. Ltd. (5 (2017) Zui Gao Fa Min Shen No. 5056), Zhongxing Lighting Company held in the retrial application that the assertion regarding the design points and features of the patent for design involved made by Sanxing Lighting Company in the litigation of this case was obviously different from that in the announcement for invalidation procedure, which violated prosecution history estoppel.

In the case of the dispute, the Supreme People's Court simply responded as follows: although Zhongxing Lighting Company believed that the design points asserted by Sanxing Lighting Company were different in the infringement litigation and in the invalidation procedure, it did not furnish evidence to prove such assertion, and thus the assertion was not supported by the Court.

In a dispute over infringement of a patent right for design between Sichuan Zhengwei Lighting Co. Ltd. and Sichuan Huati Lighting Technology Co. Ltd. (6 (2014) Min Shen Zi No. 1342), the retrial petitioner Zhengwei Company asserted that the protection scope summarized by Examination Decision on the Request for Invalidation No. 21944 of the Patent Reexamination Board and Administrative Judgment No. 2523 of the Beijing No.1 Intermediate People's Court was different from that summarized by the Courts of First Instance and Second Instance in this case. The first instance and second instance expanded the protection scope of the patent involved, which violated prosecution history estoppel.

In this regard, the Supreme People's Court believed that "in Examination Decision on the Request for Invalidation No. 21944, the Patent Reexamination Board made explanations to the reasons of the request for invalidation of Zhengwei Company. It not only determined that the invalidation reason of nonconformity of the provision regarding "a new design which is fit for industrial application" cannot be established but also described the appearance characteristics of the patent involved in the reasoning part. By comparison to the appearance characteristics summarized in the first-instance judgment of this case, the description made it clear that "the lower bottom of the lamp arm has a white pattern," and the structural part of the appearance design is described more specifically. Moreover, the Patent Reexamination Board maintained the validity of the patent right after the description was not regarded as the abandonment of a certain right by the patentee Huati Company. In this regard, the court of second instance determined that prosecution history estoppel cannot be applied in this case. It is proper to make such determination."

In this case, in fact, the Supreme People's Court still believed that by comparison to the infringement procedure, the appearance characteristics of the patent involved were described more specifically in the confirmation procedure. However, the more specific description did not lead to the abandonment of the right, and thus the patent right can be maintained valid. Therefore, prosecution history estoppel was not applicable. According to this judgment logic, one aspect that is not easy to attract attention should be the affirmative answer that prosecution history estoppel can be referred to in cases of a dispute over infringement of a patent right for design.

[B] Several Typical Cases of the Application of Prosecution History Estoppel

Deleting the parallel technical solution in the claim will lead to the application of prosecution history estoppel because the deleted parallel technical solution in the claim is abandoned by the express act of "deletion" and can no longer be reincorporated in the protection scope of the patent for protection in the infringement procedure.

In a dispute over infringement of a patent right for invention between Aonuo (China) Pharmaceutical Co. Ltd. and Hubei Wushi Pharmaceutical Co. Ltd., and

WANG Junshe (7 (2009) Min Ti Zi No. 20), the Supreme People's Court held in the review that "the amendment made by the patentee to Claim 1 in the patent granting procedure abandoned the technical solution including the technical feature "calcium gluconate." According to prosecution history estoppel, the technical solution abandoned by the patent applicant or patentee by amending the claim and the Description or making the observations in the procedures of granting or announcement for invalidation of a patent should not be incorporated in the protection scope of the patent right in the patent infringement dispute. Therefore, the protection scope of the patent right involved should not include the technical solution of the technical feature "calcium gluconate." The corresponding technical feature of the sued infringing product is calcium gluconate, which pertains to the technical solution abandoned by the patentee in the patent granting procedure and should not be regarded as being equivalent to the technical feature "active calcium" recited in Claim 1 and which is to be incorporated into the protection scope of the patent right.

Claims 1 and 2 of the publication text of the patent involved ZL 95117811.3 are as follows:

(1) A medicine for preventing and treating calcium defects, characterized in that it is prepared from the following raw materials by weight:

soluble calcium	4-8 parts
zinc gluconate or zinc sulfate	0.1-0.4 part
glutamine or glutamic acid	0.8-1.2 part(s).

(2) The medicine for preventing and treating calcium defects, according to Claim 1, characterized in that the soluble calcium is calcium gluconate, calcium chloride, calcium lactate, calcium carbonate, or active calcium.

In the process in response to the First Office Action, in order to overcome the defect that the claim is not supported by the Description, the applicant amended the above two claims as follows and finally obtained the grant:

(1) A medicine for preventing and treating calcium defects, characterized in that it is prepared from the following raw materials by weight:

active calcium	4-8 parts
zinc gluconate	0.1-0.4 part
glutamine or glutamic acid	0.8-1.2 part(s).

Obviously, in the patent granting procedure, the applicant abandoned four technical solutions in which the soluble calcium is calcium gluconate, calcium chloride, calcium lactate and calcium carbonate by the manner of "deletion."

In a dispute over the confirmation of noninfringement of patent right for invention between Guizhou Xinbang Pharmaceutical Co. Ltd. and Nanchang Hongyi Technology Co. Ltd. (8 (2011) Min Shen Zi No. 543), the Supreme People's Court held in the retrial that "the active ingredient and matrix used in the preparation method of "dropping pill of breviscapine" by Xinbang Company are 4g breviscapine and 28g polyethylene glycol 4000, respectively, and the weight ratio thereof is 1: 7. Both Hongyi Company and Xinbang Company had no objection to this. The active ingredient and matrix used in the "dropping pill of breviscapine" defined in Claim 1 of patent No. 91.0 are 20 parts by weight of breviscapine and 300 parts by weight of polyethylene glycol 6000, and the weight ratio is 1:15. It can be seen that the matrix and the weight ratio of the active ingredient and the matrix used in the dropping pill of breviscapine of Xinbang Company are different from those of Patent No. 91.0. In the granting procedure of patent No. 91.0, Hongyi Company defined the matrix to polyethylene glycol 6000 by amending the Claims and abandoned the technical solution of using polyethylene glycol 4000 as the matrix. In this litigation, Hongyi Company incorporated the technical solution of using polyethylene glycol 4000 as the formula matrix of "dropping pill of breviscapine," which had been abandoned in the process of patent granting examination, into the protection scope of the patent right, which should not be considered."

In order to more clearly show the amendment made by the applicant in the patent granting procedure, the relevant claims of the patent involved ZL 03110091.0 are listed as follows:

> Claims 1 and 2 of the publication text of the patent involved ZL 03110091.0 are as follows:
>
> (1) A dropping pill of breviscapine and a preparation method thereof, characterized in that: the dropping pill of breviscapine is prepared through adding the breviscapine to the fused matrix, stirring evenly, dropping into pills, condensing into pills in coolant, removing coolant and drying.
>
> (2) The matrix in the dropping pill of breviscapine and the preparation method thereof according to Claim 1 comprises, but is not limited to, polyethylene glycol 4000, polyethylene glycol 6000, sodium stearate, glycerol gelatin, poloxamer, stearic acid, glycerol monostearate, hydrogenated vegetable oil, insect wax, etc.
>
> Claim 1 of the publication text of the patent involved ZL 03110091 is as follows:
>
> (1) A dropping pill of breviscapine, characterized in that it is prepared from 20 parts by weight of breviscapine active ingredient and 300 parts by weight of ethylene glycol 6000 matrix.

In a dispute over infringement of a patent right for invention between Dyson Technology Limited and Suzhou Taiyikai Electronic Technology Co. Ltd., Ecovacs Robotics Technology Co. Ltd., and Ecovacs Robotics Co. Ltd (9 (2016) Zui Gao Fa Min Shen No. 2653), the Supreme People's Court held in the retrial that in the application documents of the patent involved, the additional technical feature of original Claim 5 is "the main body includes a motor and/or a battery," and the additional technical feature of original Claim 6 is "the motor and/or battery is arranged above the base surface of the main body." Dyson Company amended Claim 1 of the patent involved at the substantive examination stage, incorporating the original Claims 5 and 6 into Claim 1, and deleting the technical solutions "the main body includes a motor or a battery" and "the motor or battery is arranged above the base surface of the main body." As can be seen, it should be considered that Claim 1 of the patent involved has expressly abandoned the protection of the technical solutions "the main body includes a motor or a battery" and "the motor or battery is arranged above the base surface of the main body," and only remained the technical solutions "the main body includes a motor and a battery" and "the motor and battery is arranged above the base surface of the main body." Obviously, if the motor or battery is arranged "(diagonally) above the base surface side of the main body," " it belongs to the content explicitly abandoned by the patent involved and cannot be incorporated into the protection scope of the claim."

In a dispute over the confirmation of noninfringement of patent right for invention between Beijing Sogou Technology Development Co. Ltd., Beijing Sogou Information Service Co. Ltd. and Beijing Deepquant.Ai Technologies Co. and Beijing Jiugong Mixing Presentation Technology Co. Ltd. (10 (2019) Zui Gao Fa Zhi Min Zhong No. 74), regarding whether the input method involved has the technical feature (d) of Claim 1, the Intellectual Property Court of the Supreme People's Court held in the second instance that "the focus of the dispute between the two parties is whether the paging display mode referred to in technical feature (d) is 'full display' or 'partial display'. First, it can be determined from the technical problem to be solved by the patent involved and the disclosed technical solutions and the like that the technical feature (d) of Claim 1 should be interpreted as displaying all phrase candidates. Second, based on 'prosecution history estoppel', the patentee has explicitly abandoned the technical solution 'partial display'. Specifically, first, judging from the disclosure of the publication text of the patent involved, the technical solution disclosed in the original Description and Claims of the patent involved does not clearly define the technical feature 'partial display'. Second, the patent applicant voluntarily amended the Claims and submitted the amendment replacement sheets of the Claims, in which the technical feature 'output part or all of the phrase candidates into candidate list window of the display device' is added into Claim 1. Third, in the process of substantive examination of patents involved, item 2 of the First Office Action of the patent involved pointed out that the amendment 'output part of the phrase candidates into the candidate list window of the display device' in '(b)... and mixing together, outputting part or all of the phrase candidates into the candidate list window of the display device' recited in Claim 1 goes beyond the scope of disclosure contained in the original Description and Claims, which does not comply with the provision of Article 33 of the Patent Law. In response to the First Office Action, regarding item 2 of the examination comments, the patentee pointed out that paragraph 2 on page 7 of the Description clearly discloses that 'sorted according to the principle of phrase-length priority and usage frequency priority, and then presented in candidate list window on a page-by-page basis for choosing by the user'. When there are many candidates, one screen cannot completely display all the candidates. At this time, it is the conventional practice in the art to display them on a page-by-page basis and display some candidates on one screen. Therefore, the corresponding amendment in (b) of Claim 1 does not go beyond the scope of disclosure contained in the original Description and Claims. In addition, in response to the Second Office Action, the patentee pointed out that the content that goes beyond the scope of disclosure contained in the original Description and Claims pointed out in the First Office Action is deleted, that is, the corresponding content 'full or partial display' in Claim 1 is deleted, and it is amended as 'presented in candidate list window on a page-by-page basis', such that it becomes the technical feature recited in the patented Claim 1. In this case, in the process of patent application for the purpose of patent right granting, the patentee has clearly pointed out through observations that 'partial display' means page-by-page display and does not mean partial display of phrase candidates. Moreover, the patentee explicitly abandoned the technical solution 'partial display' through amendment. Therefore, the assertion of Deepquant Company and Jiugong Mixing Company that the technical feature is 'partial display' is contrary to 'prosecution history estoppel' specified in the above judicial interpretation."

[C] Observations and the Application of Prosecution History Estoppel

Compared with the above typical cases in which prosecution history estoppel is applied by deleting the parallel technical solution in the claim, the application of prosecution history estoppel through observations is less typical.

Whether in the granting procedure or in the confirmation procedure, the applicant or the patentee usually makes the following observations regarding the closest prior art: the claim is different from the closest prior art, and its specific distinguishing technical feature is as follows: the distinguishing technical feature performs a different function in the closest prior art as it does in the present patent; the distinguishing technical feature brings about a beneficial technical effect, even an unexpected technical effect, to the present invention. According to whether the corresponding technical feature closest to the prior art is within the literal meaning of the technical feature of the claim, the author divides the observations into the following two categories:

(1) Restrictive observations: the corresponding technical feature closest to the prior art is within the literal meaning of the technical feature of the claim, and the observations constitute restrictive observations, which will lead to the application of prosecution history estoppel.
(2) Nonrestrictive observations: the corresponding technical feature closest to the prior art is not within the literal meaning of the technical feature of the

claim, and the observations do not constitute restrictive observations, which will not lead to the application of prosecution history estoppel.

Regarding the above (1) restrictive observations, the following two paths can be followed in infringement determination:

(1)-1 First, the restrictive observations are used to interpret the claim, and the corresponding technical feature closest to the prior art is eliminated from the technical feature of the claim so as to determine the protection scope of the text. This should be the use of prosecution history estoppel to interpret the claim mentioned by some people. However, according to the understanding of the author, the accurate statement should be the use of restrictive observations to interpret the claim. At this time, the patentee can no longer assert text infringement but can only settle for second best and assert equivalent infringement. Then, when the patentee tries to reincorporate the corresponding technical feature closest to the prior art into the protection scope of the claim through the doctrine of equivalents, prosecution history estoppel is applied; that is, the application of the doctrine of equivalents is deterred by the restrictive observations.

(2)-2 The protection scope of the text is directly determined based on the literal meaning of the technical feature of the claims without interpreting the claim by using the restrictive observations. At this time, the patentee will undoubtedly claim text infringement. Correspondingly, in order to oppose the allegation of text infringement, the sued infringer can assert to apply prosecution history estoppel to the patentee, that is, to use the restrictive observations to deter the application of text infringement. This should be the use of prosecution history estoppel in text infringement mentioned by some people.

In the above two paths, the author prefers the first path because this path is more in line with the common cognition; that is, prosecution history estoppel is a necessary restriction on the doctrine of equivalents.

Regarding the above (2) nonrestrictive observations, the following path will be followed in the infringement determination: according to the "three bases" and "readily envisage" of the equivalent infringement determination, whether the corresponding technical feature closest to the prior art constitutes the equivalent feature of the technical feature of the claim will be judged. Certainly, since the applicant or the patentee has already emphasized the differences in technical means, function and effect between the corresponding technical feature closest to the prior art and the technical feature of the claim in the observations, the corresponding technical feature closest to the prior art probably does not constitute the equivalent feature of the technical feature of the claim to a large extent.

The six cases listed below belong to the situation that the above (2) nonrestrictive observations do not lead to the application of prosecution history estoppel, which also shows that the observations in the granting and confirmation procedures will not easily lead to the application of prosecution history estoppel, and it is unnecessary for the applicant or the patentee to hold back from taking action when making observations. Certainly, in the process of making observations, special attention should still be paid to avoid using negative and abandonment expressions, such as, is not, not including, etc.

In a dispute over infringement of a patent right for invention between Changsha Shenxiang Universal Machine Co. Ltd. and Hunan Guangyi Technology Co. Ltd., and XIA Jiyong (1 (2013) Min Ti Zi No. 127), the Supreme People's Court held in the review that "to apply prosecution history estoppel, it is necessary to examine the true intention of the observations made by the patentee in the examination procedure of the request for invalidation. Upon trial, according to the technical solutions disclosed in Evidence 1 (US patent No. US3339853) and Evidence 6 (US patent No. US4022387) in the examination procedure of the announcement for invalidation, the disclosed grinding surfaces are all vertically arranged, which makes the grinding roller and the grinding mill cooperate at the same horizontal height, thus embodying the position relationship that the grinding roller is on the inner side of the grinding mill, whereas the technical solution 'the grinding roller is located above the inclined side of the grinding mill' recited in Claim 1 of the patent involved can realize the beneficial effects of delaying the descending speed of materials to be ground, increasing the grinding working time and the like. The observations of Shenxiang Company in the examination procedure of the announcement for invalidation are intended to emphasize the difference between the patent involved and the prior art 'the grinding roller is on the inner side of the grinding mill' disclosed in the above Evidences 1 and 6, which only uses the expression 'upper and lower positions' within the original meaning of the relative position of the grinding roller and the grinding mill as defined in Claim 1. Obviously, in the examination procedure of the request for invalidation, the observations made by the patentee Shenxiang Company on Claim 1 of the patent involved based on the two reference documents of Evidences 1 and 6 did not further limit the literal meaning of the disputed technical feature, and did not exclude the technical solution 'the grinding roller is located above the inclined side of the grinding mill.' Therefore, the technical solution does not belong to the technical solution abandoned by amending the claims, Description or observations in the procedure of announcement for patent invalidation."

In a dispute over infringement of a patent right for invention between CAO Rongguo and Guang Zhou Pan Yu Hoyo Industrial Co. Ltd., and WalMart (Zhejiang) Inc. (11 (2014) Min Shen Zi No. 1949), the Supreme People's Court held in the retrial that "although the patent applicant of the patent involved only generally emphasized in the observations that many technical features including 'curved reinforced parts' were different from the prior art, the patent applicant did not state the difference of a certain feature and the prior art, and thus the specific technical solution abandoned cannot be determined. Therefore, prosecution history estoppel prescribed in Article 6 of *Judicial Interpretation I* cannot be directly applied. Although the patent applicant of the patent involved only generally emphasized in the observations in the process of patent right granting that many technical features including 'hinge part' were different from the prior art, the patent applicant did not state the difference of a certain feature and the prior art, and thus the specific technical solution abandoned cannot be determined. Therefore, prosecution history estoppel cannot be applied."

In a dispute over administrative handling of infringement of a patent for utility model between XAUT Crystal Growing Technology Co. Ltd. and Intellectual Property Office of Luoyang City of Henan Province (12 (2015) Xing Jian Zi No. 153), XAUT Company asserted that the third distinguishing technical feature between the alleged infringing product and the patent of Luoyang Jinnuo Company lies in: 3. The high-frequency coil of the alleged infringing product of XAUT Company has a straight opening, whereas the patented product of Luoyang Jinnuo Company has an oblique opening. The Supreme People's Court held in the retrial that "LIU Chaoxuan and Luoyang Jinnuo Company only made a beneficial feature comparison between the oblique opening and the straight opening in the patent invalidation procedure, and did not explicitly make a restriction promise or abandonment to the technical feature of the straight opening. XAUT Company believes that prosecution history estoppel should be applied in this case but does not furnish evidence to prove it, so the reason cannot be established."

In a dispute over infringement of a patent right for invention between Nanjing Changjiang Furnace Science and Technology Co. Ltd. and Yangzhou Dicastal Hub Manufacturing Co. Ltd., and Nanjing Nianda Furnace Science and Technology Co. Ltd. (13 (2017) Zui Gao Fa Min Shen No. 1312), the Supreme People's Court held in the retrial that "according to the statement 'reference document 1 does not give the technical enlightenment that the lift drive cylinder can be mounted on the top of the support frame, that is, the support column considered by the Examiner, but rather teaches that the lift drive cylinder should be mounted on the quenching frame, that is, the quenching lifting frame of reference document 1' in the *Observations* made by Changjiang Company, it can be known that Changjiang Company emphasizes that the 'support frame' of the patent involved is different from the 'quenching lifting frame' of reference document 1. Moreover, the lift drive cylinder of the patent involved is mounted on the top of the support frame, and the corresponding structure disclosed in reference document 1 is also mounted on the top. Therefore, Changjiang Company did not emphasize and restrict the feature 'top' in the granting procedure, and it is not because the 'top' is emphasized and restricted that grant is obtained. The court of second instance applied prosecution history estoppel improperly, and the court makes a correction."

In a dispute over infringement of a patent right for utility model between Wuxi Guowei Chinaware and Electric Appliances Co. Ltd., JIANG Guoping and Changshu Linzhi Electrical Heating Device Co. Ltd., and Suning.com Co. Ltd. (14 (2018) Zui Gao Fa Min Zai No. 111), the Supreme People's Court held in the review that "the so-called distinguishing feature 3 of Linzhi Company and the application of prosecution history estoppel are related to feature F 'the heat-conducting aluminum pipe forms semicircular grooves on the left side and the right side respectively after being pressed' of Claim 2 of this case. In the process of announcement for invalidation of the patent in this case, the patentee asserted that the function of the groove of the patent in the case is different from that of Evidence 5. The 'U', 'W' and 'V' grooves in Evidence 5 function as fixing elements, and the function of the semicircular shape in the patent of this case is to offset the extension in the width direction during aluminum tube pressing. The groove of the patent in this case is formed only after the heat-conducting aluminum tube is pressed, whereas the V-shaped groove of Evidence 5 has been formed before pressing. Decision No.24085 approved the above assertion of the patentee that the grooves on the left and right sides of the patent in this case have a different function from the grooves in Evidence 5. Although the patentee emphasized the function and formation time of semicircular grooves on the left and right sides of the heat-conducting aluminum pipe in the patent of this case in the process of announcement for invalidation of the patent, it did not completely exclude the existence of grooves with specific shapes on the left and right sides of the heat-conducting aluminum pipe before pressing. At the same time, Decision No.24085 clearly affirmed that the left and right sides of the heat-conducting aluminum pipe of the patent in this case can be slightly sunken before pressing. Therefore, the observations made by the patentee of this case in the procedure of announcement for invalidation did not waive the technical solution that the left and right sides of the heat-conducting aluminum pipe have grooves with specific shapes before pressing. Decision No.24085 further confirms that the patent in this case includes the technical solution that the left and right sides of the heat-conducting aluminum pipe have grooves with specific shapes before pressing. The observations made by the patentee in this case in the procedure of announcement for invalidation did not lead to the legal effect of prosecution history estoppel asserted by Linzhi Company."

In a dispute over infringement of a patent right for invention between Suzhou Yabisi Compound Materials Co. Ltd. and Zhuhai Aibei Packaging Materials Co. Ltd. (15 (2019) Zui Gao Fa Min Shen No. 905), the Supreme People's Court believed in the retrial that "regarding whether the sued infringing product has the technical feature of a heat-sealed block, Claims 1 and 5 do not explicitly define that all parts of the heat-sealed block are formed by sealing four layers of films (two inner films and two outer films). In particular, in the case that 'the top end of the heat-sealed block (5) is higher than the top end of the two inner films', the top end area does not include the inner films. In the sued infringing product, the top end of the heat-sealed coil is higher than the top end of the two inner films, but the two inner films do not fall out of the range of the heat-sealed coil. Therefore, the determination that the sued infringing product falls within the protection scope of the technical feature 'heat-sealed block' in the second-instance judgment is appropriate. In this case, the patentee involved stated the function and effect of arrangement of the heat-sealed block in the granting procedure, but the evidence in this case is insufficient to prove that the technical solution of the sued infringing product is abandoned. Therefore, the assertion of Aibei Company that prosecution history estoppel should be applied in this case cannot be established."

The Annual Report on Intellectual Property Rights Cases of the Supreme People's Court (2010) gives the typical significance of the case of infringement of a patent between Youta Company and Vanguard Company ((2010) Minti Zi No. 158) under the title "The observations of the patentee in the granting and confirmation procedures may lead to the application of prosecution history estoppel": according to the observations made by the patentee in the procedures of patent granting and announcement for invalidation of the patent involved, and the comparative analysis of the technical effects of different process conditions disclosed in the Description of the patent involved, it is determined that the relevant technical feature in the sued infringing product is not equivalent to the corresponding technical feature in the patent involved, and the sued infringing product does not fall within the protection scope of Claim 1 of the patent involved.

Specifically, in a dispute over infringement of a patent right for invention between Chengdu Youta Pharmaceutical Co. Ltd. and Jiangsu Vanguard Pharmaceutical Co. Ltd., and Sichuan Kelun Medicine Trade Co. Ltd. (16 (2010) Min Ti Zi No. 158), the Supreme People's Court held in the review that "in addition to the observations made in the procedures of granting and announcement for invalidation of the patent involved, Youta Company also emphasized in the section 'Determination of the Best Extraction Conditions' on page 12 of the Description of the patent involved that compared with 3 times of decoction, the production cost can be reduced by 2 times of decoction, so 2 times of decoction is chosen; and emphasized in the section 'Determination of Fineness of Extract Powder in Example 5' on pages 15-16 of the Description, the suspension system of soft capsule contents prepared by crushing Lamiophlomis rotata Kudo into fine powder with 200 mesh sieve is the most stable. Therefore, the features '2 times of decoction' and '3 times of decoction', 'crushing into fine powder, passing through 200 mesh sieve' and 'grinding into fine powder" do not constitute equivalent features, and do not fall within the protection scope of Claim 1 of the patent involved."

According to the above specific contents, the author holds that this title in Annual Report on Intellectual Property Rights Cases of the Supreme People's Court (2010) seems to be inconsistent with the typical significance of this case, it may be more appropriate to adjust the title to "The observations of the patentee in the granting and confirmation procedure may 'not' lead to the application of prosecution history estoppel."

[D] Several Cases of Nonapplication of Prosecution History Estoppel

[1] Nonabandonment of the Technical Solution Means Nonapplication of Prosecution History Estoppel

The essence of prosecution history estoppel lies in: the technical solution that has been abandoned can no longer be recovered and incorporated into the protection scope of the claim, whether through amendment or observations based on the principle of good faith. That is to say, only when there is the abandonment of the technical solution can prosecution history estoppel apply; on the contrary, without the abandonment of the technical solution, there is no application of prosecution history estoppel.

In a dispute over royalty for a patent for invention in the temporary protection period between GuangZhou LianRou Machinery And Equipment Co. Ltd. and Zhe Jian Intelligent Equipment Co. Ltd., and Zouping Hengsheng Metal Technology Co. Ltd. (17 (2018) Zui Gao Fa Min Shen No. 4398), regarding the problem that LianRou Company made amendment to the patent application in the granting procedure of the patent in this case, the Supreme People's Court held in the retrial that "although LianRou

Company amended the feature 'after the spring is compressed to a certain degree, the spring is disengaged from the spring conveying mechanism and is clamped and conveyed by the spring compression conveying mechanism' into the feature 'after the spring is compressed to a certain degree, the spring is disengaged from the spring conveying mechanism and is clamped and conveyed by the conveying belt body outside the two baffles', Claim 1 of the patent has stated that 'the spring compression conveying mechanism comprises baffles and conveying belts wound on the outsides of the baffles'. Therefore, the spring compression conveying mechanism is composed of baffles and a conveying belt to continue compressing and conveying the spring. Clamping and conveying the spring by the spring compression conveying mechanism is actually clamping and conveying the spring by the conveying belt. Therefore, the protection scope of the patent is not restricted by the amended technical solution. The protection scope of the sued infringing technical solution is the same as the protection scope of the patent right of this case before and after the restriction. LianRou Company does not incorporate the technical solution abandoned in the patent granting procedure into the protection scope of the patent right in the infringement litigation of the patent in this case. Prosecution history estoppel is not applicable in this case, and the sued infringing technical solution falls within the protection scope of Claim 1 of the patent in this case."

In this dispute, the Supreme People's Court first confirmed that the protection scope of Claim 1 had not changed substantially before and after the amendment and that there is no abandonment of any technical solution, and then on the basis that there is no abandonment of the technical solution, directly and clearly determined that prosecution history estoppel was not applicable in this case.

[2] *The "Passive" Invalidation of a Claim Does Not Result in the Application of Prosecution History Estoppel to Dependent Claims of the Claim*

In a dispute over infringement of a patent right for utility model between Zhongyu Electronics (Shanghai) Co. Ltd. and Shanghai Nine Eagles Electronic Technology Co. Ltd. (18 (2011) Min Ti Zi No. 306), the Supreme People's Court specifically discussed the applicable conditions of prosecution history estoppel and the criteria for determining an abandonment as follows:

> Applicable Conditions of prosecution history estoppel
>
> In general, only two forms, namely, the amendment of claims and Description or observations, can lead to the abandonment of the technical solution, and further cause the application of prosecution history estoppel. The independent claim is announced invalid, the patent right is maintained valid on the basis of the dependent claim, and the dependent claim actually replaces the status of the original independent claim. However, the content of the dependent claim or the protection scope determined by the dependent claim has not changed due to the invalidation of the original independent claim. Since each claim is a separate and complete technical solution, each claim should accurately and completely summarize the protection scope claimed by the applicant in the original application,

> regardless of whether the claim appears in the form of an independent claim. On this basis, each claim may be individually maintained valid or announced invalid. The effect of each claim shall be presumed to be independent from the effect of other claims. Even if the claim on which the dependent claim depends is announced invalid, the dependent claim cannot be considered invalid accordingly. Therefore, it should not be simply considered that the protection scope determined by the dependent claim is restricted because claim on which the dependent claim depends is invalid.
>
> The criteria for determining the abandonment
>
> The protection scope of the patent right is defined by the technical features contained in the claims, so the change of the protection scope of the patent right is also reflected in the change of the technical features in the claims. In the procedures of granting or announcement for invalidation of the patent, the patentee can, on his own initiative or at the request of the Examiner, restrict the protection scope determined by a claim by adding technical features, or make a restrictive interpretation of a claim through observations. Prosecution history estoppel is applicable to the amendment or observations that lead to the narrowing of the protection scope of the patent right, that is, the technical solution abandoned by the amendment or observations. The abandonment is a self-abandonment made by the patentee through amendment or observations. However, if the Patent Reexamination Board determines that the independent claim is invalid and maintains the patent right valid on the basis of the dependent claim, and the patentee has not made the above self-abandonment, when judging whether the "abandonment" in prosecution history estoppel is constituted, full attention should be paid to the case that the patentee does not make self-abandonment and the conditions for determining the abandonment should be strictly determined. If the additional technical feature in the dependent claim is not summarized by the independent claim, it cannot be presumed that the technical solutions in addition to the additional technical feature have been completely abandoned because the additional technical feature has no original reference.

Claim 3 of the patent involved defines Claim 2 on which Claim 3 depends by adding the technical features "carbon film and silver film" and their positional relationship with the brush and further defines Claim 1 on which Claim 2 depends. Specific to this case, the Supreme People's Court held according to the above applicable conditions and determination criteria that: both independent Claim 1 and its dependent Claim 2 are announced invalid, and the patent involved is maintained valid on the basis of the dependent Claim 3 of Claim 2. However, it does not mean that a restrictive amendment is made to Claim 1; that is, Claim 1 is further defined by the additional technical features of Claims 2 and 3. The "silver film" in Claim 3 is not mentioned in Claims 1-2. Moreover, Zhongyu Company did not amend the claims and Description in the patent granting and invalidation procedures, nor did it abandon the technical solution of using conductive materials other than "silver film" as guide strips in the observations. Therefore, it should not be considered that the additional technical feature "silver film" of Claim 3 can no longer apply the doctrine of equivalents based on the fact that Claims 1-2 are announced invalid.

Based on the case of the dispute, another situation is envisaged: Claim 3 further defines the existing technical feature in Claim 2 on which Claim 3 depends as "silver film," and further defines Claim 1 on which Claim 2 depends; similarly, independent

Claim 1 and its dependent Claim 2 are announced invalid, and the patent involved is maintained valid on the basis of the dependent Claim 3 of Claim 2. In this case, can prosecution history estoppel be applied to the additional technical feature "silver film" of Claim 3? The answer should still be no because the patentee does not make any restrictive amendment to Claim 3 to abandon the technical solution.

[3] The Addition of a Technical Feature to Make a Further Definition Does Not Cause the Application of Prosecution History Estoppel

In a dispute over infringement of a patent right for invention between Tianjin Lianli Chemical Co. Ltd. and Zhejiang Furuide Chemical Co. Ltd. (19 (2018) Zui Gao Fa Min Zai No. 387), before the patent involved was granted, Lianli Company amended Claim 1 by adding a technical feature "material level switch," which is part of the additional technical feature of Claim 11.

The Supreme People's Court held in the review that:

> In the procedures of granting and confirmation of the patent for invention, the patent applicant is entitled to submit observations or amend claims according to law. It is a common situation in patent examination practice that the patent applicant adds new technical features when amending claims and asserts that the amended technical solution is not obvious. Although the addition of technical features to the claim may further define the protection scope of the patent right, resulting in the change of the protection scope of the claim, in the case that there is no any other evidence proving that the patentee "abandons" the specific technical solution through amendment or observations, it cannot be determined that the patentee has completely "abandoned" all other technical features equivalent to the technical feature and cannot assert the application of the doctrine of equivalents to the added technical feature just because the addition of technical features in the claims causes the protection scope of the claims to be further restricted. In this way, the protection scope of claims amended by adding technical features will be excessively restricted, and the sued infringer can easily avoid infringement by amending and replacing the technical features, which will lead to the imbalance of interests between the patentee and the public. Such practice is neither consistent with the purpose of prosecution history estoppel, nor with the legislative purpose of patent law to protect the legitimate rights and interests of patentees and encourage inventions and creations.
>
> In this case, although the patentee added the "material level switch" when amending Claim 1 during the substantive examination process, the patent right involved was ultimately maintained valid. However, in the invalidation procedure, there is no evidence proving that the patentee abandoned to assert equivalent infringement to the technical solution of determining whether the aluminum powder is emptied by pressure detection according to the above amendments and observations. Therefore, the assertions made by Furuide Company that prosecution history estoppel should be applied to this case and that the "material level switch" can no longer be deemed to be equivalent to the pressure detection in technical solution A are not supported by the court.

[E] Restrictive Amendments or Observations Are Explicitly Denied

Article 6 of *Judicial Interpretation I* allows the application of prosecution history estoppel, while Article 13 of *Judicial Interpretation II* slightly restricts the application and restricts the final application conditions of prosecution history estoppel.

In a dispute over infringement of a patent right for invention between CAO Guilan, HU Meiling, JIANG Li, JIANG Haotian, and Chongqing Lifan Automobile Sales Co. Ltd., Chongqing Lifan Passenger Vehicle Co. Ltd., Jiangsu Wieson Automotive Co. Ltd., Nanjing Jiuhuashan Automobile Maintenance Co. Ltd., Lifan Industry (Group) Co. Ltd., and Hangzhou Yafan Automobile Co. Ltd. (20 (2017) Zui Gao Fa Min Shen No. 1826), the Supreme People's Court held in the retrial that "since there is continuity in the determination of the technical feature in the patent granting and confirmation procedures, whether the observations made by the patentee are 'explicitly denied' should be judged objectively and comprehensively on the examination of the technical feature at the stages of patent granting and confirmation, focusing on whether the restrictive observations made by the patentee on the technical solution is finally approved by the judge, and whether the patent application is granted or the patent right is upheld caused thereby. According to the above relevant facts in this case, in the granting procedure, the Patent Examination Department of the China National Intellectual Property Administration did not approve Jiang Xiaoping's observations on technical features a and b, and held a clear negative opinion. Moreover, the granting of the patent involved was not based on the restrictive observations on features a and b. In the subsequent invalidation examination procedure, the Patent Reexamination Board did not overturn the negative opinions held at the substantive examination stage. In commenting the inventive step of the patent involved, although the Decision on Invalidation lists the technical features a and b as the distinguishing features, the existence of technical features a and b does not affect the patent reexamination board to make the examination comment that the patent involved involves an inventive step on the basis that there is an opposite teaching in the prior art and those skilled in the art do not have the motivation of combining the feature c 'the radio receiving antenna is an AM/FM common antenna'. Since the restrictive observations made by the patentee have been explicitly denied in the substantive examination, and the invalid examination procedure has not overturned the determination and reached the opposite conclusion, in this case, it should be determined that there is a fact that the restrictive observations made by the patentee have been explicitly denied. This is consistent with the fact that the restrictive observations do not bring about the acquisition and maintenance of the patent right and is not contrary to the purpose of prosecution history estoppel to prevent the patentee from 'benefiting from both the infringement procedure and the granting and confirmation procedure'. Therefore, Jiang Xiaoping's observations regarding features a and b do not have the legal effect of the abandonment of the technical solution."

It can be seen from this dispute that: first, in view of the continuity of the determination of the technical feature in patent granting and confirmation procedures, it is necessary to examine whether the restrictive observations made by the patentee on the technical solution are "finally" approved by the judge, and the final denial or approval shall prevail; second, the "denial" must be "explicit," and the refusal of comment is not an explicit denial; third, according to the contents "whether the patent application is patented or the patent right is maintained caused thereby" and "the fact that the restrictive observations do not bring about the acquisition and maintenance of the patent right," the benefit made from the granting and confirmation procedure in the benefits made from both the infringement procedure and the granting and confirmation procedure refers to the "actual benefit" rather than "expected benefit" or "benefit expectation."

[F] The Allocation of Burden of Proof of Prosecution History Estoppel

Regarding the allocation of the burden of proof for the application of prosecution history estoppel and the nonapplication of prosecution history estoppel, the Supreme People's Court had the following discussions:

In a dispute over infringement of a patent right for invention between Tianjin Lianli Chemical Co. Ltd. and Zhejiang Furuide Chemical Co. Ltd. (19 (2018) Zui Gao Fa Min Zai No. 387), regarding the burden of proof for the application of prosecution history estoppel, the Supreme People's Court held in the review that "according to the provision of Article 13 of *Judicial Interpretation II,* in the case that the patentee has made restrictive amendments or observations, when whether the principle of estoppel is applicable is determined, it should be ascertained that whether the patentee has 'abandoned' the specific technical solution through the 'restrictive amendments or observations' rather than just considering whether the 'restrictive modification or statement' has a substantial influence on the effectiveness of the patent right. Therefore, if the sued infringer asserts the application of prosecution history estoppel, he shall prove the specific circumstances of the patentee's 'restrictive amendments or observations' and whether the patentee has abandoned the 'the sued infringing technical solution' accordingly. However, if the patentee asserts that 'it does not lead to the abandonment of the technical solution' and prosecution history estoppel is not applicable, the patentee shall bear the burden of proof for "the restrictive amendments or observations being explicitly denied."

In a word, in general, first, the patentee should submit evidence for the infringement and make infringement comparison to prove that the sued infringing technical solution falls within the protection scope of the claim of the patent involved; then, the sued infringer furnishes evidence to prove that the patentee abandons the "sued infringing technical solution" through "restrictive amendments or observations," which leads to the application of prosecution history estoppel; finally, the patentee should prove that the "restrictive amendments or observations" is explicitly denied, so prosecution history estoppel cannot be applied in the end.

§18.04 CONCLUSION

Prosecution history estoppel is applicable to the sued infringement that occurred on or after October 1, 2009. The court can voluntarily apply prosecution history estoppel, and prosecution history estoppel can be referred to in a dispute over infringement of a patent right for design. The deletion of the parallel technical solution in the claims and the restrictive observations will lead to the application of prosecution history estoppel, while nonrestrictive observations will not easily lead to the application of prosecution history estoppel. Nonabandonment of the technical solution, the "passive" invalidation of the claim, and the further definition by adding technical features do not certainly lead to the application of prosecution history estoppel. The sued infringer who asserts the application of prosecution history estoppel should furnish the evidence to prove that the patentee has abandoned the "sued infringing technical solution" through the "restrictive amendments or observations," while the patentee who asserts the nonapplication of prosecution history estoppel should furnish the evidence to prove that the "restrictive amendments or observations" are explicitly denied.